economics

by EXAMPLE

economics
by EXAMPLE

DAVID A. ANDERSON
Centre College

Worth Publishers

Aquisitions Editor: Sarah Dorger
Associate Editor: Marie McHale
Development Editor: Cecilia Gardner
Marketing Manager: Scott Guile
Associate Managing Editor: Tracey Kuehn
Project Editor: Katherine Evancie
Art Director: Babs Reingold
Senior Designer: Kevin Kall
Photo Editor: Cecilia Varas
Production Manager: Barbara A. Seixas
Composition: Matrix Publishing
Printing and Binding: RR Donnelley
Cover Art: Joe Belbruno

ISBN-13: 978-0-7167-6934-7
ISBN-10: 0-7167-6934-4

© 2007 by Worth Publishers

Printed in the United States of America

Fourteenth printing

Worth Publishers
41 Madison Avenue
New York, NY 10010
www.worthpublishers.com

To my students

ABOUT THE AUTHOR

David A. Anderson received his B.A. from the University of Michigan and his M.A. and Ph.D. from Duke University. He is currently the Paul G. Blazer Professor of Economics at Centre College, where he has taught since 1992. Dr. Anderson specializes in the economics of law, crime, and the environment. He has also published scholarly articles on futures markets, ARCH models, marriage, social insurance, instructional evaluation, childbirth, gender stereotyping, and dispute resolution, among other topics. His ten books cover the topics of dispute resolution, environmental economics, active learning, and introductory economics.

C O N T E N T S

PART 9: PUBLIC POLICY 119

PART 10: TECHNOLOGY AND INNOVATION 133

PART 11: THE MACROECONOMY 149

PART 12: GROWTH AND EMPLOYMENT 167

PREFACE

This book introduces the principles of economics with enticing, real-life applications. The goal is to help readers understand how their lives are immersed in economics as they learn critical concepts. The thirty chapters address hot topics such as globalization, Internet piracy, legal reform, outsourcing, environmental policy, immigration, and big-box retailing, all within the framework of economic principles.

In a refreshing pedagogical approach, stories rather than diagrams explain economic concepts in the context of choices and policies relevant to today's students. The explanations are lively, surprising, and replete with solid economic content. Each chapter ends with a set of discussion-starting questions to encourage in-class reflections and debates.

In traditional principles courses, this book can be used as a supplement to any principles text, serving as a source of additional explanations, applications, and provocation. Chapter subtitles identify the emphases of each chapter for easy pairing with assignments of material in the core textbook. The book can also stand alone for use in one-semester survey courses and others requiring minimal mathematics or graphical analysis. Whether used on its own, as a companion to a standard text, or as summer reading for AP students, *Economics by Example* sheds new light on the exciting applications of economics that are so important to the success or failure of public policies and to the happiness or discontent of us all.

A SUMMARY OF EACH CHAPTER'S COVERAGE

Here is a closer look at chapter content to assist with reading selections and pairings between chapters in this book and in others.

Part 1: Introduction

Chapter 1, What's to love about economics? *Virtues of the Economic Way of Thinking*: Motivates the study of economics and introduces efficiency, marginal analysis, social welfare maximization, and simplifying assumptions as foundations for critical economic findings. Examples involve skipping class, punishments for those who download music illegally, the cost-benefit analysis of wildlife preservation, the benefits of higher education, and cyclist Lance Armstrong.

Chapter 2, Why did the cashier let Biff Henderson eat all the free mints? *An Introduction to the Power of Incentives*: Explains the quintessential finding of economic research: that people respond to incentives in rational ways. Examples involve a stunt by David Letterman's stage manager Biff Henderson, salary incentives in sports, automobiles and oil prices, a variety of types of government policy, and numerous sources of perverse incentives.

Part 2: Supply and Demand

Chapter 3, The coffee market's hot, why are bean prices not? *Insights into Supply and Demand*: Explains the shapes and functions of supply and demand curves. The primary examples revolve around coffee as the world's second most traded commodity (after oil) and second most popular beverage (after water). Other examples include equilibrium prices as motivators for Columbus and Magellan, the increasing opportunity cost of babysitting and solar panel installation, the increasing marginal cost of fish, and the diminishing marginal benefits of water.

Chapter 4, Why was the great newspaper heist so easy? *Diminishing Marginal Utility and the Price Elasticity of Demand*: Uses the example of a theft of thousands of newspapers by a college fraternity to discuss the underpinnings of demand, the implications of diminishing marginal utility, and the elasticity of demand.

Part 3: Markets and Decisions

Chapter 5, How can economics influence your choice of a spouse? *Supply, Demand, and Price Signals in the Marriage Market*: Explains how markets work and how prices affect decisions, focusing on the example of the market for marriage partners.

Chapter 6, Is Adam Smith rolling over in his grave? *Perfect Competition, Efficiency, and the Father of Modern Economics*: Discusses the most famous teachings of Adam Smith about product markets and private consumption decisions. Also deals with the virtues of perfect competition, efficiency conditions, ethics, and the theory of second best.

Part 4: Production

Chapter 7, Why are there more members of a band than professors in a class? *Diminishing Marginal Returns and the Demand for Labor*: Explains diminishing marginal product and the derived demand for inputs. The primary example involves the marginal product of rock musicians and economics teachers

Chapter 8, Could the future cost of energy change life as we know it? *Production Costs and the Inescapable Demand for Energy*: Discusses production costs in the crucial and timely context of energy market regulation.

Part 5: Consumer Choice

Chapter 9, Why is cash the ultimate gift? *Optimal Consumption, Deadweight Loss, and the Virtues of Flexible Spending*: Explains utility maximization, consumer surplus, and producer surplus in such contexts as holiday gift giving.

Chapter 10, Why should we pay for what we throw away? *Incentives for Efficiency from Pay-Per-Unit Pricing*: Discusses preferences for consumption as they relate to budget constraints. Examples include "pay-per-throw" programs in which households pay a fixed amount per bag of trash left on the curb, amusement parks, and all-you-can-eat restaurants.

Part 6: Efficiency

Chapter 11, Why not split the check? *A Briefing on Market Failure*: Describes sources and solutions for market failure. The importance of internalizing costs is explained using the example of splitting the check for a restaurant meal. Applications include the high cost of health care.

Chapter 12, How gullible are we? *Information Problems and Their Applications to Schools of Economic Thought*: Examines institutional, informational, and cognitive constraints on efficient market decisions through the examples of exonerated death row inmates, urban legends, and the origins of war.

Part 7: Market Power

Chapter 13, What's behind the music industry's woes? *The Sound of Market Power:* Explains the influence of market power in the context of Internet music downloads and lawsuits against those involved in the illegal sharing of music files.

Chapter 14, Wal-Mart: Friend or foe? *Economies of Scale, Low Prices, Low Wages, and Thinking Outside the Box*: Looks into the world of big-box retailers, delving into issues of economies of scale, predatory pricing, and market structure.

Part 8: Risk, Uncertainty, and the Market

Chapter 15, What is the value of human life? *Reasons and Methods for Placing Finite Values on Unidentified Human Lives*: Explains how risk and uncertainty enter into individual decisions and how economists use responses to the risk of death to assess the statistical value of human life.

Chapter 16, Do potential criminals contemplate their fate? *Making Incentives Matter in the Face of Risk and Uncertainty*: Discusses risk and uncertainty in the context of crime and law enforcement. The primary examples involve research findings on whether various types of criminals consider the consequences of their actions and their likelihood of being apprehended and convicted.

Part 9: Public Policy

Chapter 17, Should damage awards in lawsuits be capped? *Benefits and Costs of Limiting the Burden of Litigation*: Presents pro and con arguments on the hot economic topic of placing caps on punitive and compensatory damages awarded in lawsuits involving medical malpractice and product liability.

Chapter 18, What's to love about taxes? *Free Riding on Public Goods, Deadweight Loss, and the Lesser of Two Evils*: Explains the history and realities of our love-hate relationship with taxes. Included are discussions of public goods, tax regressivity, deadweight loss, and methods of taxation.

Part 10: Technology and Innovation

Chapter 19, Will technology put us all out of work? *Unemployment, Creative Destruction, and Quality of Life*: Examines the myth that technological innovations will lead to the replacement of human workers. Explains the types of unemployment and discusses such technological innovations as the automation of motor vehicle manufacturing and the mechanization of farming.

Chapter 20, Do pharmaceutical patents cost lives or save them? *Balancing Incentives for Innovation with Prices More Disease Victims Can Afford*: Covers both sides of the debate over patents and other barriers to competition as incentives for innovation, specifically in the pharmaceutical industry.

Part 11: The Macroeconomy

Chapter 21, Why do we neglect leisure and cheer for divorce? *The Divergence of Gross Domestic Product and Measures of Well-Being*: Explains the reasons and methods for calculating gross domestic product. Discusses the income, consumption, and value-added approaches. Highlights the weaknesses of GDP as a measure of welfare and presents alternative measures, such as the Index of Sustainable Economic Welfare.

Chapter 22, Does the money supply matter? *Money, the Fed, and the Debate over Optimal Monetary Policy*: Provides an overview of the major schools of thought in regard to monetary policy. Explains the structure and purpose of the Federal Reserve System.

Part 12: Growth and Employment

Chapter 23, What's to like about outsourcing? *The Influence of International Labor Markets*: Investigates outsourcing as an alleged boon to growth and bane to domestic employment. The pro-outsourcing remarks of Council of Economic Advisers chairman Greg Mankiw are discussed in the light of statistical evidence and economic reasoning.

Chapter 24, Do tree huggers deter growth and employment? *Myths, Labor Markets, and Environmentalism*: Highlights myths and realities in the debate over economic growth and environmental protection.

Part 13: Macroeconomic Policy

Chapter 25, How much debt is too much? *Expenditure Smoothing, Ricardian Equivalence, Crowding Out, and Investments for the Future*: Presents the weightiest pro and con arguments in the debate over debt creation, including explanations of Ricardian equivalence and crowding out.

Chapter 26, What is the role of government? *Political-Economic Systems, Snags in Private Solutions, and Remedies with a Role for Government*: Explains the various forms of government and the role of government in a successful economic system. Topics include the Coase Theorem, the enforcement of property rights, and government remedies for market failure.

Part 14: International Economics

Chapter 27, Is globalization a bad word? *Comparative Advantage, Culture Clashes, and Organizations Meant to Make the Most of Global Markets*: Demystifies the nebulous concept of globalization, explaining benefits such as the economic incentives for cooperation and toleration, and costs such as exploitation and homogenization.

Chapter 28, Why are some nations rich and others poor? *Growth Models, Miracles, and the Determinants of Economic Development*: Discusses the question that weighs on the minds of developmental economists: What is the cause of poverty? Major theories are explained and available solutions are considered.

Part 15: Global Issues

Chapter 29, Pollution: How might economics help save the planet? *Cap and Trade Programs as a Market Solution to Problems Small and Large:* Explains how tradable emissions permits can provide efficient incentives for pollution abatement while allowing flexible solutions, and how cap-and-trade programs are being applied to myriad problems—environmental and otherwise—around the globe.

Chapter 30, Immigration: How welcoming should Lady Liberty be? *The Costs and Benefits of Relatively Open Borders*: Presents the arguments for and against relatively open immigration. Discusses the effects of immigration on domestic employment and productivity, as well as the connections between immigration, on the one hand, and inflation, population growth, public assistance, skills gaps, and cultural diversity, on the other.

ACKNOWLEDGMENTS

I am indebted to Cecilia Gardner, Marie McHale, and Katherine Evancie for editing and pre-press work of the highest quality. Several colleagues provided valuable feedback on various drafts of this text. I'd like to specifically thank Ronnie Liggett, University of Texas–Arlington; Debra Israel, Indiana State University; Sally Adamson, Duncanville High School; Roger Meiners, University of Texas–Arlington; Kenny Christianson, Binghamton University–Ithaca College; and Craig M. Newmark, North Carolina State University. For assistance in developing the concept for this book I am grateful to Michael Brody, Menlo School; James Chasey, College of DuPage; Eric Dodge, Hanover College; Woodrow Hughes, Jr., Converse College; Joy Joyce, Willowbrook High School; Matthew Pedlow, Jackson High School; Fred Smith, Davidson College; Shaun Waldron, Niles West High School; and Alene Zimmer, Katy Independent Schools. None of this would have been possible without the loving support of my wife, Donna, and my children, Austin and Ally, who tolerated my late nights of prose polishing and fact checking. Most importantly, I want to thank you, the reader, for being open to exploring a discipline that offers new perspectives on the betterment of society.

David A. Anderson

economics

by EXAMPLE

CHAPTER 1

WHAT'S TO LOVE ABOUT ECONOMICS?
Virtues of the Economic Way of Thinking

Once a year, 100 fun-loving individuals descend on a college town for a week of work and play. The group includes surfers, Ironman triathletes, hula dancers, weight lifters, vegetarians, musicians, world travelers, and water polo coaches. They frequent local ballgames, racetracks, and karaoke nights, where songs such as "Sweet Transvestite" and "New York, New York" are belted out with gusto. They flood the sushi bars, bistros, and trendy cafés. What's the common denominator among this crowd of hip, talented women and men? They're all economics instructors like your own, gathered to grade a standardized national economics exam. What makes economics so exciting that it inspires all sorts of people to devote their lives to conveying its wisdom? There are many answers to that question; what follows is the tip of the iceberg.

ECONOMICS IS EVERYWHERE

Economics doesn't simply appear in books or lurk in bank vaults. Economics is above you in airplanes, below you in coal mines, behind the fabric content of your clothing, and underpinning the politics of your nation. Economics is the study of limited resources and unlimited wants. The broad scope of this discipline results from the limits on virtually every human want. Beyond money, there are limited supplies of time, information, clean water and air, potential spouses, employers, employees, NCAA Final Four basketball tickets, and everything you would buy if you won the lottery. Economics is behind your choice to go to school, the cinnamon in your latte, your adherence to laws (or lack thereof), and the public policies of your government. Economics is also the lens through which people who seek happiness should look before making decisions. Consider an example: Have you ever skipped class? Skipping is an option you confront daily, and you must decide how often to tempt fate with truancy. Economists explain that firms confront their production decisions by considering the additional cost and benefit of each unit and manufacturing more units until the additional benefit no longer exceeds the additional cost. If you're maximizing your happiness, you do the same thing when deciding whether to attend class.

Centre College student Adair Howell skipped class recently for a *Today Show* interview as the winner of the *Cosmo* Cover Model Contest. If skipping one class allows you to launch a new career, like Adair, or to get treatment for a deadly illness, the substantial benefit exceeds the limited cost of the first class missed, which might be a few hours of extra reading and note copying. The second most important reason to skip class might be that your sports team has a competition. The third best reason might be that you're simply not in the mood. As the reasons to skip become more trivial, the costs of additional misses mount. In running, they say that if you miss 1 day of training, only you know it; if you miss 2 days, the competition knows it; and if you miss 3 days, the crowd knows it. In education, an analogous story might be that missing 1 day of class affects your conscience; missing 2 days affects your grade; and missing many days affects your future.

In order to determine the number of skips that will make you as well off as possible, you should skip until the additional benefit no longer exceeds the additional cost. (Don't get the wrong impression; if you're not interviewing, ill, or bereaved, the optimal number of skips may well be 0.) With the additional benefit falling and the additional cost rising, any subsequent skips do more harm than good. Economists call the additional benefit from 1 more of something the *marginal benefit* and the additional cost of 1 more of something the *marginal cost*. Thus, you should skip until the marginal cost equals the marginal benefit.

You weigh marginal costs against marginal benefits every day. You know that eating too much pie can make you gain weight, but the first few bites create a lot of pleasure and not a lot of weight. As your hunger is satisfied, the benefit of each additional bite decreases and its cost (in terms of excessive caloric intake) increases. Eventually, the marginal cost of another bite of pie will exceed its marginal benefit, and it's time to stop eating. If it's the best pie you've ever tasted, the marginal benefit is higher, and you'll eat more of it. Sometimes even indigestion is well justified. In 2011, high marginal benefits led Joe Menchetti to eat 2.5 apple pies in one sitting—he won $500 and fame in the New York City Apple Day Festival pie eating contest.

The study of where marginal benefit meets marginal cost leads to the efficient outcomes that economists cherish. How many hours should you spend in the library? How many laps should you swim in the pool? How much time should you spend in the shower? The answer is always the same: Just do it until the marginal benefit equals the marginal cost and you couldn't do any better.

ECONOMIC TOOLS CAN ADDRESS WEIGHTY ISSUES

It's no secret that economic theory helps businesspeople make decisions about prices, production levels, and manufacturing methods that maximize profits. The economic way of thinking also applies to the most difficult dilemmas facing society. Economic theory can address troubling problems with poverty, crime, pollution, education, health care, the legal system, child care, transportation systems, water shortages, population growth, biodiversity loss, sustainable development, and energy, to name a few.

Consider the issue of how to punish people who break the law. Suppose that each song illegally downloaded from the Internet costs society $1 in lost wages for sound mixers, CD store employees, advertisers, musicians, and others in the recording industry. As mentioned in the preceding truancy example, efficiency dictates that each activity should continue until the additional (or marginal) benefit equals the additional (or marginal) cost. For simplicity, we're assuming that the marginal cost of downloading a song remains constant at $1 and that the value of the time spent downloading is negligible. If the benefit to the recipient from downloading another song exceeds the cost to society, the download creates a net gain for society and it is efficient (although still illegal) to carry it out.

How can we bring about the efficient level of downloading? One way would be to successfully enforce a penalty of $1 for each download. If music lovers had to pay a $1 fine per download, they would download only songs that were worth at least $1 to them. Inefficient downloads that were worth less than the $1 cost to society would not occur. The trouble is that it would be dreadfully expensive to provide the level of policing required to detect every download.

Economic theory can help with that problem, too. Suppose that downloads were monitored only half the time, but only the monitors knew which half, meaning that half of all downloads were caught. With a fine of $2 that was paid half the time, downloaders would expect to pay an average of $1 per song downloaded. That is, with a 50 percent chance of having to pay $2, the expected fine per song downloaded would be one-half times $2, or $1. Music lovers who made decisions on the basis of the expected fine would still download only when their benefit from a song exceeded the cost to society.

The expected fine would also be $1 if there were a 1-in-10 chance of paying $10, a 1-in-100 chance of paying $100, or a 1-in-1,000 chance of paying $1,000. For music lovers who don't have a particular preference for, or aversion to, risk taking, any of these combinations would provide the proper incentive to limit downloads to the efficient number. With this in mind, law enforcement costs can be reduced without altering the incentives to obey the law by charging higher fines and only spending enough on enforcement to catch a smaller number of offenders. You'll read more about the economics of risk and uncertainty in Part 8.

ECONOMIC FINDINGS CAN BE SPECIFIC AND COMPELLING

What special powers do people trained in economics have that allow them to make strong arguments and precise recommendations? They may not be superheroes, but they brandish advanced quantitative tools, detailed methods of reasoning, the high-road goal of maximizing social welfare, and the use of assumptions to leap tall complexities in a single bound. Let's look at each of these powers in turn.

Quantitative Tools

Economists delve deeply into quantitative methods that yield precise answers to important questions. Because economics is about the realities facing each of us on a daily basis, the meatiest topics within economics are concrete and visible and can be discussed without advanced math, as is the case in this book. If this exposition whets your appetite for an understanding of the more rigorous side of economics, you will encounter mathematical models in other textbooks—but they will turn out to be more straightforward than they look, again because they are simply representations of situations that we all experience in daily life. As you read on about economic findings, you may well become persuaded that the evidence gained by applying quantitative tools provides benefits that far exceed any associated costs.

For example, you have probably heard people debating whether forests should be cut for lumber or preserved to protect species such as the spotted owl. Thanks to quantitative tools, economists can advance this debate from "Gee, the birds are great, but we want more homes and jobs, so we're confused" to "The long-term cost of saving the owl in terms of logging jobs and timber prices is $0.62 million, whereas the long-term value of owl preservation to humans is $1.84 million, so there's a $1.22 million net gain from saving the owls" (paraphrased from a 1991 study by Rubin, Helfand, and Loomis; figures adjusted for inflation). Sure, estimates may differ, depending on the research method and the underlying assumptions, but it is useful to obtain objective estimates of the costs and benefits of such decisions as an alternative to acting purely on the basis of gut feelings and stabs in the dark. The quantitative tools of economics make these estimates possible.

Economic Reasoning

The crux of economic reasoning, as you've already read in this chapter, is that any activity should be continued until the additional benefits from doing so no longer exceed the additional costs. Consideration of these costs and benefits can yield specific estimates of just how loud a sound system should be, how long one should sunbathe on the beach, how low a thermostat should be set, and how far one should go in school. The availability of specific answers to common puzzles is one reason why some people get excited about economics.

Here's an example: Using information on the costs and benefits of going to school for each year, students can pinpoint the best plans for their formal educations. Jennifer Day and Eric Newburger studied the average annual income of full-time workers in the United States.[1] Relative to a person with some high school education but no diploma, they found that the average worker with a high school diploma earns about $7,000 more each year. Workers with bachelor's degrees earn $22,000 more than the high school graduates, and those with professional degrees earn $57,000 on top of that.[2] These financial benefits are augmented by any nonfinancial benefits a particu-

---

[1] See www.census.gov/prod/2002pubs/p23-210.pdf.
[2] The learning associated with diplomas is only part of the reason for higher earnings. Employers use educational attainment as an indication or "signal" of associated attributes, such as intelligence and diligence, that make for more productive workers.

lar person would receive from the higher-paying jobs to which education provides access, such as more job security, lighter physical burdens, and cleaner working conditions. For comparison, the direct costs of going to school for another year are readily available—typically about $25,000 for each year of college. These costs can be combined with the cost of forgoing work to go to school and with the nonfinancial burdens of school to determine the appropriate educational goals for a particular student.

Clear and Defensible Objectives

Economic analysis can be applied in myriad contexts to pursue objectives ranging from profit maximization to everlasting bliss. When economists consider public policy, the default goal is the greatest possible net gain to society. This goal is achieved by addressing questions of what, how, and for whom to produce with an eye on *efficiency*. Think of efficiency as maximizing the size of the "pie" that represents social well-being, profit, personal happiness, or any other particular objective. As we'll discuss in greater detail in Part 6, efficient outcomes exhaust all opportunities for net gains.

Once the net gains from government policies are maximized, society must grapple with the *equity* consideration of how to divide the pie among potential recipients. For example, public lands could be opened to loggers, sold to developers, maintained as parks for tourists, or donated to the homeless. It would be efficient to use the land for the purpose that provides the greatest overall net benefits, but the most efficient outcome often conflicts with equity considerations. The greatest net benefits might come from a park, but interests in equity point toward helping the homeless. Economists study taxes, subsidies, and entitlement programs that can distribute the gains from efficiency in a more equitable manner. For example, if a particular tract of public land would be more valuable to park visitors than to the homeless, the best solution might be to create a park on the land, impose a tax on visitors, and use the tax revenues to pay for homeless shelters elsewhere.

In 2006, the U.S. Forest Service sought the sale of 200,000 acres of public land to raise about $800 million for schools and road maintenance in underprivileged rural areas.[3] The Wilderness Society argued that the land would be more valuable to the country if it remained in public hands.[4] Suppose the land is worth $800 million to the private individuals who would purchase it and $1 billion to the broader U.S. citizenry. In that case, the efficient solution is to maximize the size of the pie—the benefits from this land—by maintaining public ownership. With creative slicing of the pie, the goals of the land sale can be achieved even if the land is not sold. For example, the public beneficiaries of the $1 billion worth of land could be taxed $800 million to pay for rural schools and roads. In this way, the land would be used for its most valued purpose, the rural areas would benefit as under a land sale, and the U.S. public would receive a $200 million net gain equal to the $1 billion in benefits from the land minus the $800 million in new taxes.

---

[3] See www.msnbc.msn.com/id/11257181/.
[4] See http://action.wilderness.org/campaign/forestselloff.

Simplifying Assumptions

Sometimes less is more. Just as it's easier to follow a map that isn't muddled with markings for every tree, telephone wire, and parking space, researchers find simplifications useful when studying cause and effect. Consider the common assumption of *ceteris paribus,* a Latin phrase meaning that influences other than the one being studied remain unchanged. Suppose Lance Armstrong is biking down a mountain at 40 miles per hour (mph) and gets a flat tire. How will his speed be affected? Admittedly, many elements might come into play. If the tire blew out as Lance flew over a guardrail and went into a free fall, his speed would increase. Wet roads, a collision, or fatigue would all reduce his speed and reinforce the influence of the flat tire. Some people might throw up their hands and say it's impossible to determine for sure what would happen to Lance's speed when his tire went flat.

An economist is more likely to say, "*Ceteris paribus,* the bike will slow down." The economist is assuming that, except for the blowout, all elements of the situation—the weather, the biker's upright position, and so on—will remain the same. The *ceteris paribus* assumption allows the economist to address the issue in question without being hampered by complexities. Rather than neglecting other influences while making an estimate of speed, the economist can study each influence independently, with the assumption that the others remain unchanged. Economists use the *ceteris paribus* assumption when studying, for example, the effect of consumer demand on prices or the effect of labor unions on employee benefits. In reality, demand changes often coincide with changes in production costs that also affect prices, and unionization is one of many determinants of employee benefits; however, it is useful to isolate influences and assess them one at a time. In the end, economists can combine their data on individual influences to determine the result of several simultaneous changes, whereas skeptics who don't like to make assumptions are in free fall with a headache.

Another noteworthy and controversial assumption is that individuals behave rationally. In Chapter 2, we consider compelling evidence and implications of rational responses to incentives. Associated with the rationality assumption are expectations that people prefer more of a good thing, have goals, learn, and are consistent enough in their behaviors to exhibit *transitive preferences*. Suppose you prefer jazz to reggae music and you prefer reggae to classical music. Given a choice between jazz and classical, which type of music would you select? If the answer is jazz, you are exhibiting the rationality of transitive preferences because your response is consistent with your preference ordering of jazz first, then reggae, and then classical music. An answer of classical music would violate that rationality. More generally, economists assume that individuals will make the appropriate decisions to maximize their happiness and that firms will likewise act to maximize their profits.

Is it rational to assume that people behave rationally? Economists think so for several reasons. Without transitive preferences it would be painfully difficult to make common decisions. If you liked cola better than water, juice better than cola, and (in violation of transitivity) water better than juice, you would cycle through these choices endlessly and spend far too much time in the beverage aisle of the grocery store. Firms with managers who behave irrationally are unlikely to last long, and the same could be said of people. Anyone who eats nails and sleeps in swimming pools is unlikely to survive to pass his or her irrational genes on to the next generation. Do business managers study the graphs and equations that indicate profit-maximizing prices and quantities? Sometimes they do, and other times they may use less formal analyses to derive similar conclusions. Likewise, Nobel laureate Milton Friedman notes that although expert pool players don't really measure all the angles and distances between billiard balls on a pool table or make complex mathematical calculations to find the speed and trajectory with which to strike the ball, they often take their shots as if they did.

Of course, all of us have those mornings when we start to brush our hair with our toothbrushes and pour orange juice into our cereal. Economic theory can endure a few missteps by individuals or even a few people who never get things right. Economic theory yields useful conclusions as long as, on average, people's decisions are more rational than random, and that's true for most of us even on a bad day.

There are a number of schools of thought in economics that place different emphases on potential limits to human rationality. The institutionalists, inspired by the likes of Thorstein Veblen and Wesley Mitchell, emphasize social, institutional, and historical constraints on rationality, including predatory and acquisitive drives and instincts for workmanship and parenting. They argue that many decisions are made on the basis of rules of thumb and that there are bounds on rationality. In contrast, the Chicago school, whose current patriarchs include Milton Friedman and Gary Becker, is more optimistic that humans can reliably be treated as rational actors. Chicago school economists defend the rationality of everything from family dynamics to drug addiction. As usual, each side makes valid points, and the truth probably lies somewhere in the middle. Either way, rest assured that the importance of economic theory does not require humans to be perfect.

CONCLUSION

Thanks for giving economics a try. With these readings and this course under your belt, you will become more adept at making wise decisions, allocating resources, and maximizing the satisfaction of yourself and society. Regardless of whether you choose to join the surfers, singers, jocks, and karaoke singers who have devoted their professional lives to the science of economics, it's a good bet that the benefits you receive from this course will exceed the costs, and that makes it a most efficient and worthwhile undertaking.

DISCUSSION STARTERS

1. Do law enforcement agencies really seek an efficient amount of lawbreaking rather than no lawbreaking? Consider some illegal activities that might sometimes create more good than harm. How do the penalties for these crimes compare with the penalties for crimes that are less likely ever to be efficient? How much should people be fined for doing something that we really want to prohibit from ever happening?

2. Is it common for marginal costs to increase and marginal benefits to de-crease? What is the marginal benefit from the first, second, and third prac-tices for the swim team in a day? What is the marginal cost of the first, sec-ond, and third swim practices? (It is important to remember that costs and benefits are not strictly financial.) How are you at carrying out activities until the marginal cost equals the marginal benefit?

3. How would economists go about analyzing the likely influence of a fore-cast of heavy snow on the quantity of tickets sold for the *Nutcracker* ballet? What other changes could influence ticket sales? What assumptions should be made? Why?

4. Is it rational for some people to end their formal education with high school degrees, some to finish with college degrees, and some to obtain graduate degrees? Beyond the ability to pay tuition, what are some other reasons why different people stay in school for different lengths of time? How might the nonmonetary cost of college differ among individuals? How might the ben-efits differ?

CHAPTER 2

WHY DID THE CASHIER LET BIFF HENDERSON EAT ALL THE FREE MINTS?

An Introduction to the Power of Incentives

In a recent segment on the *Late Show with David Letterman*, stage manager Biff Henderson meandered around Manhattan timing things. How long would it take a shop owner to stop Biff from drawing faces on watermelons? When would someone say "Bless you" as Biff sneezed in Central Park? How long would a restaurant cashier let him graze on the bowl of mints at the counter? In most of these experiments, the answer was "Not long," but the cashier never stopped the mint bowl raid. Biff eventually poured the remaining mints into his pocket and left the restaurant scot-free. In this chapter we'll solve the mystery of the cashier's indifference and learn some secrets to success based on the underappreciated importance of incentives.

INCENTIVES MATTER

Economists provide a critical clue to the cashier's complacency: Incentives matter. As economist Steven Landsburg writes in *The Armchair Economist* (1991, p. 3), "Most of economics can be summarized in four words: 'People respond to incentives.' The rest is commentary." Biff's defacing (or should I say facing?) of the melons was soon halted because the shop owner was standing guard. Every melon Biff blemished represented a direct financial loss to the man who would pocket the profits from the fruit stand. If the cashier had a stake in the restaurant, perhaps she would have said something to Biff about going easy on the mints. The cashier's duty was to maximize her employer's profits, but her incentive was to avoid hassles and collect a fixed wage. She lost nothing from Biff's pilferage of the candy, and her best interests differed from those of her employer. So she failed to fulfill her duty, responding to incentives instead. For similar reasons, U.S. businesses lose an estimated $40 billion annually as a result of internal theft. Toyota, Microsoft, and Wal-Mart are among companies that use performance-based bonuses to bring the interests of employees and stockholders into closer alignment. Anyone who shares in the profits has a reason to watch out for the company's interests.

According to skeptics, people care about their employers anyway and don't need work incentives. Indeed, many workers do care about their workplaces; the issue is that even the most loyal workers also care about other things, such as their families, hobbies, gardens, and churches. We act with our hearts, but our hearts are divided among many competing objects of affection. Those pro athletes who love their teams and talk about giving "110 percent" also love their spouses, their favorite charities, and their vacation homes; consequently, even though they are truly dedicated to their sports, it takes monumental performance incentives to get a mere 100 percent out of them. A professional football player might stand to earn an extra $100,000 for rushing more than 1,000 yards in a season, $10,000 for catching 6 touchdown passes, or $300,000 for being on the roster for at least 14 games. As an example, Tampa Bay Buccaneers wide receiver Michael Clayton was eligible for a roster bonus (for showing up for enough games) of $460,000 in 2005.

Incentives matter for coaches, too. University of Maryland football coach Ralph Friedgen receives an extra $50,000 each year if his program avoids legal and NCAA infractions, $75,000 if at least 75 percent of his senior players graduate, and $225,000 if the team goes to a bowl game. University of Hawaii football coach June Jones's performance incentives include $17,500 for every victory more than 6 in a season and up to $10,000 annually if first-year scholarship players receive at least a 2.7 grade point average (GPA).

Those who pay the bills for sports teams apparently believe that incentives make a difference, and evidence supports them. Joseph Boyer and Jeffrey DeSimone,[1] among other researchers, find that performance incentives have a meaningful influence on game outcomes. There are bonuses for good grades, too, but coaches seldom shorten practices to extend study time. That's because, when confronted by conflicting incentives, it is rational to respond to the largest one. Noting that university coaches' incentives to win games far exceed their incentives to promote academic achievement, economist Andrew Zimbalist writes, "You look at the proportional size of each bonus, and it's not very hard to see where, over the long term, the priority and focus are going to be."[2] In other words, if college athletes aren't meeting expectations in the classroom, rather than criticizing coaches for holding practices long into the evening, it might be more effective to rewrite their contracts.

---

[1] This article is available for download at http://ideas.repec.org/p/wop/eacaec/9908.html.
[2] See www.washingtontimes.com/national/20040428-120939-8135r.htm.

INCENTIVES DRIVE MARKETS

In the marketplace, prices provide incentives for the allocation of scarce resources among competing interests. When oil prices set record highs, as they did in 2006, more resources are devoted to oil prospecting, more acres of land and ocean floor are set aside for drilling, and more money is spent to research and develop alternative sources of energy. What we now call "oil" was called "rock oil" in the nineteenth century, and whale oil was the lamp fuel of choice. With high prices for whale oil came strong incentives to replace it with petroleum products.[3] Similarly, if oil prices rise high enough, it will become financially viable to obtain oil from oil shale and tar sand, and the new price incentives will spawn industries that mine and refine oil from new sources.

What incentives drive your choice of a vehicle? Desires for status and sex appeal are important motivators for car buyers, and oil prices also have an influence. A General Motors (GM) Hummer gets about 11 miles per gallon of gasoline, whereas a Toyota Prius gets about 50 miles per gallon.[4] In 2003, 35,259 Hummers and 20,387 Priuses were sold. As oil prices soared to record highs in 2004, Hummer sales slumped, prompting GM to cut its Hummer sales forecast from 40,000 to 30,000 cars. Meanwhile, Toyota, with many customers willing to pay more than the suggested retail price for a Prius, increased 2004 sales to 54,000 cars. Fueled by continued oil-price incentives, which only increased after Hurricane Katrina crippled 10 U.S. refineries,[5] Toyota sold 108,000 Priuses in 2005 and projected further sales growth in 2006.[6] Consumers responded to the incentive to buy fuel-efficient cars in order to save money at the gas pump and to help protect the environment, and Toyota responded to the incentive to produce more Priuses in order to profit from the car's growing popularity and premium prices.

Because prices and the incentives they create are so important, you can look forward to more discussions of market prices later in this book. In Chapter 3, we discuss the determinants of prices, Chapter 5 explains how a special type of price might play into the selection of a spouse, and Chapter 6 considers how market prices can lead us to efficient outcomes.

INCENTIVES UNDERPIN EFFECTIVE POLICY

Appropriate incentive structures can be used to address many policy dilemmas. How could we get more people to clean up and recycle bottles and cans? Place a dime deposit on them.[7] How do we try to curtail potentially deadly habits, such as smoking and drinking? We increase so-called sin taxes on the associated products. How do we motivate employers to create safer workplaces? We base the cost of workers' compen-

---

[3] See www.energyquest.ca.gov/story/chapter08.html.

[4] See http://hybridcars.about.com/od/toyotaprius/fr/2005toyotaprius.htm.

[5] See www.chron.com/disp/story.mpl/special/05/katrina/3332630.html.

[6] See www.nctd.com/review-intro.cfm?Vehicle=2006_Toyota_Prius&ReviewID=1890.

[7] For information on existing bottle deposit legislation, see www.toolkit.container-recycling.org/GetTheFacts/other/nickel.htm. Michigan's 10-cent deposit on bottles helps it top other states to achieve a bottle return rate that is consistently about 95 percent.

sation insurance on each firm's history of injuries. More generally, how can we get ourselves to study more, procrastinate less, tidy up, or slim down? We can dangle a proverbial carrot by promising ourselves rewards.

Many states have passed legislation similar to the Kentucky Education Reform Act instituting performance incentives for public school teachers. One controversial result is higher standardized-test scores among students in public schools. Some parents and observers say the incentives are so effective that they motivate educators to make the school year too long. Grassroots groups, such as SummerMatters!!, are now organizing to create incentives against extensions of the school calendar. There is also concern that incentives for high student test scores steer schools away from subjects such as music and art, in which individual achievement is hard to measure using standardized tests, and encourage states to set low standards so that more of their students "succeed."[8]

When you purchase tickets for an airplane flight or a movie, you are subjected to a common incentive scheme called *peak-load pricing*. The idea of peak-load pricing is to create incentives for customers to demand goods and services when supply is ample and not when supply is short. Taking this approach, restaurants often provide lower prices before 6 P.M. and tropical resorts offer discounts in the summer to spread their patronage out—a cheaper solution than expanding to accommodate more customers during the peak season. The cost of building and maintaining a power plant depends on the amount of energy output required during peak hours of production, and higher daytime rates encourage customers to delay as much usage as they can until evening. There are cyber cafés in Amsterdam whose hourly rates at any given time depend on the number of workstations currently being used. And happy hour drink prices in bars would more aptly be called quiet hour prices because they create incentives for patrons to visit during what otherwise would be slow periods.

Governments at every level use the incentive of tax breaks to encourage business growth. When the board of governors of the U.S. Federal Reserve System (the "Fed," for short) wants to spur the economy, it provides incentives for growth by lowering the interest rate that firms pay on their loans. When the Fed wants to cool the economy down and stem inflation, it engineers the opposite incentive, discouraging investment by imposing higher interest rates.

Despite their promise, adequate incentive structures are often absent from policy measures. Too many pay scales are driven by seniority alone, and too many service providers have insufficient incentives for quality or frugality. The sales clerk who won't get off the phone to help a customer, the instructor who won't give students the time of day, and the politician who doesn't vote to balance the budget are all symptomatic of misplaced incentives.

PERVERSE INCENTIVES MATTER, TOO

Incentives can have both intended effects and unintended effects, which is all the more reason to study them. For example, subsidies encourage production and consumption of the subsidized products, which is good if too few are being made but bad if

---

[8] See, for example, www.washingtonmonthly.com/features/2005/0510.toch.html.

the starting point is an adequate or excessive supply. Biff's melons, along with oil, education, and automobiles, are subject to various subsidies. The pollution-reduction benefits from Priuses might justify the roughly $3,700 in tax-based subsidies available to businesses (private individuals receive about $2,000), but the potential $10,500 tax savings for purchasers of Hummers may be a bad idea because of their relatively large environmental impact.

Perverse incentives are those that create unintended consequences. Hummers come with such a large tax break because vehicles weighing at least 3 tons receive favorable tax treatment not afforded to "luxury autos."[9] The weight limit, which was established to provide special tax status for construction, farming, and hauling vehicles, provides incentives for the production and purchase of oversized sport utility vehicles (SUVs) and pickup trucks. Today dozens of vehicle models used for light-duty transportation get this exemption because of their tremendous weight. Here are a few more examples of perverse incentives:

- Executive salaries that increase with a corporation's size may encourage excessive mergers. More than 60,000 mergers took place between 1980 and 2000.

- Plaintiffs' attorneys' fees that grow in proportion to the amount received at trial or settlement may encourage litigation. Between 1960 and 2003 the number of U.S. civil court cases filed increased more than fourfold, from 59,284 to 252,962.

- The relatively large donations received by crippled beggars in India have led some beggars to injure themselves or their children deliberately in order to gain the sympathy of passersby and thus increase their incomes.

- The Endangered Species Act of 1973 has led some landowners to destroy wildlife habitats so that no discovery of endangered species can be made that would trigger a loss of development rights.[10]

- Owners of stock in companies that sell antivirus software have an incentive to propagate viruses in order to motivate purchases of the software.

- Paying for tasks on an hourly basis may encourage workers to work too slowly, whereas paying by the job can encourage workers to work too quickly.

- "Three-strikes" laws mandating that three-time felons be given the maximum sentence may provide incentives for criminals to kill witnesses to their third offenses because the murders might prevent their convictions and, in any case, won't increase their punishments.

- Price ceilings (limits on how high prices can go), intended to make goods and services more available to underprivileged customers, cause shortages. For example, rent controls on apartments increase the quantity of apartments demanded and reduce the incentives to maintain existing apartment buildings or build new ones.

[9] Specifically, the heaviest vehicles are not subject to the $7,660 limit on first-year depreciation that applies to some other classes of vehicles. See www.bankrate.com/brm/news/auto/car-guide-2004/tax-SUVs1.asp.
[10] See www.journals.uchicago.edu/JLE/journal/issues/v46n1/460103/460103.html.

- Price floors (limits on how low prices can go), intended to help sellers of goods and services earn more money, create surpluses. For example, minimum wage laws, which create a floor (minimum) for the price of labor, decrease the number of workers hired and increase the number seeking work. The result is an increase in the unemployment rate.

- Restrictions on the legal supply of products such as marijuana and alcohol create illegal markets in which suppliers earn high profits and have strong incentives to get potential customers hooked on the products.

INCENTIVES ARE MORE THAN MONEY

In Chapter 1, I explained that economics isn't all about money; neither are incentives. Money is a means toward ends such as power, respect, security, and acquisition—but it isn't the only means of achieving these objectives. Managers of businesses and institutions often entice outstanding employees with the power of lofty titles, such as vice president or distinguished professor. Volunteers gain respect in their communities. Many workers in Japan accept relatively low wages in exchange for lifelong job security. Trips, presents, and services from government lobbyists and pharmaceutical company sales representatives are strictly regulated because of the dangerous incentives of biased advocates bearing gifts.[11] And in Leadville, Colorado, every year, people run 100 miles at high altitude in less than one day to earn a belt buckle.[12]

CONCLUSION

Biff discovered the kind of void in proper incentives that permeates policymaking at many levels. An understanding of the degree to which incentives matter is a secret to success in policymaking, politics, motivation, management, and virtually every other walk of life. Take it from former economics majors, such as Presidents Ronald Reagan and George H. W. Bush, Governor Arnold Schwarzenegger of California, retired Supreme Court justice Sandra Day O'Connor, rocker Mick Jagger, and former Harvard University president Lawrence Summers, to name only a few. These people have used their knowledge of incentives, among other talents, to achieve great things.

Economists routinely confirm what great sleuths have known all along: Actions and motives are seldom separated. When detectives can't solve a crime by screening suspects according to motive, alibi,[13] and ability to commit the crime, they frequently turn to another type of incentive—the reward. In the Old West, "Wanted Dead or Alive" posters offered bounties of $100 and up for the capture of criminals.[14] In the new West, the Los Angeles City Council offers rewards of $25,000 and up for tips leading to convictions for rapes, murders, and hate crimes.[15] For bounty hunters, like bottle deposit hunters and almost everyone else, incentives have proven to be a powerful tool. Whether you intend to influence the writing of legislation, legal decisions,

[11] See, for example, www.ama-assn.org/ama/pub/category/4263.html.
[12] See www.skyrunner.com/story/2004lt100.htm.
[13] An *alibi* is a defense that the suspect was not at the scene of the crime when it was committed.
[14] See www.larned.net/rogmyers/NWBH.htm.
[15] See www.physsci.uci.edu/psnews/?id=16.

rock lyrics, or university policies, remember that the pen may be mightier than the sword, but incentives set both of those instruments into motion.

DISCUSSION STARTERS

1. How do incentives influence your study habits? Why do students so often ask, "Is this topic going to be on the test?" Why would it be unwise for an education-maximizing instructor to reply, "No, it isn't"?

2. Can you tell when a sales clerk works on a commission basis? Do people who work for tips behave differently from those who do not? Can you tell from an instructor's behavior whether he or she has tenure?

3. What are some examples of perverse incentives that are not discussed in the chapter?

4. How might incentives be used to encourage volunteer work and community service?

5. What incentives might help to explain why consumers support abusive "sweatshop" manufacturing operations? Can you think of other examples of outwardly inappropriate behavior that is well explained by underlying incentives?

CHAPTER 3

THE COFFEE MARKET'S HOT; WHY ARE BEAN PRICES NOT?
Insights into Supply and Demand

Under fifteenth-century Turkish law, a wife could divorce her husband if he failed to provide her with a daily quota of coffee. Coffee is no longer grounds for divorce, but it is the world's most popular beverage after water and a common element of cozy getaways and productive workdays. Diamonds are another element that cements marriages, but although the price of diamonds drives people to steal, coffee beans have become a steal, costing only a few dollars a pound in the retail market. The fall of coffee prices as popularity rises can be explained with the allied concepts of supply and demand. Supply and demand are so critical to economics that they're the only concepts with their own diagram in this otherwise graph-free book. This chapter describes the graph that economists can't live without and explains what all the fuss is about in the context of Christopher Columbus, cans of tuna, and coffee beans.

SUPPLY, DEMAND, AND THE GREAT EXPLORERS

The story of supply and demand began long ago. Let's pick it up with the great explorers of the fifteenth and sixteenth centuries. In 1492, Christopher Columbus sailed the ocean blue in search of a westward route to Asia and its gold. In 1519, Ferdinand Magellan proved that the earth is round on an expedition to the Spice Islands, where cinnamon, nutmeg, and cloves were abundant. The royalty of Spain paid generously for these trips because gold was precious and, at that time in Europe, some spices were worth more than their weight in gold. Why were these products so expensive? This chapter explains how the combination of high demand and limited supply leads to high prices. Thanks to the incentives that high prices provide, new trade routes were established, supply increased, and spices became affordable. In other words, Europeans came to America and you can have cinnamon in your latte thanks to the workings of supply and demand.

Because they explain so much, let's explore the concepts of supply and demand. We'll refer to them and their famous graph again in later chapters.

Supply

The supply curve exhibits the relationship between price and quantity supplied. According to the *"law" of supply*,[1] as price increases, the quantity suppliers would be willing to supply increases, and as price decreases, the willingly supplied quantity decreases. This suggests, for example, that the Reno Philharmonic Orchestra[2] would be willing to put on more performances per week if it could command an $80 ticket price than if it could command a $60 ticket price. This positive relationship between price and quantity is illustrated by the upward slope of the supply curve in the accompanying diagram.

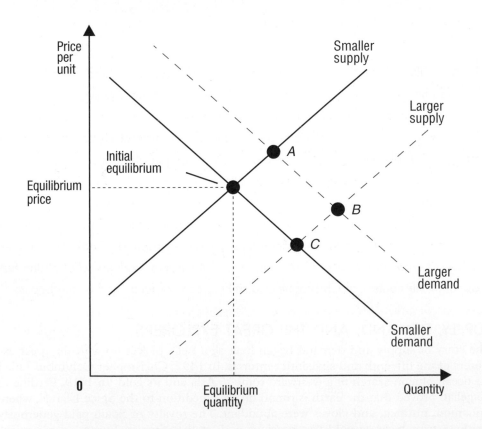

[1]Like other laws, the relationships that economists refer to as laws are sometimes broken.
[2]See www.renophilharmonic.com/.

It is likely that the law of supply describes your own behavior as well. Think about how many hours of burger flipping, lawn mowing, or babysitting you would supply per week at various prices. If you would supply more hours for $50 per hour than for $5 per hour, your supply curve resembles the one in the diagram. Let's examine why you probably would, using the economic concept of opportunity cost.

The *opportunity cost* of a particular action is the value of the next-best alternative you gave up to take that action instead. Part of the opportunity cost of going to college is the money you could have earned working at McDonald's instead. The opportunity cost of an hour of babysitting is the value you would have received from your next-best use of that hour. Your first hour of babysitting would substitute for the least valuable alternative activity—perhaps watching reruns on television. Additional hours of babysitting must be carved out of more and more valuable alternatives, such as watching your favorite television program, sleeping, and (as a last resort!) studying economics. The loss of these activities is the opportunity cost of babysitting, and you are rational to babysit until the opportunity cost exceeds the hourly wage for babysitting. The first few hours of babysitting might have an opportunity cost below $5 each, but many more hours have an opportunity cost below $50 each. Thus, the law of supply holds: As the price for babysitting increases, so does the quantity of babysitting hours supplied.

It's not only babysitting services that exhibit increasing opportunity costs. Consider items produced for sale, which economists refer to as *goods*, made with productive resources—such as labor, machines, and natural resources—known collectively as *inputs*. As manufacturers make more and more of a good, they must use inputs that are less and less specialized for that purpose. The use of less appropriate inputs leads to increasing opportunity costs. Consider the U.S. Department of Energy's goal of having solar panels on 1 million rooftops by 2010.[3] Plan participants began by employing the few experienced panel installers, who worked quickly using specialized trucks and installation equipment. The cost per installation increased as available specialists were snapped up and additional progress required training for roofers and others who felt comfortable climbing ladders but had no experience with solar panels.[4] Inexperienced workers naturally complete tasks more slowly, and they might occasionally break panels because their vehicles aren't made to carry fragile glass. In order to further increase the number of installations, even less appropriate workers and equipment would have to be employed. By the time the participating firms started hiring accountants with no ladders and fears of heights, the marginal (additional) cost of each solar panel installation would become very high indeed. In a country with hundreds of millions of barren rooftops, the goal of 1 million solar installations reflects, in part, recognition of increasing opportunity costs.

Increasing marginal costs cause suppliers to require higher prices in exchange for greater quantities. Thus, the supply curve, which shows the relationship between price and quantity supplied, is generally upward sloping. Marginal costs rise with production levels in many contexts and for many reasons. For example, it becomes increasingly expensive to obtain larger quantities of natural resources, such as fossil fuels and fish, as

---

[3]See www.millionsolarroofs.org/.
[4]For example, www.kysolar.org describes new solar installation training programs to handle the "shortage of trained, active installers."

suppliers must tap more distant and less productive areas of the land and sea. And according to the *"law" of diminishing marginal returns*, if you add more and more of an input that is easily varied, for example fishers, to an input that is relatively fixed in quantity or size, such as a boat, the additional number of fish caught by each new fisher will eventually fall. Congestion decreases the contributions of new fishers, as do decreasing opportunities for specialization. A single fisher in a boat would have to navigate, tend the nets, and manage the catch. She or he might not become particularly good at any of these varied tasks. With three fishers, each could specialize in 1 of the 3 tasks and become particularly skilled and effective in that area. As more fishers are added, there are no new opportunities for specialization, redundancy sets in, and it becomes more costly to increase production levels. The classic example of diminishing marginal returns is about adding seeds to a flowerpot: If you keep adding seeds to a fixed amount of soil, the additional returns in terms of flowers will eventually decrease, and, at some point, there will be so many seeds in the pot that another seed will find no soil.

The market supply curve is simply the sum of individual firms' supply curves, which is determined by adding up the quantities supplied by all the suppliers at each price. Suppose the fish market consists of 2 suppliers, Fred's Fish and Fay's Fish. If Fay would supply 10 fish for $1 each and 15 fish for $2 each, whereas Fred would supply 6 fish for $1 each and 12 fish for $2 each, then the market supply is 16 fish at $1 (10 from Fay plus 6 from Fred) and 27 fish at $2 (15 from Fay plus 12 from Fred). This information is summarized in the following table. The supply at any other price can be determined in the same way—that is, by adding up the quantities supplied by all fishers.

PRICE	FAY'S SUPPLY	FRED'S SUPPLY	MARKET SUPPLY
$1	10	6	16
$2	15	12	27

Because the supply curve reflects the marginal cost of production, the entire curve will shift downward and to the right, as from the solid supply curve to the dotted supply curve in the figure, when the cost of producing each additional unit decreases. For example, it would become cheaper to catch fish if there were an improvement in fishing technology, better weather, a reduction in fishing taxes, an increase in restocking subsidies, or higher catch limits. As the sum of all the fisher supply curves, the market supply curve will also shift downward and to the right when new fishers enter. The opposite of any of these changes will shift the supply curve upward and to the left, as from the dotted supply curve to the solid curve.

Note that a change in the price of fish does not change the marginal cost of catching fish and will, therefore, not shift the supply curve. Rather, it will cause a movement to a new point along the existing supply curve, as from the point labeled "Initial equilibrium" to point *A* in the figure. To distinguish between these two types of changes, we call a movement along a stationary supply curve a *change in the quantity supplied* and a shift in the supply curve itself, as from the solid supply curve to the dotted supply curve, a *change in supply*.

Demand

The demand curve shows the relationship between the price of a good or service and the quantity demanded. The demand for a good or service depends on the benefits it conveys. Whether it is fish, clothing, coffee, or almost anything else, the *marginal benefit*—the benefit gained from 1 more—generally decreases as quantity increases because needs become satisfied and desires become satiated.[5] The 1st beverage you drink in a month keeps you alive, whereas the 100th provides no such benefit. The height of the demand curve at each quantity indicates the most that anyone would be willing to pay for that unit of the good. With benefits decreasing as individuals receive more and more of a good, the height of the demand curve decreases, giving it a negative slope, as illustrated in the figure. The result is referred to as the *"law" of demand*: As the price of a good or service decreases, the quantity demanded increases.

Consider your demand for cans of tuna fish. Your 1st can in a week provides the important benefits of protein, minerals, omega-3 fatty acids (to reduce the risk of heart disease), and a welcome break from peanut butter and jelly. Perhaps you would be willing to pay up to $5 for the benefits of a first can of tuna if you had to.[6] If so, your demand curve has a height of $5 at the quantity of 1. A second can of tuna provides a little more variety and more of the same nutrients. Getting those benefits for the second time in a week isn't as essential as getting them the first time, but perhaps a second can is worth $1 to you. In that case, your demand curve has a height of $1 at a quantity of 2. A third can is even less important and may have you craving a break from tuna fish. Let's say you would pay up to 30 cents for a third can, and you wouldn't pay anything for any more tuna. Your demand curve thus has the height of 30 cents at a quantity of 3 and a height of 0 at every higher quantity.

As explained in Chapter 1, economists assume that people behave rationally. It is rational for you to buy cans of tuna fish until the benefit you receive from 1 more can is no longer worth at least as much as the price you must pay for it. If the price were $6, you wouldn't buy any tuna fish because even the first can is only worth $5 to you. If the price were $4, you would buy 1 can because it's rational to pay $4 for some-

PRICE	YOUR DEMAND	MY DEMAND	MARKET DEMAND
$6	0	0	0
$5	1	0	1
$4	1	0	1
$3	1	1	2
$2	1	1	2
$1	2	2	4
$0.30	3	2	5
$0	3	2	5

[5] This concept, called *diminishing marginal utility*, is explained in greater detail in Chapter 4.
[6] Of course, you are unlikely to need to pay $5 for a can of tuna, but the demand curve describes the most you would pay if you had to, not what you must or do pay.

thing that's worth $5. At a price of $1 or less, you would buy the second can, which is worth $1 to you, and if the price were 30 cents or less, you would buy 3 cans but no more.

The market demand curve is found by adding up the quantities demanded by all individuals in the market at each price. Suppose I would be willing to pay up to $3 for my first can of tuna fish, $1 for a second, and nothing for a third, and that you and I are the only consumers in the tuna fish market. The table on page 21 illustrates the demand schedules for you, me, and the market. The quantity demanded in the market would be 1 can at a price of $5 because at that price you would demand your first can. At $3 the market demand would increase to a quantity of 2 because I would buy my first can at that price. The quantity demanded would increase to 4 at a price of $1 because each of us would buy our second can if the price fell to $1. At a price of 30 cents the market demand would increase to 5. After that point, neither of us would purchase another can of tuna fish at any price. Thus, the market demand curve falls to a height of 0 after the quantity of 5.

Because the demand curve reflects consumers' willingness to pay for each additional unit of a good or service, the curve will shift upward and to the right, as from the solid demand curve to the dotted demand curve in the figure, when the willingness to pay increases. This could result from

■ a change in income

■ a successful advertising campaign

■ expectations of an upcoming increase in prices

■ an increase in the price of substitutes, such as peanut butter and jelly

■ a decrease in the price of complementary goods, such as bread

■ an increase in the number of tuna fish consumers

The opposite of these changes would cause the demand curve to shift downward and to the left. The effect of a change in income depends on the type of good in question. A *normal good* is one that consumers buy more of when their incomes increase, and an *inferior good* is one that consumers buy less of when incomes increase. Whether a good is normal or inferior depends on individual preferences. For some people, tuna fish might be a normal good. Other people might buy more steak and less tuna fish when their incomes increase, so for them steak would be normal and tuna fish would be inferior. Other examples of goods that are inferior for some people include secondhand clothing, rides on public buses, store-brand soda, and Spam. After an increase in income, the demand curves for normal goods shift upward and to the right and the demand curves for inferior goods shift downward and to the left. Again, the opposite is also true.

The Marriage of Supply and Demand
Referring to the figure, note that the supply and demand curves reside on the same graph, with the price per unit measured on the vertical axis and the quantity of a particular good measured on the horizontal axis. Supply and demand meet at the equi-

librium point, which is so named because it represents a balance between the quantity demanded and the quantity supplied. The price directly to the left of the equilibrium point is the equilibrium price, and the quantity directly below the equilibrium point is the equilibrium quantity. If the price is initially set *above* the equilibrium price, the quantity supplied will exceed the quantity demanded, and the resulting surplus will lead suppliers to lower their price. If the price begins *below* the equilibrium price, the quantity demanded will exceed the quantity supplied, and the resulting shortage will motivate an increase in the price. Thus, we expect the price to reach the equilibrium level and stay there until there is a shift in either the supply curve or the demand curve. With knowledge of a shift in one of the curves, we can learn how price and quantity are affected by drawing the shift and comparing the new and old equilibrium points.

Now we are equipped to explain the happenings in the spice and coffee markets of the past and present. In the sixteenth century, the supply of cinnamon in Europe was very small. Because quantities are measured on the horizontal axis and the smallest quantities are farthest to the left, we represent a relatively small supply with the solid "smaller supply" curve on the left side of the graph. Suppose demand is represented by the solid "smaller demand" curve. To discover the influence of supply fluctuations on price, we compare the price level (height) at the initial equilibrium of the solid supply and demand curves and at equilibrium point *C* at the intersection of the dotted "larger supply" curve and the solid demand curve. With limited supply, the price is higher, which helps to explain the high equilibrium price fetched by cinnamon and other spices imported by Europeans 500 years ago. The supply of spices to Europe and America increased dramatically after Columbus, Magellan, and other explorers established faster and safer trade routes to Asia. As more and more ships brought spices to Western shores, the supply curve shifted from left to right and the equilibrium price fell.

THE COFFEE CRISIS

In the spice example, we left the demand curve unchanged, but to examine recent activity in the coffee market, we must consider the effect on prices of changes in demand. Starting again at the equilibrium of the solid demand and supply curves in the figure, an increase in the popularity of coffee shifts the demand curve to the right. This demand shift indicates that people are willing to buy more coffee at any given price. What happens to the equilibrium price as a result of this increase in demand? It rises to the level of equilibrium point *A,* and higher prices entice an increase in the quantity of coffee supplied. Note that the change in demand has not affected the cost of producing coffee, which depends on input costs rather than demand, so the supply curve does not shift. Point *A* is on the same supply curve that we started with, but the price has risen because the demand curve shifted outward.

Today, U.S. consumers demand roughly $1.3 trillion worth of imported goods annually. The United States is the largest importer of coffee, which, after oil, is the most traded commodity in the world. More than 400 billion cups of coffee are consumed worldwide each year. But as increasing demand led Starbucks, Inc., to open 5,700 new retail outlets during the past 5 years, the price of coffee beans declined by half. Let's examine the paradox of coffee prices in the context of supply and demand.

In the 1980s, coffee sold for about $1.20 per pound on the world market. This price provided healthy profits for coffee growers and led to a rapid expansion in the allocation of land to coffee farming in countries such as Vietnam and Brazil. The fruits of these plantings became available in the 1990s. Although coffee demand was robust during that period, supply increased by even more than demand. The dotted curves in the figure represent the larger demand and the much larger supply of coffee experienced in the 1990s. An increase in demand lifts prices, but an increase in supply lowers them, and the downward effect on prices was dominant. Despite the large demand, prices were depressed by the overarching supply glut.

In the early 2000s, coffee prices languished at about 50 cents a pound, a 100-year low when adjusted for inflation. Unfortunately for farmers, it is difficult to switch abruptly from growing coffee to cultivating some other, faster-growing crop. With millions of farmers committed to coffee production, the supply was slow to decline in response to the depressed prices. During the past decade the glut of coffee has impoverished some 25 million farmers in 50 countries.[7] In 2004, the level of world coffee production finally fell, and prices crept up to about 60 cents per pound. This supply response may mark the beginning of the end of the coffee crisis.

CONCLUSION

Supply is determined by the marginal cost of production, which generally increases with quantity. Demand is determined by marginal benefit, which tends to fall as quantity increases. The price-setting teamwork of supply and demand, along with the predominant influence of a large supply of coffee beans, explains why coffee prices are low despite the long lines at Starbucks. Similar paradoxes abound. Why are essentials, such as food and water, inexpensive, whereas nonessential jewels and professional ball players command lofty prices? The answer lies in the abundant supply of food and water and the limited availability of jewels and great ball players. Sometimes it is the demand side of the price-setting duo that is neglected. Struggles to combat high oil prices have focused on the supply side—seeking new sources, asking oil-rich countries to increase production, and tapping into the Strategic Petroleum Reserve.[8] A decrease in the demand for oil would also lower prices, but fuel-economy standards for cars have remained unchanged since 1990. Whether trying to explain, predict, or influence prices, keep in mind that supply and demand work together to determine price and that both are available to be influenced by policy.

[7]See, for example, www.oxfamamerica.org/newsandpublications/press_releases/archive2004/press_release.2004-09-16.0588754646.
[8]The Strategic Petroleum Reserve is a collection of more than 700 million barrels of oil for use primarily in emergencies. After Hurricane Katrina knocked out many oil-pumping and refining operations in the Gulf of Mexico in 2005, President George W. Bush authorized the sale of 30 million barrels from the Strategic Petroleum Reserve to avoid price spikes at the pump.

DISCUSSION STARTERS

1. In Chapter 2, I explained that in 2005 Toyota doubled the supply of Priuses, and yet people were paying higher prices than ever for those cars. Using a supply-and-demand graph, explain how an increase in price can accompany an increase in supply.

2. As your income increases, what do you think will happen to your demand curve for Folgers coffee? What will happen to your demand curve for Starbucks coffee? Are these goods, therefore, normal or inferior?

3. How do you think Magellan's discoveries affected the market demand curve for spices? What do you think is the main reason for any change in the market demand curve for cinnamon during the past 500 years?

4. An organization called TransFair certifies a "fair trade" designation for coffee beans purchased at a wholesale price of $1.26 or more per pound. What do you think would happen to the quantity of coffee beans supplied and demanded if the government mandated a minimum wholesale price of $1.26 for all coffee bean purchases?

CHAPTER 4

WHY WAS THE GREAT NEWSPAPER HEIST SO EASY?
Diminishing Marginal Utility and the Price Elasticity of Demand

In the 1980s, members of a fraternity at Michigan State University allegedly tied a pledge to a flagpole and slung mud on him. When the school newspaper published an unflattering photograph of the incident, thousands of copies of the newspaper went missing from distribution sites across campus. Someone had stolen the papers in an effort to keep the photo from being seen. Why had this theft been so easy? Sodas and candy bars cost as much as newspapers, but candy vending machines have elaborate mechanisms to prevent the removal of more than 1 item at a time. In contrast, newspaper vending machines allow the entire stack of papers to be taken after only 1 has been purchased, and school newspapers are often set out for free with little fear that someone will take the whole pile. This chapter explains how differing demands for various goods shape public policy and pricing decisions, as well as the design of vending machines. (By the way, even when theft is easy, crime doesn't pay: The great newspaper heist caught the attention of newspapers across the country, and the photo of the dirty deed was republished from coast to coast for millions to see.)

THE MEANING OF LIFE

Economics has been called the dismal science,[1] but it is really about the meaning of life. The Dalai Lama, exiled Tibetan leader and winner of the 1989 Nobel Peace Prize, writes in *The Meaning of Life* (2000, p. 29) that "it is a fact that everybody wants happiness." The demand curve is simply a reflection of what makes us happy. The happier something makes us, the more we would be willing to exchange for it and the higher is our demand for it. Other things being equal, relatively high demand boosts prices and spurs suppliers to provide more of what pleases us. This chapter explains the demand curve's foundation in measures of happiness and some of the reasons for the demand curve's importance.

There is no obvious measure of happiness. The benefits that consumers receive from goods and services could be measured, for example, in terms of giggles, goose bumps, satisfaction points, or smiles. Economists measure happiness in terms of *utility*, which they measure in units called *utils*. In agreement with the Dalai Lama, economists assume that human nature guides individuals to seek happiness. In economic terminology, the quest to be as happy as possible means that it is better to have more utils than fewer and that we make decisions with the goal of maximizing our utility.

The sources of utility are subjective and result from personal tastes and preferences. Some people like sushi; others like their fish cooked. Some people like to shoot wild animals with cameras; others prefer to use rifles. These differences and the arbitrary nature of utility measurement make interpersonal utility comparisons impossible because there is no concrete gauge for such comparisons. You might report a gain of 100 utils from a day at the Five Flags theme park, whereas I reported a gain of 1,000 utils, but who is to say that I really gained more happiness than you did? Fortunately, the simple fact that more utils are better is sufficient in many important areas of economic analysis, some of which this chapter explores.

The additional utility gained from 1 more unit of a good is called the *marginal utility* of that good. According to the *"law" of diminishing marginal utility,* each additional unit of a good or service consumed provides less happiness—that is, fewer utils—than the 1 before it. This law explains the demand curve's negative slope. You learned in Chapter 3 that the height of the demand curve at each quantity indicates the most that consumers would be willing to pay for 1 more unit of the good. The demand curve's height at quantities of 1, 4, and 17, for example, is thus the number of dollars worth of marginal utility that the 1st, 4th, and 17th units provide. The height of an individual's demand curve decreases because the utility from 1 more unit decreases as more units are consumed. As explained in Chapter 3, the market demand is simply the sum of each individual's demand, so it, too, takes its negative slope from diminishing marginal utility.

EXAMPLES OF MARGINAL UTILITY AND DEMAND

Variations in the marginal utility of goods yield a varied crop of demand curves. A dollar will get you a soda or a can of soup, but the average American purchases 19 cans

---

[1] See www.econlib.org/LIBRARY/Columns/LevyPeartdismal.html.

of soda and only 1 can of soup per week.[2] For a typical consumer of refrigerators, the marginal utility (and, therefore, demand) starts relatively high and plummets after a quantity of 1. Thus, owners of a good refrigerator are unlikely to respond to even the deepest discounts in refrigerator prices. For candy bars, marginal utility and demand typically begin low and fall gradually as more bars are consumed, depending on the sweet tooth of the consumer. The characteristic demand for these goods explains why you'll see "buy one, get one free" sales on Rolo's chocolates and RC Colas but not on refrigerators: The marginal utility of the second fridge doesn't warrant the promotion.

The marginal utility of newspapers is similar to that of refrigerators but lower. Your first copy of the daily newspaper provides the latest information on current events, entertainment, sports, and any storms that are brewing. All this gives the first newspaper considerable marginal utility. Consequently, millions of people buy subscriptions to newspapers. For example, about 1.8 million people pay $200 a year to subscribe to the *Wall Street Journal*. Here's the twist: The average U.S. citizen consumes 49.2 gallons of soft drinks, 67 pounds of poultry, and 12,406 kilowatt-hours of electricity in a year, but have you ever heard of anyone with more than one subscription to the same newspaper? Unless you're an art teacher in the midst of a large papier mâché project or the owner of a new puppy, the marginal utility of a second newspaper is minuscule. Although there might be some benefit from selling or giving extra papers to others, the marginal utility of a second paper is usually so low that newspaper vending machines can give customers access to the entire box of papers without creating great losses. Many school papers are stacked around campus with no supervision—a strategy that works because of a lack of interest in obtaining multiple copies.

Suppose the value of your marginal utility from today's newspaper drops from $3 for the first newspaper to 0 for the second. This precipitous drop in marginal utility means that the quantity of papers demanded is unlikely to change when the price changes. A change from one price above $3 to another price above $3 would not trigger a purchase because both prices exceed a newspaper's value to you. A change from one price below $3 to another price below $3 would not cause you to buy another newspaper because you don't want a second paper at any price. Only if the price changed from above $3 to below $3 would any change take place: You would then make your first purchase. Once you've shelled out the cash to open the box and gain access to the newspapers, you have no interest in a second copy.

When the value of multiple copies increases as the result of, say, a desire to protest or cover up a story, newspapers are especially vulnerable to large-scale thievery. On the day the *Crimson White*, the student newspaper of the University of Alabama at Tuscaloosa, reported the firing of the head football coach for expenditures at a strip club, about 1,500 copies were stolen. After an article in the *Michigan Journal* reported that four fraternity members had been found in possession of alcohol and marijuana, 1,400 copies of the paper were stolen. Across the country, liberal and conservative groups have accused each other of stealing thousands of newspapers to suppress the "truth." Politics aside, the truth is that potential embarrassment breeds consumers who suddenly place a whole lot more value on a stack of identical newspapers.

---

[2] See www.bottledwater.org/public/InfoForRepNatFactSheettest.htm and www.campbellsoupcompany.com/atw_usa.asp?cpovisq=.

PRICE ELASTICITY OF DEMAND

The rate at which marginal utility falls as the quantity of a good rises determines other information critical to economists and businesses: consumers' sensitivity to price changes. The level of this sensitivity helps determine whether a price hike will cause many customers to leave or profits to leap. Economists call the sensitivity of quantity demanded to price changes the *price elasticity of demand*. If you buy a lot more movie DVDs when the price goes down a little, and a lot fewer when the price goes up, your demand for DVDs is relatively elastic. If you persist in purchasing only 1 cell phone when the price goes up or down, your demand for cell phones is inelastic. To be precise, the value of the price elasticity of demand is

$$\frac{\text{percentage change in quantity demanded}}{\text{percentage change in price.}}$$

Consider a few real-world examples: A 10 percent increase in the price of coffee leads to about a 2.5 percent decrease in the quantity demanded, so coffee has a price elasticity of 2.5/10, or 0.25.[3] A 10 percent increase in the price of restaurant meals leads to about a 23 percent decrease in the quantity demanded, so the price elasticity of restaurant meals is 23/10, or 2.3. When coffee and other goods have a price elasticity between 0 and 1, demand for them is described as *inelastic* because it is not particularly sensitive to price changes. When restaurant meals and other purchases have a price elasticity greater than 1, demand for them is described as *elastic* because it is highly sensitive to price changes.

Don't make the common mistake of confusing elasticity with the slope of the demand curve. At a given quantity and price, a steep demand curve is less elastic than a relatively flat demand curve, but there's more to elasticity than slope. The slope of the demand curve is found by dividing the change in price by the change in quantity; elasticity is found by dividing the percentage change in quantity by the percentage change in price. A straight demand curve with a constant slope has a different elasticity at every point because, even though price and quantity are changing at a constant rate, the *percentage* changes in price and quantity are not constant. For example, an increase in quantity from 100 to 101 represents a 1 percent increase in quantity, whereas an equivalent increase in quantity by 1 from 10 to 11 represents a 10 percent increase in quantity. Thus, moving rightward along a straight demand curve, the slope stays the same but elasticity decreases as the percentage change in quantity falls and the percentage change in price rises.

In general, the quantity demanded is more responsive to price changes, and, therefore, more elastic, for goods and services that

- have many substitutes
- are not essential to daily life
- require a large share of our wealth
- can be purchased at a later time

---

[3] Because the price change is negative and the quantity change is positive, the price elasticity is actually a negative number. However, for simplicity, most economists discuss elasticities in *absolute value* terms, meaning that the negative signs are removed.

The opposite is also true: Goods and services have a relatively inelastic demand when they have few substitutes, are necessities, require a small share of our wealth, or must be purchased without delay.

Consider the price elasticity of demand for taxi rides in New York City and for the *New York Times*. Substitutes for taxis include buses, subways, bikes, and feet. Many New Yorkers don't own cars, getting around just fine with alternative forms of transportation and considering it a luxury to hire a taxi. A taxi ride from one borough of New York to another can easily cost $20 or more. It's common for visitors to take taxis from the airport to their hotels but then to take mass transit or walk to places such as Central Park, Ground Zero, and Wall Street. It's not that the marginal utility of another taxi ride is 0, but the fare exceeds their willingness to pay for a second ride. When demand is elastic, consumers are on a thin margin between buying more and not buying more. Minor temperature fluctuations or a bit of rain can make the critical difference in the marginal utility of a taxi ride, and available taxis become a rarity in extreme weather. When New York City taxi fares increased by 25 percent in 2004, riders spoke of switching to public transportation for borderline situations, such as nonemergency doctor visits and dinners with married ex-girlfriends. (I'm not making this up; see http://www.nymetro.com/nymetro/urban/features/taxi/n_20286/.)

In contrast, the *New York Times* faces a relatively inelastic demand. The steep drop-off in marginal utility that occurs after the 1st newspaper is bought prevents more copies from being sold to existing customers as prices fall, and the price is low enough that modest price fluctuations involve only a small fraction of most people's income. Indeed, when the daily *New York Times* raised its newsstand price by 33 percent to $1 in 2003, circulation hardly budged.

THE DEMAND FOR HEART SURGERY AND SIN

Talk-show host David Letterman had heart bypass surgery in 2000, as did former president Bill Clinton in 2004. In a way, the demand for open-heart surgery is similar to that for newspapers: Most people don't need more than 1, although those who require surgery would be willing to pay a lot more than $3 to get it. The marginal benefit of necessary surgery is life, and most people would pay whatever they could beg, borrow, or steal to get that benefit. Heart bypass surgery costs about $50,000. Cancer treatment can cost $100,000 or more, and a bone marrow transplant can cost $500,000. For anyone who would pay everything possible to stay alive, the demand curve for these treatments is vertical at the quantity needed for survival, up to the maximum amount of funds that the person can obtain through all means.

The demand for lifesaving surgery is inelastic because it is a necessity. Addiction can create a perceived necessity for drugs. Without discounting the deadly repercussions of illegal drug use, economists, including Nobel laureate Milton Friedman, have used the concepts of supply and demand to argue for drug control via legalization. The legalization of drugs would increase the supply and cause the price to fall, but if the demand curve for drugs were vertical at the quantity users needed for their fixes, the quantity consumed would not change as prices changed. Lower prices would reduce profits for drug sellers and cut back on sellers' incentives to get people hooked on their products with free samples and other aggressive marketing techniques. This could result in fewer people becoming addicted while allowing taxation and more effective regulation. Similar arguments have been made for the legalization of prostitution, as has occurred in Germany, Sweden, and most of Nevada. Opponents argue that legalization can increase the demand by attracting consumers who don't currently use drugs or prostitutes out of respect for the law. Whichever side is right, the demand curve is at the crux of the issue.

The debates about legalizing drugs and prostitution are among many policy controversies that revolve around demand. Suppose we want to reduce drinking or smoking by imposing so-called sin taxes on alcohol or tobacco. Taxes lead to higher prices, but higher prices may or may not lead to substantially lower consumption levels, depending on the elasticity of demand. Studies suggest that a 10 percent increase in price leads, on average, to roughly a 4 percent decrease in the number of cigarettes smoked and a 3 percent decrease in the amount of beer consumed. From these numbers, it appears that sin taxes wouldn't take a large bite out of drinking and smoking unless the tax rate were enormous. However, these habits are usually begun at a young age when expenditures on alcohol and tobacco make up a relatively large portion of the consumers' incomes, and, therefore, demand for the products is more elastic. For example, the price elasticity of demand for young smokers is about 3 times that for the average smoker. Demand is also more elastic in the preaddiction phase of consumption because there is no perceived need for a certain minimum quantity, or "fix."

The price elasticity of demand is critical to the pricing decisions of firms. If demand is inelastic, more revenue is gained by raising prices because the quantity demanded decreases proportionately less than the price increase. Suppose a baker selling 100 loaves of bread per day for $1 per loaf could double her prices and lose only one-quarter of her business. Rather than receiving $1 × 100 = $100 per day in revenues, she would receive $2 × 75 = $150. With larger revenues and fewer goods to produce, the firm will certainly earn higher profits. Thus, a firm should raise prices whenever the demand for its product is inelastic. Analysts predicted that, because the demand for newspapers is inelastic, the increase in the price of the *New York Times* that was discussed in an earlier section would increase revenues by more than $5 million a year.

If demand is elastic, a higher price will result in lower revenues because demand decreases proportionately more than the price increase. In this case profits might increase or decrease, depending on whether the reduction in costs (thanks to decreased production) is larger or smaller than the reduction in revenues. For example, an increase in the price of pizza that decreased revenues by $1,000 but, because fewer pizzas were made, decreased costs by $1,200 would provide a net increase in profits of $200. In Part 7 (Chapters 13 and 14), we'll see how the relatively inelastic demand that monopolies face allows them to charge higher prices and results in lower quantities than would be produced in competitive markets.

CONCLUSION

Your study of the underpinnings of demand will help you determine what shifts and shapes demand curves. Given the imminent relevance of this knowledge to you as a future policymaker, businessperson, or economics test taker, let's review it.

Diminishing marginal utility is the reason for the negative slope of the demand curve. As you get more of something, you generally receive less utility from the last unit received, and you are, therefore, willing to pay less for additional units, as indicated by the decreasing height of your individual demand curve. Because the market demand curve is the sum of all the individual demand curves, its shape, too, is dictated by diminishing marginal utility.

The price elasticity of demand measures the responsiveness of quantity demanded to price. Formally, price elasticity is the percentage change in quantity demanded divided by the percentage change in price. The sharp drop-off in the marginal utility of newspapers and refrigerators, for example, makes their demand curves relatively steep and unresponsive to price changes (inelastic). The gradual decline in the marginal utility of candy bars and sodas makes their demand curves relatively flat and sensitive to price changes (elastic). The elasticity of demand influences the effect of taxes on quantities purchased, the likely result of legalizing marijuana or prostitution, the wisdom of raising product prices, and the differing optimal designs for candy and newspaper vending machines (unless the news stories have raised enough dander to warrant mass theft!). These are among the important implications of supply and demand. Chapter 5 explains that these concepts apply to things even more important than money.

DISCUSSION STARTERS

1. How would you characterize the demand for illegal drugs among your friends? Is that demand (or lack thereof) determined by the fact that the drugs are illegal? What implications does this have for the government's drug enforcement policy?

2. What are some other examples of goods with relatively high and relatively low price elasticity of demand?

3. Summarize in your own words the links among diminishing marginal utility, demand, and elasticity.

4. Explain whether you would expect the demand for the following goods to be elastic or inelastic and why: software programs, cameras, notebook paper, peaches, textbooks, Thanksgiving turkeys, all carbonated beverages, A & W root beer.

CHAPTER 5

HOW CAN ECONOMICS INFLUENCE YOUR CHOICE OF A SPOUSE?

Supply, Demand, and Price Signals in
the Marriage Market

It's an age-old story, as sung by Emile in Richard Rodgers and Oscar Hammerstein's musical *South Pacific*:

> Some enchanted evening you may see a stranger . . . and somehow you know, you know even then, that somewhere you'll see her again and again. Who can explain it?

Marcellus in Meredith Willson's *The Music Man* thinks he can explain a thing or two about attraction. He sees kissing on a first or second date as a signal of low standards,

> But a woman who waits 'til the third time around . . . She's the girl he's glad he's found. . . . The girl who's hard to get!

Marcellus has a point, and it applies equally to men and women. As in markets for goods and services in which rare stuffed animals and exclusive doctors are prized, judgments about whom to pursue may rest on signals of quality, such as how hard people are to attract. That is the crux of the social price theory, as explained in this chapter, which considers marriage through an economic (but human) lens.

MARKETS AND MARRIAGE

It may surprise you to learn that marriage is the topic of dozens of important economics articles. However, economics isn't only about money; economics is also about scarcity, choice, and utility maximization, and marriage has much to do with all of these concerns. Nobel Prize–winning economist Gary Becker wrote an entire book, *A Treatise on the Family* (1981), about the economics of marriage and families. Remember that economists model markets, and a *market* is any mechanism or institution that brings buyers together with sellers. Ninety-five percent of Americans marry, so most of us become buyers and sellers of marital partners at some point. The *marriage market* is simply the mechanism that brings us together.

The marriage market is a valuable case study because it exemplifies three seldom-recognized characteristics of markets. First, not all markets have a fixed location. Many products, from Girl Scout cookies to illegal drugs, are bought and sold far from "bricks-and-mortar" stores, and the Internet brings markets for virtually everything right into your home. Likewise, the marriage market is alive and well in residence halls, nightclubs, churches, and workplaces.

Second, markets don't necessarily involve money. Tickets for a taping of *The Tonight Show* have no monetary cost, but successful consumers pay the high price of waiting in long lines early in the morning. The price of dining at all-you-can-eat buffets can include indigestion in addition to dollars, and the price of a stolen car can include prison time. When making decisions, it is perfectly rational for consumers to consider such factors as risk, health effects, time spent, and opportunities lost in addition to monetary prices. In the game of love, some potential partners are easier to attract than others, and the time and effort that go into relationships are relevant parts of the price paid by participants in the market for companionship.

Third, markets assist consumers in dealing with uncertainty. When you're shopping for items such as scarves, paintings, and dictionaries, what you see is what you get. Uncertainty creeps in, however, when you're looking for a quart of ice cream, a physician, or a bottle of wine. From the outside, consumers may not know the inner qualities of the products and services: Is the ice cream made with high-quality ingredients? How skilled is the doctor? How superb is the wine? In a market economy, prices can be critical indicators of information that is otherwise unavailable. Decisions to buy and sell products are guided by prices, which reflect both the value of goods to society and the cost of providing those goods. High prices spur producers to make what society most wants. This chapter focuses on how prices can signal quality in the absence of better information.

THE UNCERTAINTIES OF LABOR AND OF LOVE

Consider the pairing of an employer and an employee in the labor market. Some aspects of a potential work relationship are clear from the beginning. Job candidates can usually find out about salary, working conditions, and the prospects for promotion. For employers, a résumé and an interview typically provide glimpses into the suitability of a prospective employee. Both sides must wonder whether a more suitable match could be made with further searching, and each must grapple with uncertainty about commitment from, and compatibility with, the other.

Participants in the marriage market face the same ambiguity about the marginal benefit of additional search efforts. Uncertainty regarding commitment and compatibility is of even greater concern in the marriage market than in the labor market because, if a better candidate comes along after a spouse is chosen, the situation cannot be remedied simply by saying, "I quit" or "You're fired." Further, the gains from marriage depend on offerings that are less certain than a salary offer, such as affection, parenting skills, fidelity, ambition, patience, and other things that are difficult to predict on the basis of promises or appearance. For these reasons, the estimation of unknown qualities is central to the search for a spouse.

This is the information age, and we don't like to be uninformed, particularly about someone we might hire or wed. A majority of employers now require drug tests, and a growing number are performing criminal background checks on job applicants. In extreme cases, people hire detectives to track a prospective spouse's history and current behavior. A matchmaking service in Boca Raton, Florida, advertised that a client's potential spouse would be scrutinized by an "independent worldwide investigation company," by psychologists, by an astrologer, and by a handwriting analyst to boot. Such information seeking isn't usually so intense, but some degree of inquiry is a natural part of the market process for goods with high prices and uncertain value.

THE ROLE OF PRICES

Searching for a marriage partner involves making a decision about whether to pursue a relationship on the basis of an initially meager number of signals. As in the choice of a doctor, a college, or a bottle of wine under uncertainty, consumers seek indicators of the relative value of the available alternatives. Suppose your boss asked you to buy an outstanding bottle of wine to impress a new client, and you didn't know much about the choices. To pick a winner, you might look at the bottles, survey the knowledge and opinions of friends, look into the reputations of various vineyards, and sample a few vintages. You would probably also use price as a guide.

Prices embody information about the value of goods to unseen individuals in the market, they reflect expected returns on investments, and they lead individuals toward optimal choices regarding resource allocation. Chapter 3 explained how price is determined by the intersection of supply and demand. A high price indicates that demand for the product is high, supply is low, or both.

If substitute goods have similar supply curves[1] and differing prices, these price differences indicate different levels of demand. Relatively high demand and correspondingly high prices reflect interest from informed consumers and provide a valuable basis for judging quality. If the demand for one doctor allows her to successfully charge $80 per physical, whereas another can charge only $50, other things being equal, the doctor with the higher demand is probably doing a better job of satisfying her patients. Differences in demand also help explain why some universities can charge more than $40,000 in tuition, whereas others cannot.

When it is impossible to learn everything about a good or service before making a commitment to buy it, the price may serve as the best possible, and sometimes the only, gauge of quality. This is the case even when the price involves more than money. For example, the price of a school, a doctor, and a bottle of wine includes admissions standards, the length of the waiting list, and the availability of a particular wine, re-

---

[1]Chapter 3 explained that supply curves indicate the additional cost of providing more of a good or service, so goods with similar supply curves require similar costs of production.

spectively, in addition to the monetary price. A good student can satisfy higher admissions standards and thus gain admission into better schools. If a student is accepted immediately into 1 school and placed on a waiting list for admission to another school of similar size, the student is getting an important signal regarding the quality of the 2 schools.

SOCIAL PRICE

Before we plunge into the marriage market, please understand that the economic analysis of marriage need not be dehumanizing. The benefits that economists assume we seek from marriage have little to do with cold, hard cash. Instead, they consist of love, compassion, self-esteem, companionship, and other genuine reasons for marriage. Subjecting the institution of marriage to market analysis simply permits a better understanding of typical human behavior.

What does it take to win someone's heart? For some people the answer may involve money, but for many, successful courtship has more to do with things such as kindness, intellect, humor, romantic gestures, appearance, and the ability to contribute to a happy marriage. People being courted must decide what efforts and qualities will win them over; such a standard for successful courtship has been called a *social price*. As extremes, someone with high standards has a high social price; someone who acts desperate has a low social price.

When the supply of a good is fixed, as is the case for a college with fixed enrollment, an actor such as Johnny Depp, an athlete such as Mia Hamm, or a marital prospect, the supply curve is vertical at the quantity available. No matter how many directors want Johnny Depp to act for them today, only 1 day's performance can be supplied, so his supply curve is a vertical line at the quantity of 1. When the supply curve is vertical, supply is the same regardless of price, so the level of demand determines the price that can be charged. When it comes time to charge tuition or negotiate salary, colleges, actors, and athletes use information on their value to consumers to anticipate demand and establish the appropriate price. The trick is to receive the highest payment possible without asking too much, which would put a damper on interest. Likewise, individuals use knowledge of their own abilities and potential to set the social prices they expect from suitors.

Sometimes another person, such as a parent, does know an individual's prospects better than the individual does. That person is likely to set a *price floor* (a minimum price) for the individual until age and maturity allow a better personal assessment. Imagine teenager Terri announcing to her parents that she intends to begin a relationship with inferior Ivan. Terri's parents are likely to forbid her to see Ivan because, they decide, she has set her social price too low by hanging out with an unworthy suitor.

As with the prices of goods and the salaries of workers, the social prices of individuals are bid up or down by high or low demand. In other words, the social prices of individuals will rise and fall with their popularity, as determined by friends who know the individuals well and by the relative scarcity of other individuals with comparable qualities.

Economists use the term *marital income* to describe the gains from marriage. *Marital income* encompasses all the real-world reasons for getting married, such as opportunities for laughter, home-cooked meals, children, cozy late-night conversations, and help taking the dog out on cold winter mornings. An individual's contribution to marital income is determined by such things as his or her self-discipline, intentions, moral standards, prospects, plans, inner strength, experience, and prior successes. Potential mates pay the resulting social price via courting efforts and, in some cases, prenuptial agreements. As part of her social price and as a means of reducing uncertainty associated with her third selection of a spouse, superstar Jennifer Lopez required actor Ben Affleck to sign a contract indicating he would receive none of her wealth on divorce, and if a divorce involved cheating on his part, she would receive one-half of his wealth.

As with doctors, schools, and wines, potential mates exhibit only a fraction of their promise through observable traits. Social prices provide additional clues to the marital income that would follow from prospective pairings. Social prices are not monetary in most societies.[2] Instead, an individual's social price is reflected in the ease with which he or she can be courted. Depending on the context, social price could be conveyed by the amount of eye contact made, the receptiveness to initial dating propositions, popularity in desirable social circles, or the interval of time before sexual intimacy is accorded. Among individuals with similar outward traits, a marriage market participant with imperfect information is likely to expect greater marital income from prospects with higher social prices. In other words, Marcellus of *The Music Man* was right about us prizing those who are hard to get.

Skeptical about the workings of the marriage market as expressed here? Consider some of the rationality behind the use of social prices:

- After attracting a potential mate easily, a searcher could reason that by putting forth more effort, he or she could attain an even higher quality mate.

- On observing that a candidate has a low social price, a searcher may assume the existence of unobserved traits that make it impossible for this candidate to maintain higher standards. The extreme case would be a desperate individual with a social price near 0.

- Included in marital income is a sense of accomplishment. Someone who requires little courting effort makes for a less exciting search and a less prized catch.

- Unrealistic prospects will have prohibitively high standards, meaning that they are uninterested and the searcher can't afford their social price.

- Having more men than women results in relatively more competition among men and, therefore, relatively high social prices for women, whereas having more women than men increases competition and social prices for men. For example, in New York City and Washington, DC, a dearth of eligible men intensifies women's efforts to find suitable mates, whereas in China, Alaska, and some rural areas of the United States, disproportionately low numbers of women result in greater competition among men for marriage partners.

---

[2]Bride payments called *dowries* are still common in some parts of the world. See http://www.infoplease.com/spot/dowries1.html.

MARITAL SEARCH STRATEGIES

It would be an understatement to say that uncertainties inherent in the marriage market lead to considerable frustration. Some discouraged searchers resort to the strategies of traditional markets, including newspaper advertising and large expenditures of money. Marriage brokers make fortunes with promises to facilitate the search process, sometimes with tragic consequences. In 2003, U.S. Senator Maria Cantwell introduced the International Marriage Broker Regulation Act to oversee the many brokers operating in the United States and to prevent the trafficking and abuse of vulnerable women.[3]

Thousands of marital searchers have turned to classified ads, or "personals," to seek spouses. Experimentation with personal messages in mock ads supports the social price theory. When about 100 students at Centre College were shown personal ads and asked with whom they would most like to pursue a marital relationship, the most alluring ads were those that expressed high social prices with statements such as "I only go out with people who treat me well." Those exhibiting a low social price with lines such as "I'm having a hard time finding a date" received less interest.

Fee-based matchmaking services are exploding on the Internet, and some consumers are willing to pay $50,000 or more to matchmakers, one of whom was accused in 2004 of defrauding single women out of $2.8 million. Given the economics of the marriage market, searchers themselves may be tempted into fraud as well. Knowing that social prices are important in the evaluation of potential mates, some individuals appear to have incentives to overstate their social prices. This might work initially, but it is not a successful long-term approach. As in the search for doctors, colleges, and wine, in time, each participant in a relationship begins to see the same predictors of unseen traits—signs of initiative, inner strength, aspirations, and success rates in achieving goals—that the other has used to set a social price. Personal appraisal gradually replaces the importance of price signals and corrects for misrepresentation of social price. The inevitability of the truth coming out, the availability of divorce, and the costs of repeated searches make deception an unwise and inefficient strategy.[4]

CONCLUSION

Markets can exist virtually anywhere and, although money may not be involved, almost everything has a price. Uncertainty rears its ugly head when looks can be deceiving, as with schools, workers, and bottled spirits, but markets offer assistance. For a given supply, a relatively high price indicates a high demand from those who know the product. High prices provide a signal for suppliers to produce more when possible, and a supplier's ability to charge high prices is an indication of quality to consumers.

Related uncertainty exists in the market for spouses. Marital searchers, as if choosing a fine wine, look to the wealth of information that is embodied in prices. Although

[3]This act was approved by the Senate Judiciary Committee in September 2005. At this writing it had not yet been voted on by the full Senate. See http://www.capaa.wa.gov/IMBR_act.html.
[4]For supporting theoretical arguments, see David A. Anderson and Shigeyuki Hamori (2000), "A Theory of Quality Signaling in the Marriage Market," *Japan and the World Economy, 12:*3, 229–242.

marital searchers have imperfect information about themselves as well as their suitors, they are the best assessors of their own aspirations and potential, and they use this knowledge to set standards for courtship and marital offers. Searchers use these standards, or social prices, to estimate unseen qualities in potential mates.

Advice to the lovelorn: Don't sell yourself short, but don't price yourself out of the market, either.

DISCUSSION STARTERS

1. What evidence can you offer to support the chapter's suggestion that a marriage market exists?

2. Do you ever use price as an indicator of quality? If you had friends call you from the hospital asking you to pick out the best cigars available to hand out in celebration of the birth of their baby, might you use price as a signal of cigar quality? Why or why not?

3. When is it wise to play hard to get? When is it unwise? What economics-related warnings should marital searchers be aware of as they play the delicate cat-and-mouse game of courtship?

4. Does it ever seem as if the people you like the most are the least attracted to you? Could this be the result of crush-related discounts in social prices? What is a remedy for this source of frustration?

5. What would happen to social prices if cultural stereotypes diminished the self-esteem of one sex and inflated that of the other? Could this explain the imbalanced distribution of marital income within some marriages?

6. Do you agree that social prices work as explained in this chapter? What are your thoughts on the marriage market as discussed here?

CHAPTER 6

IS ADAM SMITH ROLLING OVER IN HIS GRAVE?

Perfect Competition, Efficiency, and
the Father of Modern Economics

The celebrated eighteenth-century political scientist Adam Smith worshipped the workings of free markets, and his words are still quoted in support of unbridled capitalism. However, Smith's role as the patron saint of unconstrained markets may be unwarranted: Smith abhorred market power, and the market efficiency he glorified was achieved only by perfectly competitive markets that were unlike most that have ever existed in the real world. Do a few detours from Smith's market model matter? In a word, yes. And if you've seen prices that differ between gas stations or between burger joints, you've seen evidence that competition is seldom perfect. This chapter explains the splendor of markets at their best and presents some neglected truths about Adam Smith and his notion of the invisible hand.

THE BEAUTY OF PERFECTLY COMPETITIVE MARKETS

Adam Smith is often proclaimed the patriarch of modern economics. His most famous saying appeared in his 1776 book, *The Wealth of Nations*, in which he wrote that the individual decision maker

> *intends only his own gain; and he is in this, as in many other cases, led by an invisible hand to promote an end which was no part of his intention. . . . By pur-*

suing his own interest, he frequently promotes that of the society more effectually than when he really intends to promote it.[1]

The notion of the market embodying an "invisible hand" by which self-interested behavior yields socially desirable outcomes has captured the fancy of generations of economists and policymakers. As discussed in Chapter 1, efficiency is a matter of attaining the largest possible gains with the least possible waste. The efficiency of markets stems largely from desirable conditions that occur at market equilibrium, where the supply-and-demand curves intersect to establish quantity and price (see Chapter 3). Smith explained how a competitive market tends toward a price that is fair to both buyers and sellers, and that this price allocates resources as well as possible from the broad standpoint of society. At their best, markets can achieve conditions bordering on the ideal. Suppose you were a benevolent, all-knowing dictator. After eliminating war and hunger, and banishing the word *widget* from economics textbooks, you could advance the well-being of society by allocating resources to achieve three types of efficiency:

- *productive efficiency*, meaning that firms minimize the average cost of producing their goods
- *allocative efficiency*, meaning that each type of good is produced until the benefit from another unit of the good no longer exceeds the cost of producing another unit
- *distributive efficiency*, meaning that goods go to those who value them the most

Remarkably, perfectly competitive markets achieve all three of these outcomes without your help as dictator. The following sections explain how that happens.

Under conditions that resemble *pure* or *perfect competition* as Smith imagined it, a large number of sellers sell the same good to a large number of buyers. Competitors can enter and leave the market easily, and everyone involved in the market has full information about what is available from whom at what price. Under these conditions, no consumer would pay more than the lowest available price; a firm that charges more than its competitors would get no business. Firms need not charge less than the equilibrium price because they can sell all they want at the equilibrium price (by virtue of demand equaling supply at equilibrium). Thus, each firm in a perfectly competitive industry ends up as a *price taker*, taking on the equilibrium price determined by the balance of supply and demand in the market.

Consider (as a real market that provides a break from routine) the on-line market for rubber clown noses—those bright-red semispheres that fit over a real nose and make onlookers smile. There are many buyers and sellers, the noses are all pretty much the same,[2] ample information on prices and suppliers is available through a quick Internet search, and it's possible for almost anyone with access to a computer to enter or exit

---

[1] All quotes from Adam Smith's *Wealth of Nations* are from http://www.online-literature.com/adam_smith/wealth_nations/ unless otherwise noted.

[2] Assume they are the same for the purposes of this example. As with most things, you can find variations such as custom-made clown noses or foam noses, but they can be considered different products.

the Internet market.[3] Perfect competition isn't all funny business; markets for agricultural products, such as corn and sugar, also approximate the perfectly competitive model.

Productive Efficiency

Firms seek *economic profits*, calculated by subtracting all costs, including the value of entrepreneurs' time and the opportunity costs of using capital,[4] from revenues. Entrepreneurs would accept 0 economic profits if necessary because they could not earn anything more in their next-best work opportunity. For example, if your highest-paying alternative job were as a marketing manager earning $80,000 per year, you would subtract $80,000 as the value of your time when calculating economic profits in the clown nose industry. So earning 0 economic profits implies that you are covering all of your costs, *including the $80,000 opportunity cost of your time*, and you couldn't earn another cent doing anything else.

Productive efficiency is achieved in perfectly competitive markets thanks to the ease of entry and exit by similar firms seeking economic profits. If ClownAntics.com isn't using the lowest-cost methods of clown nose production, competitors, such as TheClownShop.net, will.[5] Rival firms can undercut the price charged by an inefficient firm and steal its business. If the market price for clown noses exceeds the average cost of producing them, other fully informed entrepreneurs, such as Betty at ClownCostumes.com, will be attracted to the market by the smell of profits, and the entrance of new firms will increase the supply and lower the equilibrium price. This pattern will continue until the lowest-cost process of nosemaking no longer provides economic profits. Similarly, if the market price for clown noses falls below the minimum average cost of producing them, nose sellers, such as TwinklesTheClown.com, will start going out of business. As these firms exit, supply will decrease and the equilibrium price will rise until the remaining firms are earning just enough to cover all their costs. In the long run, firms in a perfectly competitive industry will receive a price equal to their minimum average cost and will earn 0 economic profits. This situation leaves no room for the use of inefficient production methods in a perfectly competitive industry.

Allocative Efficiency

Remember that the supply curve represents the increasing marginal cost of producing each unit and that the demand curve represents the decreasing marginal value of each unit to consumers. At quantities of production below the equilibrium quantity, the demand curve is above the supply curve, indicating that the value of 1 more unit will exceed the cost. If the marginal value of another clown nose is $7 and the marginal cost is $3, more noses should be produced. However, it would be inefficient to produce beyond the equilibrium quantity because marginal value falls below marginal

[3] For example, there are 10 individual sellers and 68 "eBay stores" at www.ebay.com selling clown noses as of this writing. If you saw those stores earning worthwhile profits, you could start up a competing Internet "store" at almost no expense.
[4] For example, even if the owners of a pizza shop have purchased their pizza oven, by using it, they forgo the opportunity to rent it out to someone else. Thus, the rental rate of an oven is a cost of using it for owners and renters alike.
[5] In this reality-based book, all Web addresses are real.

cost at the point of equilibrium. If another clown nose would cost $4 to make and it would be worth only $2, it would be unwise for society to allocate resources for another nose. It follows that to produce the equilibrium quantity is to produce all those units that are worth more than they cost to provide.

Like the equilibrium quantity, the equilibrium price is established at the intersection of supply and demand, meaning that the price equals both the marginal cost and the marginal value of the last nose sold. The condition for allocative efficiency is often stated as the equality of marginal cost and price because if the price that buyers are willing to pay is above the marginal cost, consumers must value another nose at more than the cost of making one, and too few clown noses are being made. Conversely, if buyers are not willing to pay a price as high as marginal cost, marginal value is below marginal cost and too many noses have been made.

Distributive Efficiency

The well-being of society is maximized if clown noses go to those who value them the most—presumably clowns. A perfectly competitive market is up to the task of maximizing well-being. Consider a simplified market with 5 potential buyers: Abe, Ben, Clem, Dot, and Ernest, each of whom is interested in, at most, 1 clown nose. The values these clowns receive from a rubber nose are, respectively, $12, $8, $6, $3, and $1. Suppose the marginal cost of producing the first 5 clown noses is $2, $4, $6, $8, and $10, as shown in the accompanying table.[6] Three noses should be produced, because any additional noses would be valued at less than the cost of producing them.[7]

BUYER	BUYER'S MARGINAL VALUE	SELLER'S MARGINAL COST
Abe	$12	$?
Ben	$ 8	$ 4
Clem	$ 6	$ 6
Dot	$ 3	$ 8
Ernest	$ 1	$10

In our example, the equilibrium price will be $6 because that is the only price that equates supply and demand. As explained in the first section of this chapter, expect perfectly competitive firms to conform to the equilibrium price. Three of the clowns—

[6] These numbers are simply made up to comply with the law of supply (see Chapter 3), which indicates that supply curves are upward sloping as a result of increasing marginal costs. The rate at which marginal costs increase is exaggerated here for the purpose of illustration.

[7] It might be tempting to say that 4 noses should be produced because Dot would be willing to pay the $2 cost of the first nose, Clem would pay the $4 cost of the second nose, Ben would pay the $6 cost of the third nose, and Abe would pay the $8 cost of the fourth nose. Here's the catch: No matter which clowns got which noses, the cost of making the fourth nose would be $8, and the combined benefit that the clowns receive would increase by only the $3 value that Dot receives when 4 rather than 3 are made. So making a fourth nose leads to a net loss of $8 − $3 = $5. Aside from this loss of efficiency, there's also the problem that each good in a perfectly competitive market sells for the same price.

Abe, Ben, and Clem—will be willing to pay the $6 equilibrium price. Because those who place the highest value on noses are willing to pay the highest price, clown noses will be rightly allocated to true nose lovers.

In contrast, imagine that a lottery rather than a market is used to allocate 3 noses. If names are drawn out of a hat, the recipients are equally likely to be any of the 5 clowns. Suppose Ben, Dot, and Ernest win the lottery. The total value created by the noses is the sum of the recipients' marginal values: $8 + $3 + $1 = $12; this amount falls below the $12 + $8 + $6 = $26 worth of value obtained through the market allocation. In both cases the cost of producing 3 noses would be $2 + $4 + $6 = $12, but the net gain is the highest with the help of the market. Nonetheless, lotteries are common for allocating dorm rooms and student tickets for popular football games, among other valuable goods and services.

TROUBLE IN PARADISE: MARKET FAILURE AND IMMORALITY

The previous examples demonstrate how buyers and sellers can enhance the well-being of society merely by acting out of self-interest. Adam Smith marveled at the potential for markets to allocate resources efficiently without government assistance, as if they were guided by the invisible hand of a benevolent dictator. To Smith, competition was the great enforcer that held greed at bay. Should 1 merchant decide to charge an excessive price, another merchant would swiftly provide the same product for less money. This is the case under perfect competition. Those who cite Smith's work to support a more general disdain for government must be aware of two issues about which Smith is often misinterpreted: market failure and morality. This section introduces the sources of market failure, each of which is covered in a full chapter later on, and discusses the overlap between markets and morality.

Market Power Matters

> *The cruelest of our revenue laws, I will venture to affirm, are mild and gentle, in comparison to some of those which the clamor of our merchants and manufacturers has extorted from the legislature, for the support of their own absurd and oppressive monopolies.*
>
> *—Adam Smith,* The Wealth of Nations

Although Smith venerated competitive markets, he abhorred monopoly power and trade secrets. In *The Wealth of Nations*, Smith wrote of "the mean rapacity, the monopolizing spirit, of merchants and manufacturers, who neither are, nor ought to be, the rulers of mankind." The celebrated efficiency of competitive markets is jeopardized when individual sellers or buyers have *market power*, meaning that they can restrict supply and increase prices, or when any of the other conditions for perfect competition are violated.

Legal, technical, and economic barriers are among the deterrents to potential competitors in many markets, as a few examples will demonstrate. Pfizer, Inc., holds a patent on Viagra and ships the medication in bottles with radio frequency identification tags so that bottles coming from Pfizer can be distinguished from bottles coming from counterfeiters. In 2004, the De Beers Corporation, which controls much of the world's diamond industry, paid a $10 million fine and pleaded guilty to criminal price fixing. Members of cartels, such as the Organization of Petroleum Exporting Countries (OPEC), collude to reduce production and raise prices. The Recording Industry Association of America (RIAA) has sued individuals for illegally using peer-to-peer file-sharing systems to swap recordings of copyrighted songs and to distribute public-domain music that competes with music industry offerings. Advertisements showing car engines flying in pursuit of name-brand gasoline trucks and resorts that take Visa but not American Express credit cards exemplify attempts to reduce the influence of competitors via product differentiation. And in the third-largest retail merger in history, Kmart and Sears joined forces, eliminating price competition between them.

Neglected Costs and Benefits

In order for the equilibrium quantity of a good or service to be efficient, buyers and sellers must also bear, or *internalize*, the full cost and benefit of that product. Otherwise, the market equilibrium formed by the marginal costs and marginal benefits that market participants perceive differs from the true equilibrium of marginal costs and marginal benefits felt by society. Consider the following examples:

- As the Anheuser-Busch brewery makes beverages in St. Louis, it releases more than 450,000 pounds of suspected pollutants, such as hydrochloric acid, into the air in a typical year. Because beer-market participants don't bear the full health cost of these emissions, without intervention, the equilibrium quantity would be too large.

- The movie *Supersize Me* (2004) and the book *Fast Food Nation* (Schlosser, 2001) suggest that the overconsumption of fast food may cause more health problems than most consumers realize. If buyers don't have full information on the health costs associated with their food, or if some of those costs are paid by other taxpayers via Medicaid or Medicare, then the demand curve will overstate the true benefits of fast food to society and, again, the equilibrium quantity will be too large.

- If studying economics increases people's contributions to society by making them wiser voters and more productive workers, the demand curve for economics classes will understate the value of economics to society, and the equilibrium number of students will be too small.

Such benefits and costs that aren't borne by those making decisions about the products are called *externalities*. What is to be done when the assumptions of perfect competition are violated, as in these examples? Economists Richard Lipsey and Kelvin Lancaster advanced the general theory of second-best, which demonstrates that, when 1 of the conditions for perfect competition is not met, intervention to remedy the situation can lead to a better outcome than a hands-off approach, even if every other condition is met. Thus, if free markets cultivate market power, pollution, and study benefits that aren't internalized, then antitrust legislation, environmental regulations, and funding for education may be warranted to achieve the best possible situation. Do you have full information on the prices of competing doctors, restaurants, or hotels where you live and travel? If not, policies requiring the posting of prices could improve efficiency and social well-being, and such policies do exist for restaurants and hotels in some countries.

Potential sources of market failure, including externalities, imperfect information, imperfect competition, and public goods, are the topics of Chapter 11. The remainder of this chapter focuses on another widely misunderstood area of Adam Smith's work.

Morality and the Market

Smith believed that markets would overcome immoral behavior. He believed that benevolence would spring from market forces because, through trade, people gain in proportion to what they give and thus are prompted to develop ways to give more. But as with market failure, problems with morals have persisted in a way that Smith hoped they would not. Recent examples include the corporate ethics scandals at Arthur Andersen, Enron, Adelphia, ImClone, Citigroup, Qwest, WorldCom, and Tyco.

Tension exists between the desire for complete freedom and the desire to avoid the moral bankruptcy that threatens the efficiency of markets. The contemporary Adam Smith Institute is a self-proclaimed "free-market think tank,"[8] but Smith himself was a moral philosopher, and his theories assumed a foundation of righteousness and human decency. He wrote of every person being "left perfectly free to pursue his own interest in his own way" on the premise that markets compel ethical behavior.

Smith wrote at length about the morality that underpinned his laissez-faire disposition. In the context of children whose parents are poor role models, Smith wrote that "the example of that bad conduct commonly corrupts their morals; so that, instead of being useful to society by their industry, they become public nuisances by their vices and disorders." In his book *The Theory of Moral Sentiments* (1759), Smith argued that an individual should examine his or her behaviors as would an impartial spectator. By Smith's standard, an action is wrong if an individual feels a sentiment of disapproval when she or he considers that action. Several other schools of thought provide questions that assist decision making when markets and morals intersect:

Utilitarianism: Does this action bring the greatest good to the greatest number of people?

Ethical egoism: Is this action good for me?

The common good: Is this action good for society as a whole?

Virtue: Does this action reflect balance between vices?

Rights: Does this action respect the moral rights of everyone?

Kantianism: Would I want everyone to perform this action?

Justice: Is this action fair and just? Does it treat equals equally?

Role models: What would my hero do?

The newspaper test: Would I be embarrassed if this action appeared in a newspaper headline?

Smith would have us ruled neither by big government nor by big business. And he would have us behave in such ways as to win the approval of impartial observers. Would

[8] See www.adamsmith.org/.

these observers approve of the exploitation of labor, the neglect of health and environmental concerns, exorbitant prices, or pressure on buyers to purchase items they don't really need? Probably not—meaning that the progenitor of modern economics would disapprove of the license for unbridled greed that some see as his legacy.

CONCLUSION

Saying "Smith says" lends credibility to actions in much the same way that saying "Simon says" does in the popular children's game of that name. Smith may not be rolling over in his grave in response to becoming a laissez-faire icon, but he would certainly be glad that you have read this chapter so as to better understand the caveats that underpin his oft-quoted views. If we are to take our cues from the father of economics, it is important that we know what Adam Smith really said.

Smith said that markets can achieve miraculous efficiency and that constraints on otherwise efficient markets can distort the incentives for socially optimal behavior. Smith would not have liked artificial controls on prices, quantities, or wages; nor would he have advocated government subsidies or tax breaks. However, the markets that should not be distorted are those that involve many informed sellers of an identical product and no barriers to entry or exit by competitors. Smith probably would have appreciated such measures as nutrition information labels on food packages, restrictions on monopoly power, and harsh punishments for deceptive advertising. Likewise, the enforcement of health and environmental standards that prevent firms from imposing pollution costs on society are in the spirit of Smith's sensibilities.

Many people study supply and demand without understanding that only firms in perfectly competitive markets have supply curves. Monopolies will charge different prices for the same quantity, depending on what the demand curve looks like. Like the lessons of Adam Smith, much of what is learned in economics classes is contingent on perfectly competitive markets. Given market imperfections, individuals should relish free markets within reason while maintaining high moral standards and accepting measures that deal with market failure in order to attain the highest possible level of social well-being.

DISCUSSION STARTERS

1. What markets in your local economy most closely resemble Adam Smith's ideal of perfect competition?

2. Summarize Adam Smith's message about the potential virtues of free markets.

3. What characteristics does the hamburger market in your area share with a perfectly competitive industry? What conditions for perfect competition does it violate?

4. Given that the Justice Department and the Federal Trade Commission seek to promote competition between firms, what arguments do you suppose were used to gain their acceptance of the Kmart–Sears merger? That is, how might this merger increase the level of competition in the long run?

CHAPTER 7

WHY ARE THERE MORE MEMBERS OF A BAND THAN PROFESSORS IN A CLASS?

Diminishing Marginal Returns and the Demand for Labor

Guitarist Eric Clapton was inducted into the Rock & Roll Hall of Fame as a solo artist, and yet he seldom plays alone. He was also inducted into the Hall of Fame as a member of both the Yardbirds and Cream. Ladysmith Black Mambazo tours with 10 singers, whereas their friend Paul Simon often performs solo. Like any employer, bands could always add more people to their workforce or lay a few people off, or a band member could go it alone as a professor does. In this chapter you will learn how these decisions are made, and how rockers and professors differ in spite of the remarkable similarities in their lifestyles, wardrobes, and value to society.

WHAT CAN YOU DO FOR ME?

When bandleaders, businesses, and colleges contemplate taking on new personnel, they want to know what hiring additional workers could do for them. The contribution of 1 more worker to the level of output per period is called the *marginal product of labor*. If adding a professor at a college with 100 professors allows 30 more students to be taught each year, the marginal product of the 101st professor is 30 students per year. If another *barista* (coffee bartender) at Starbucks allows the store to serve 12 more lattes per hour, those 12 lattes are the last-hired barista's marginal product. And if a new band member would improve the band's sound and lead to 1,000 more CD sales per year, the marginal product of that band member is 1,000 CDs per year.

The Rise of Marginal Product

In the classic film *Mary Poppins*, actor Dick Van Dyke becomes a one-man band by strapping instruments onto his body. Modern one-man bands, such as Bernard Snyder,[1] appear at popular tourist destinations. The problem with such bands is that the one player is unlikely to gain mastery of the many instruments. Likewise, if you were the only worker in an espresso bar, you would have to divide your efforts among making coffee, serving customers, cleaning, stocking, running the cash register, and the many other tasks involved. With the first worker wearing many hats, each of the first few additional workers might contribute more to *total product* (the total number of drinks made per hour) than the previous worker, meaning that marginal product is increasing.

If going from 1 to 2 workers allows 1 person to get really good at making drinks while the other person can develop cash register and cleanup efficiency, the marginal product of the second worker can exceed that of the first. On working-joe.com, the staff of Working Joe Espresso suggests that a worker with divided attention can serve 10 drinks an hour, whereas a focused barista can serve 40 drinks an hour. The marginal product of the first worker is 10 because the total product increases from 0 to 10 when the first worker is hired. The second hire allows 1 person to focus on espresso-making skills and deliver 40 drinks per hour. The marginal product of the second worker is 30, because total product increases by 30, from 10 to 40, when the second worker is hired.

Diminishing Marginal Returns

Alas, marginal product can't keep increasing forever. According to the *"law" of diminishing marginal returns,* as more of one input—such as land, labor, or equipment—is added to fixed amounts of technology and other inputs, the marginal product must eventually fall. The *short run* is defined as the period of time during which the quantity of at least one input cannot change. The amount of *fixed inputs,* including machinery and buildings, is fixed in the short run because of the length of time it takes to make such changes as installing new equipment, building buildings, and getting out of leases. The amount of *variable inputs,* such as labor and ingredients, is always adjustable. It doesn't take long to hire or fire an employee or to order a new sack of coffee beans. Every input is variable in the long run.

In accordance with the law of diminishing marginal returns, the path of marginal benefits from myriad economic pursuits turns downward sooner or later. Efficiency dictates that each activity should be carried out until the marginal benefit no longer exceeds the marginal cost, and it is the fall of marginal benefits that brings a halt to many a virtuous endeavor. Other chapters in this book discuss how the marginal utility that consumers seek and the marginal revenue that firms seek generally fall. Marginal product falls sooner or later, too, as opportunities for specialization run out, redundancy sets in, and the usefulness of fixed inputs (such as stages, espresso bars, and classrooms) is spread thin by growing quantities of variable inputs (such as musicians, baristas, and professors).

Let's extend the previous section's example of the espresso bar, in which the marginal product is 10 for the first worker and 30 for the second. The accompanying table

[1] See www.onemanband.org.

presents production levels for each quantity of workers. With 1 person already working the cash register and another working the espresso machine, a third worker may be useful for keeping beverage ingredients stocked and helping to make drinks, contributing a marginal product of 20. A fourth worker wouldn't have a lot of equipment to work with but could increase sales by 15 espressos per hour by covering other workers' breaks, wiping tables, and helping the other workers stay focused on their specialized roles. A fifth worker would have less important tasks to complete but might increase sales by 5 espressos per hour by helping to take customer orders, checking in new shipments, and washing dishes. In similar ways, diminishing marginal product would be observed as more band members were added to a stage with a fixed number of instruments and as more professors were added to a fixed number of classrooms. Notice in the table that total product increases even as marginal product decreases; any positive marginal product represents a contribution to the total level of production.

WORKERS	MARGINAL PRODUCT OF LABOR	TOTAL PRODUCT OF LABOR
1	10	10
2	30	40
3	20	60
4	15	75
5	5	80

Don't Be Negative

Can marginal product be negative? Yes, indeed: At some point another worker simply gets in the way. A second barista at the drive-through Java Hut in the mall parking lot would make things cozy, and a third might deny all of them enough space to take a deep breath. When additional workers don't have much to do, their boredom invites distracting conversations and horseplay. When office workers are bored, they go online, often to send messages to other people who should be working. As evidence that such problems are real, increasing numbers of employers are using filtering services from companies such as Websense.com to block employees' access to anything from instant messaging and Internet porn to eBay and peer-to-peer services for sharing music files.

ALL EMPLOYERS ARE NOT CREATED EQUAL

Seventy-six trombones led the big parade,
With a hundred and ten cornets close at hand.
They were followed by rows and rows of the finest virtuosos—
The cream of every famous band.

—*From "76 Trombones" in* The Music Man

Not all bands, espresso bars, colleges, and factories are alike. The rate at which marginal product decreases depends on the situation and the amount of the fixed input. There may be 76 trombones in the big parade, but a folksinger can sing and play the guitar with little need for accompaniment. One player cannot make an orchestra, however, and the marginal product of the players needed to fill out the critical strings, brass, percussion, and woodwind sections is large. The contribution of a guitarist, backup vocalist, or drummer for singer Alanis Morrisette is positive but not so large. If you're looking for really big sound, consider William Havergal Brian's "Gothic" symphony (Symphony No. 1, 1919–1927), the largest symphony ever written. It requires 200 players in the orchestra itself, plus 4 brass bands and 4 large mixed choirs, for a total of more than 1,000 musicians and singers.

Why does guitarist Keith Richards appear with Mick Jagger and the other Rolling Stones, whereas Brandeis University professor and former U.S. Labor Secretary Robert Reich takes the stage alone at his lectures? It's not because additional professors cost more than additional rock stars; it's because additional professors contribute less than additional rockers do. That is, professors' marginal product plummets as more of them are added. The first professor brings intellectual intrigue to the audience. A second professor at a lecture could perhaps take over the diagram-drawing duties of the first and prevent those awkward moments when the speaker's back is turned to the audience. A third could run around glaring at students who aren't paying attention. These extra professors may not be worthless, but their contributions aren't on the same scale as adding a drumbeat and harmony to vocals. The negligible marginal product of professors beyond the first in a classroom explains why there are more members of a band than professors in a class.

THE DEMAND FOR LABOR

No employer wants to hire another worker after marginal product has become negative, meaning that additional workers will actually reduce output levels. However, there's a big difference between *negative* marginal product and *diminishing* marginal product. Employers generally do want to keep hiring after marginal product starts falling. The important reason is that any positive marginal product represents a contribution to total product. Employers are wise to keep hiring as long as the marginal product of an additional worker brings in at least as much money as that worker must be paid.

The amount of money that an additional worker brings in is found by multiplying the marginal product of that worker by the marginal revenue of the good or service (meaning the additional dollars gained from each new unit sold). If another band member increases CD sales by 1,000 and each CD sells for $10, that last-hired band member contributes 1,000 × $10 = $10,000 to the revenues of the band. Economists call the additional revenues from hiring one more worker the *marginal revenue product*. As marginal product decreases, so does marginal revenue product. In order to maximize profits, an employer will hire until the marginal revenue product equals or falls below the wage rate.

Consider an espresso bar whose first 5 workers have marginal products of 10, 30, 20, 15, and 5 drinks per hour, respectively. If each espresso sells for $2, the marginal revenue product for these workers is $20, $60, $40, $30, and $10 per hour, respectively. If the wage rate is $12 per hour, 4 workers should be hired. The revenues generated by the first 4 workers exceed their $12 cost per hour, but there's no sense in paying $12 for a fifth worker who will only bring in $10!

The demand for workers is linked directly to the demand for products. If the demand for espresso increases and drives the price up to $3 per espresso, the marginal revenue product of the first 5 workers will increase to $30, $90, $60, $45, and $15 per hour, respectively. With this higher demand for espresso, the fifth worker will be worthwhile to hire because he or she will bring in $15 worth of sales for a $12 wage. Because the demand for labor is based on the marginal revenue product of labor (the marginal product of labor times the output price), and the output price component of marginal revenue product is derived from the demand for the output, the demand for inputs is called a *derived demand*.

CONCLUSION

This chapter explains the reasons for diminishing marginal product and provides several real-world implications. You will find more applications of this concept everywhere you look. Let's consider one more example: Would you, could you, find diminishing marginal product in a boat?

If you've spent much time in a rowboat, you've probably seen that 1 person can row gently down the stream at about 2 mph. With 2 rowers in a boat with 2 oars, each can take an oar and the speed may increase to 3 mph, making the marginal product of the second rower a 1-mph increase in speed. A third person in the boat has no oar to work with but might increase the speed by 0.5 mph up to 3.5 mph by directing the back-facing rowers and preventing them from veering off course. A fourth person simply gets in the way and weighs down the boat, perhaps slowing the speed back down to 3 mph for a marginal product of −0.5 mph.

Diminishing marginal product affects everything from the speed of our progress while rowing to the decision about how many musicians the folk band Beggars Row should hire. And no matter what your economics professor's ratings are on www.rate myprofessor.com, a second professor in the same classroom probably wouldn't be nearly as valuable.

DISCUSSION STARTERS

1. In what situations have you seen diminishing marginal product in action?

2. Have you ever seen an employee who added nothing to the productivity of a business? Why do you suppose such workers are sometimes hired?

3. If you were the president of a consulting firm, how would you decide how many consultants to hire? Please be specific.

4. What could explain the fact that the band White Stripes has 2 members and the band Linkin Park has 6 members?

5. Imagine you are the owner of an espresso bar. Your first 5 workers have hourly marginal products of 10, 30, 20, 15, and 5 drinks, respectively, as in the example used in the chapter. You can sell as many espressos as you want for $1 each, labor constitutes the only nonnegligible marginal cost of selling espressos, and the wage rate in your area is $8 per hour. How many employees would you hire for your bar?

CHAPTER 8

COULD THE FUTURE COST
OF ENERGY CHANGE LIFE
AS WE KNOW IT?
Production Costs and the Inescapable
Demand for Energy

Researchers at the Post Carbon Institute (www.postcarbon.org), a nonprofit energy think tank, suggest that energy costs will increase dramatically as the supply of fossil fuels (oil, coal, and natural gas) decreases.[1] Among other things, skyrocketing energy costs would spell doom for transportation systems and the suburban neighborhoods, shopping malls, factories, and schools they serve. Energy costs are already built into the price of almost everything we buy because energy is consumed in the production, transportation, use, and disposal of most products. A spike in oil prices in the 1970s was followed by double-digit inflation rates throughout the economy. New technology will temper energy costs to a greater or lesser extent, depending on the level of investment in this technology.

At present, energy from renewable sources, such as the sun, wind, earth (geothermal), plants (biodiesel), and water (hydroelectric), costs significantly more than energy from fossil fuels. Even with the cheap stuff, 29 million households are eligible for financial help from the federal Low Income Home Energy Assistance Program

---

[1] This view is shared by other groups. The U.S. Army Corps of Engineers reports that once oil production peaks, "geopolitics and market economics will result in even more significant price increases and security risks" (see www.cecer.army.mil/techreports/Westervelt_EnergyTrends_TN/Westervelt_EnergyTrends__TN.pdf). See also www.msnbc.msn.com/id/4287300/, www.peakoil.net/, and www.lifeaftertheoilcrash.net/.

(LIHEAP), and home energy costs take about 17 percent of the income of LIHEAP re-cipients (www.liheap.org/background.html). This chapter discusses the nature, cost structures, and market structures of this most critical of inputs.

AN INTRODUCTION TO ENERGY

Energy is the amount of physical work a system is capable of performing. *Power* is the rate of energy transfer per unit of time. The first law of thermodynamics implies that energy cannot be created, consumed, or destroyed because the amount of energy in the universe is fixed. Thus, energy "production" refers not to the creation of energy but to its conversion into a usable form, and energy "use" does not mean that energy is destroyed but that it is dissipated into heat or other unusable forms.

Most of our efforts to harness energy for commercial electricity production involve making turbines spin to create electrical currents. Nuclear fission and coal combustion create steam that turns turbines. Wind and flowing water apply direct force on turbines. You may have created electricity yourself by turning a crank or a bicycle wheel rigged for that purpose. An exception is solar energy collected by a photovoltaic cell, which converts light energy into direct-current electricity without moving a thing.

From Where Does Energy Come?

The sun is the original and ultimate source of energy, fueling the plant life that feeds other living things, as well as the ancient plant life whose fossilized remains are burned as oil, natural gas, and coal. The water wheel was invented in 350 C.E. as a way to capture energy from flowing water. Windmills were used to harness wind energy beginning about 950 C.E. James Watt used wood and coal fires to power the first modern steam engine in 1765, and to this day the standard unit of power, equal to 1/746 of a horsepower, or 1 amp times 1 volt, bears his last name. Gottlieb Daimler inaugurated the gasoline-powered automobile engine in 1884. The first nuclear power plant went on-line in 1954.

Rocky Mountain Institute founder Amory Lovins describes two paths for energy dependence. The first is a "soft path" of many renewable energy sources, such as solar panels on millions of roofs or wind turbines on thousands of "wind farms." The second is a "hard path" of relatively few centralized fossil-fuel–based producers. Although Lovins made this observation in the context of environmental concerns, the distinctions between the two paths are also useful for discussions of market structures and production costs.

In 1850, the United States obtained most of its energy from decentralized sources—the muscles of humans and animals, followed by wood, water and wind, and coal. In 2006, the United States received more than 90 percent of all its energy from large, centralized sources. Most of our energy comes from petroleum products (40 percent); natural gas (23 percent); coal (22 percent); nuclear power (8 percent); and renewable sources, including flowing water, wind, and the sun (7 percent). Electricity is a secondary source of energy because another source of energy must be harnessed to make it. The primary fuel sources for making electricity in the United States are coal (52 percent), uranium (20 percent), natural gas (16 percent), flowing water (7 percent), oil (3 percent), and other renewable sources (2 percent).

Where Does Energy Go?

Like the demand for labor, the demand for energy is derived from the demand for the services this input provides. Industry creates 32 percent of U.S. energy demand, transportation creates 30 percent, residential users create 20 percent, and commercial users create 18 percent.[2] Global growth in the number of homes, businesses, industrial plants, and vehicles leads to corresponding increases in the demand for energy.

Much of the energy that is tapped by consumers literally goes up in smoke or is lost to heat or respiration. *Energy conversion efficiency* refers to the percentage of energy from a source that is converted into useful energy rather than being spent in the process of making energy useful. Wind turbines convert about 30 percent of the wind's energy into electricity. Coal-fired power plants convert 30 to 35 percent of the energy in coal into electricity. The energy conversion efficiency of standard solar cells is about 15 percent, although experimental solar cells have reached efficiency levels in excess of 30 percent.[3] If we could capture one-half of 1 percent of the energy the earth receives from the sun with 15 percent energy conversion efficiency, no other energy source would be required.

Sometimes the power goes out entirely. On August 14, 2003, an estimated 50 million people in eight U.S. states and the Canadian province of Ontario lost power, in some areas for up to 4 days. Estimates of the financial burden of this blackout in the United States approach $10 billion. Canadians lost 18.9 million work hours, and manufacturing shipments in Ontario fell by $1.9 billion. A U.S.–Canadian government investigation placed blame for the massive blackouts on the cascading effects of operators' mistakes, computer failures, rule violations, and inadequate equipment maintenance by FirstEnergy Corporation of Ohio. For many, this event was a wake-up call about the importance of energy as an input and about the vulnerability of the large, interconnected energy grids that are involved in the current structure of our energy market.

WHAT DOES ENERGY COST?

In 2006, Americans spent almost 9 percent of gross domestic product, amounting to more than $1 trillion, on energy.[4] Energy costs also include important environmental and health costs, which are addressed in Chapter 29. Here we examine the cost structure of energy production for large and small electricity producers. Several critical types of cost are explained in this context. Their meanings are summarized here for convenience:

> **Fixed cost:** a cost that does not change as more of the product is made
>
> **Variable cost:** a cost that increases as more of the product is made
>
> **Total cost:** fixed costs plus variable costs
>
> **Marginal cost:** the cost of making 1 more unit of the product

[2] See www.eia.doe.gov/emeu/mer/pdf/mer.pdf, p. 23.
[3] For example, see www.spectrolab.com/com/news/news-detail.asp?id=152.
[4] See www.eia.doe.gov/emeu/steo/pub/gifs/Slide24.gif.

Average fixed cost: the total fixed cost divided by the number of units made

Average variable cost: the total variable cost divided by the number of units made

Many Small Producers

The cost structure in an energy market depends on the scale of the production facilities, which tends to be either very large or very small. The 16,000-plus wind turbines in California produce about as much energy as 1 mid-size nuclear power plant does.[5] The U.S. Department of Energy is sponsoring a Million Solar Roofs initiative, with the goal of having 1 million rooftops outfitted with solar panels in the United States by 2010. The roofs of the Zeeland Middle School in Michigan, a Harley-Davidson dealership in Hawaii, and the home of Minnesota resident Todd Volkmeier exemplify thousands of participants in this soft-path effort.

Mr. Volkmeier installed 10 165-watt solar panels on his roof. Why 10 and not 15 or 25? The answer is that diminishing marginal returns set in for panels, just as they do for workers, as explained in Chapter 7. The marginal product of another rooftop panel (that is, the additional output received by installing 1 more panel) will decrease as the roof becomes crowded and panels must be placed in less sunny spots, and it will fall to 0 when there is no more open space for another panel.

Let's consider the cost picture for energy producers, such as Mr. Volkmeier. The $2,500 cost of the equipment—the energy inverter that makes the solar energy usable by household appliances, the wiring, and the battery pack for storing energy—is a *fixed cost* because the expenditure on these items does not change as more capacity is produced. In order to produce more energy in a given period with a given amount of sunlight, more panels must be added. Because solar panels are the input that is varied in order to produce more electricity, their cost is a *variable cost*, which amounts to $600 per panel. The *total cost* is the sum of the total variable cost and the total fixed cost for a given amount of output. Mr. Volkmeier's total cost was $2,500 + (10 × $600) = $8,500.

The determination of the best number of panels for Mr. Volkmeier requires a closer look at marginal cost and marginal benefit. We know that, in general, *marginal cost* is the cost to producers of 1 more unit of a good. The marginal benefit for producers is the *marginal revenue*—the additional revenue they take in from 1 more unit. As explained in Chapter 1, if something is worth doing, it should be done until the marginal benefit no longer exceeds the marginal cost, and that holds true for producers as well: If it is worthwhile to produce a good or service, it should be produced until marginal cost equals marginal revenue.

Marginal cost is closely tied to marginal product, although the two measures move in opposite directions. As explained in Chapter 7, the marginal product of labor generally increases and then decreases. In such cases, marginal cost falls and then rises. The explanation is straightforward: As marginal product increases for the first few workers, it takes fewer additional workers to make another unit of output, so the mar-

[5] See www.gracelinks.org/energy/wind/.

ginal cost of making that additional output falls. As the marginal product of workers falls, it takes more workers and thus more wage payments to make more units, and marginal cost increases. Likewise, as the marginal product of solar panels decreases as a result of roof crowding, it takes more additional panels to increase energy capacity by a given amount, and the marginal cost of energy capacity increases.

Let's track Mr. Volkmeier's marginal cost as he decides how many solar panels to install. Given the capacity of individual panels, in this example we will consider 165-watt increments in energy capacity. As long as there is unobstructed, sun-facing space on the roof, the marginal cost of adding 165 watts of energy capacity is $600—the cost of 1 panel—or $600/165 = $3.64 per watt. If the best available space requires that additional panels obstruct one-half of an existing panel, then it takes 2 additional panels to add 165 watts of capacity, bringing the marginal cost to $1,200 for 165 watts, or $7.27 per watt. If the best remaining roof space only gets one-third of the amount of sun necessary to bring a panel to its productive capacity, it will take 3 panels to increase Mr. Volkmeier's capacity by 165 watts, and the marginal cost is $1,800 for 165 watts, or $10.90 per watt. Finally, if the only place to put another panel is on top of an existing panel, the marginal cost of energy capacity becomes infinite: There is no amount that can be spent on additional panels to increase capacity.

Average fixed cost is total fixed cost divided by the quantity of output. To find the average fixed cost of producing 165 watts of capacity, we divide the total fixed cost of $2,500 by 165 and find $15.15. As output increases, average fixed cost invariably decreases because the same total fixed cost is divided by a larger and larger quantity. For example, the average fixed costs of producing capacities of 330, 825, and 1,100 watts are $7.57, $3.03, and $2.27, respectively. When a capacity of 250,000 watts is being produced, the average fixed cost is 1 cent.

Average variable cost is the cost of the variable input (panels) divided by the quantity of output (watts). Suppose that the first 4 panels have prime locations in the sun, the next 1 create 50 percent obstruction for other panels, the 4 after that must go on the side with one-third as much sun, and additional panels provide no net gain. The average variable cost of producing 330 watts is (2 × $600)/330 = $3.64. The production of 825 watts requires 4 panels at full capacity plus 2 panels at half capacity, so the average variable cost is (6 × $600)/825 = $4.36. The production of 1,100 watts requires 4 panels at full capacity, 4 panels at half capacity, and 2 panels at one-third capacity, for an average variable cost of (10 × $600)/1,100 = $5.45.

Producers compare average total cost with price to determine whether profits or losses are in store. Average total cost is the sum of average fixed cost and average variable cost. It can also be found by dividing total cost by the quantity of output. Because

WATTS	MARGINAL COST	AVERAGE FIXED COST	AVERAGE VARIABLE COST	AVERAGE TOTAL COST
330	$ 3.64	$7.57	$3.64	$11.21
825	$ 7.27	$3.03	$4.36	$ 7.39
1,100	$10.90	$2.27	$5.45	$ 7.72

the total cost of producing 330 watts is ($2,500 + [2 × $600]) = $3,700, the average total cost is $3,700/330 = $11.21. Likewise, the average total cost of producing 825 and 1,100 watts is $7.39 and $7.72, respectively.

The accompanying table summarizes the marginal and average cost levels. Notice that as output increases, the average total cost decreases and then increases. Average total cost will generally fall as output increases at small levels of production because decreases in average fixed cost are initially dramatic (for example, going from 1 watt to 2 watts cuts the average fixed costs down from $2,500 to $1,250), and these decreases are larger than the increases in average variable cost. At higher output levels, average fixed cost decreases more gradually than average variable cost increases, and average total cost begins to rise at precisely the quantity at which marginal cost rises above average total cost.

With millions of small producers of identical units of energy, the energy market would resemble the perfectly competitive model that Adam Smith described as being efficient, as discussed in Chapter 6. In such a market, it would be impossible for any one producer to maintain a price for energy in excess of average cost because competitors would be willing and available to sell energy for a price as low as average cost. However, the energy market in the United States does not, in fact, resemble the competitive model.

Few Large Producers

Eleven hundred coal-fired power plants and 103 nuclear reactors provide 72 percent of the United States's electricity needs. In 2004, Colorado regulators approved plans for the state's first new coal-fired power plant in 23 years. This addition to the Comanche Generating Station in Pueblo will cost an estimated $1.3 billion and produce 750 megawatts (a megawatt is 1 million watts). The Watts Bar Nuclear Power Plant in Tennessee, the most recent reactor to go on-line in the United States, began operation in 1996 with a capacity of 1,138 megawatts after a painful 23 years of construction delays at a cost of $8 billion.[6]

Although there is diminishing marginal product from coal and uranium, the overarching cost of these types of operations is the cost of building the power plants themselves. The enormous fixed cost of these facilities makes the cost structure of coal-fired and nuclear energy producers different from that of soft-path producers. Consider the average cost of nuclear power. The average fixed cost of the first million watts produced at the Watts Bar plant is $8 billion/1 million = $8,000 per watt. In contrast, variable costs and marginal costs are relatively small. The fuel cost in coal production is about two-thirds of the variable cost; the remaining one-third is for things such as labor and plant maintenance. Uranium fuel represents one-third to one-half of the variable cost of nuclear power. As Ron Hagen[7] of the U.S. Department of Energy commented, "This is important, because if you want to operate in a market, what matters is marginal cost; how much will it cost to sell extra power?"

The fixed costs of coal and nuclear power are prohibitive for any modest level of production. A competitive market divided among many coal or nuclear power pro-

[6] See www.energybulletin.net/5950.html.
[7] See http://archive.salon.com/tech/feature/2001/12/10/nukes/index2.html.

ducers could not survive because none of the plants would sell enough energy to cover fixed costs. The only way for such a plant to break even is to serve a large region and to sell mass quantities of electricity. When high fixed costs effectively eliminate access to the market by competing firms, the result is a *natural monopoly*—a single firm that is more efficient than any number of competitive firms would be. Water utilities are also natural monopolies because the enormous cost of a water system infrastructure causes average fixed cost to eclipse marginal and average variable costs; the solutions described in the next section apply similarly to water suppliers.

IS ENERGY REGULATION A GOOD IDEA?

Our reliance on natural monopolies for power raises the prospects for regulation to achieve both monopoly production and moderated prices simultaneously. As explained in Chapter 7, competition keeps prices in check, whereas a monopoly can garner lasting profits at the expense of consumers. The importance of energy to production, transportation, food supplies, and winter heating, among other essentials, makes price moderation a concern of government legislators. Given that a monopoly will exist naturally, regulation can limit prices and increase output. By restricting prices to the level of average cost, lawmakers can ensure that consumers pay the smallest amount possible without sending the power utility into debt.

Regulations must be applied and removed with care. In the summer of 2000, people in California began to experience an electricity shortage after power plants in that state were deregulated and sold to private energy wholesalers. The wholesale price of power was uncapped, but limits remained on retail prices. Thus, the power utilities purchased power from the deregulated wholesalers and sold it to customers at regulated retail prices. As cold snaps and heat waves increased electricity demand, production was constrained by plant closings and by increased temperatures that caused more precipitation to fall as rain rather than snow, leaving less snowmelt to fuel hydroelectric power stations.

Increased demand and decreased supply caused the wholesale energy prices in California to exceed the regulated retail prices. The inability to pass higher costs on to consumers resulted in electricity shortages and multibillion-dollar debt among the power utilities. The state experienced *brownouts* (periods of low voltage in power lines that cause lights to dim and equipment to malfunction) and *blackouts* (complete power outages as a result of overburdened power grids). Factories and stores closed; traffic signals faltered. In the end, it was necessary to increase retail electricity prices across the state by 12 to 55 percent.

CONCLUSION

Energy can be produced centrally by natural monopolies using fossil fuels or uranium, or locally by small producers of energy from alternative sources. There has been considerable interest and growth in alternative fuels during the past several decades, but, pollution costs aside, fossil fuels are still far less expensive and provide the large majority of energy in the United States. Dwindling stocks of oil and coal, dilemmas over the safe and secure storage of nuclear waste, ethical interests in conserving energy resources for future generations, and the demands of worldwide development force users to grapple with the spectrum of energy options. The high fixed costs of hard-path solutions invite monopolistic market structures and contentious regulations. Looking ahead, improvements in alternative energy technology could lower the costs of decentralized soft-path sources, such as wind and solar, and change both the structure of energy markets and the price of power.

DISCUSSION STARTERS

1. The Castle River Wind Farm in Alberta, Canada, operates 67 wind turbines and produces 125 million kilowatt-hours of electricity—enough to serve 20,000 homes. Why do you suppose the company erected 67 turbines, rather than, say, 50 or 100?

2. According to warnings from the Post Carbon Institute, fossil-fuel supplies will bring about "relocalization"—a return to communities with local economies, housing, schools, and amenities. Other people expect that technological advances will lower the cost of alternative fuels to the vicinity of fossil-fuel costs. How much reliance do you believe can be placed on high-tech solutions to the energy problem?

3. Which of the following power sources are most likely to come from natural monopolies? Which could be set up either as centralized power sources or as decentralized, soft-path sources? What are the advantages and disadvantages of each type of setup?
   a. wind turbines
   b. hydroelectric power generation along a river
   c. coal
   d. oil
   e. solar
   f. nuclear

4. Of the six types of costs discussed in this chapter, which type is the most important to the decision as to how much of a good or service to produce? Why?

5. Draw supply-and-demand curves on a graph to illustrate what you think happened in the alternative energy market as a result of skyrocketing retail energy prices in California.

CHAPTER 9

WHY IS CASH THE ULTIMATE GIFT?
Optimal Consumption, Deadweight Loss,
and the Virtues of Flexible Spending

The U.S. Census Bureau reports that the average citizen spends $26,650 in a typical year. This includes average expenditures of $177 on shoes, $159 on computers and software, $360 on higher education, $184 on jewelry and watches, and $252 on furniture. If money grew on trees, then people would all purchase more of most of these goodies, but in reality money is scarce and they must make difficult choices guided by personal preferences. Buying gifts to suit other people's preferences becomes even trickier. According to the Coinstar National Currency Poll, the typical individual spends almost $900 a year on gifts. As an example of the potential difficulties, one woman attacked her husband on Valentine's Day after he bought her a dozen roses because she thought the family would have been better served if the $50 the roses cost had been spent on food and clothing. This chapter explains how individuals should make decisions about personal consumption and why so many people leave the purchasing decisions to others at holiday time by giving gift certificates or cash.

LIVING WITHIN LIMITS
Cyndi Lauper sings that "girls just want to have fun." Economists see the same goal in a broader light: All consumers just want to be as happy as possible given the cards they've been dealt and the money they've acquired. At the same time, even the most

comparable consumers have widely divergent preferences and make correspondingly dissimilar purchases in the pursuit of happiness. As singer Alanis Morissette invested in guitars and stage equipment to launch her musical career, her twin brother, Wade, bought a yoga studio and traveled to India to practice the art of chanting. The Olsen twins of *Full House* fame seem to live and work in unison and face similar budget constraints, but Ashley chose to major in psychology in college, whereas Mary Kate majored in cuisine.[1] Despite similarities in the way people use preferences to make utility-maximizing choices, the fact that people's preferences differ makes flexibility in spending a virtue and has implications for gift giving and policymaking, which are discussed later in the chapter.

Author Samantha James divides the earnings from her best-selling books among savings and millions of available goods and services in an effort to maximize her happiness. The owners of Sam's Burger Joint in San Antonio, Texas, make decisions about investments and inputs in order to maximize profits. And Uncle Sam, also known as the U.S. government, works with an annual budget of about $2.5 trillion to improve the welfare of society. Although loans and the sale of stocks and bonds offer some flexibility in the amounts available for Samantha, Sam, and Uncle Sam to spend, individuals, firms, and governments all face insurmountable limits that necessitate strategic spending.

Financial constraints force an opportunity cost on every purchase. For Samantha, a dollar spent on books can't be spent on clothes. For Sam, a dollar spent on buns can't be spent on ketchup. For Uncle Sam, a dollar spent on bombs can't be spent on classrooms. Budget managers at every level labor to adjust allocations to better suit their goals, be they utility, profit, or social well-being. In 2005, President George W. Bush proposed cuts in funding for 150 programs,[2] including Amtrak, veterans' benefits, and community development grants, while suggesting increased expenditures on other programs, such as Pell education grants, the military, and homeland security. Likewise, in recent years the typical consumer has chosen to spend more on bus rides and physicians' services and less (after adjusting for inflation) on taxi fares and funerals. In this chapter, the method behind the madness of consumer choices and a bit of the madness behind our method of gift giving is explained.

THE OPTIMAL CONSUMPTION RULE

With the goal of gaining as much utility as possible, optimal consumption comes from spending each dollar on the item that brings the greatest "bang per buck," meaning that the largest possible marginal (additional) utility is obtained from each dollar spent. Consider the popular digital music player called the iPod. On average, a consumer could afford to buy about 100 iPods a year if he or she bought nothing else. Avid music listeners can get a lot of utility out of their first iPod, as 22.5 million of them did in 2005, but few purchased a second iPod, let alone 99 more. As suggested by the law of diminishing marginal utility, a first iPod satisfies more critical needs and is, therefore, more valuable to a particular consumer than is a second unit, which

---

[1] See www.answers.com/topic/the-olsen-twins.
[2] See www.abc.net.au/am/content/2005/s1298145.htm.

might be fun to have but serves fewer unmet needs. It's likely that the marginal utility from the purchase of a second music player would be lower than that from an initial expenditure of the same amount on, say, cashmere sweaters.

Formally, the *optimal consumption rule* states that money allocated among several goods should be divided so that the marginal utility per dollar is the same for each of the goods. If the marginal utility per dollar spent on the last unit of good A is higher than that for good B, more utility could be gained by increasing expenditures on good A and spending less on good B. As more is spent on good A, the law of diminishing marginal utility holds that the marginal utility of good A will fall. As less is spent on good B, the marginal utility of that good will rise. This reallocation of money to the good that provides the most marginal utility per dollar should continue until the marginal utility per dollar is the same for all goods.[3] (Note that it may be impossible to fine-tune allocations to equate the marginal utility per dollar for goods such as automobiles that come in large increments; in that case, the goal is to come as close to equality as possible.)

Let's examine the workings of the optimal consumption rule using a realistic example. Remembering that utils are a convenient measure of happiness, suppose that your first 2 iPods would give you 900 and 300 utils, respectively, and your first 4 cashmere sweaters would give you 600, 450, 350, and 300 utils, respectively. Let's say that an iPod costs $300, a cashmere sweater costs $150, and you have $600 to spend on these options. If you spent your budget on 2 iPods, your total utility would be 1,200 and the utility from the last (marginal) iPod would be 300, or 300/300 = 1 util per dollar. By giving up the last iPod, you could purchase a first and second sweater that provide 600/150 = 4 and 450/150 = 3 utils per dollar, respectively—an improvement in marginal utility per dollar, or bang per buck. The result is an increase in total utility to 900 + 600 + 450 = 1,950.

At the other extreme, if you spent your $600 on 4 sweaters, your total utility would be 1,700 and the marginal sweater would provide 300 utils, or 2 utils per dollar. By giving up the last 2 sweaters, you could purchase the first iPod and receive 3 utils per dollar. This reallocation would increase your total utility to 1,950, as calculated previously. With 1 iPod and 2 sweaters, the marginal utility per dollar is 900/300 = 3 for iPods and 450/150 = 3 for sweaters. As the example shows and as the optimal consumption rule suggests, working toward equality maximizes utility in marginal utility per dollar.

THE VIRTUES AND VICES OF VARIETY IN CONSUMPTION

The optimal consumption rule guides us toward balance in our consumption. A wardrobe consisting only of shirts is bettered with fewer shirts and more pants because the marginal utility per dollar from the first few pairs of pants exceeds that from the last few of many shirts. It's the same story when allocating funds between food and shelter, electronics and linens, and most other common goods. Naturally, people don't want balance in all things. When allocating a travel budget between trips to Europe

---

[3] In formal notation, the optimal consumption rule is

$$MU_A/P_A = MU_B/P_B$$

and trips to the South Pole, most of us would allocate all our money toward the former. Seldom does the appropriate balance mean equal numbers of two items. People don't purchase equal numbers of shoes and bicycles, although they have a strong preference for equality between left and right shoes and front and back bicycle tires.

Variety is a virtue when it comes to exciting the mind with a mix of purchases; eating a balanced diet; and juggling our attention among home, family, work, and recreation. In other contexts, preferences for balance among varied possibilities can lead to trouble. During finals week a student's unsatisfied desire for balance between work and play can be a lure out of the library. In marriage the temptation to seek a variety of romantic partners can be a lure out of fidelity—and, ultimately, out of marriage. And the quest for variety in our daily lives can lead us out of financial solvency and into debt if one seeks expensive foreign travel, new cars, home renovations, and extensive wardrobes.

THE PURPOSE OF PURCHASES

Previous chapters have explained that efficiency is about maximizing net gains. The net gains from sales can be divided into what are called consumer surplus and producer surplus. *Consumer surplus* is the difference between the values consumers place on a good and the amount they must pay for it. People buy things for the consumer surplus they receive, not for the portion of value that is offset by price. If you would be willing to pay $60 for a new jacket and the price is $50, you enjoy $10 worth of consumer surplus from that jacket. If the jacket were priced at $60, you would be indifferent between buying it and not buying it because you would gain no consumer surplus from the purchase—payment of the price would eat up all the value you would receive from the jacket.

Sellers are similarly motivated by the prospect of net gains. *Producer surplus* is the difference between the price of a good and the marginal cost of making it. If it costs $35 to make another jacket and that jacket sells for $50, the producer surplus from that exchange is $15.

Deadweight loss is a loss of benefit that does not become anyone else's gain. In 1878, Black Bart (also known as Charles E. Boles) robbed California's La Porte to Oroville stagecoach to obtain a Wells Fargo express box containing $500 in gold and a silver watch. This transfer of gold and silver did not represent a deadweight loss because Wells Fargo's loss was Black Bart's gain. Crimes such as this do create deadweight loss as the result of time and money spent carrying out and defending against the offenses. When the *Titanic* hit an iceberg and sank in 1912, it was a loss to the victims who perished and to the Oceanic Steam Navigation Company, which owned the ship. Because no one received benefits in exchange for this vessel and its victims, those losses represent deadweight loss.

In the context of buying and selling, deadweight loss is the loss of consumer or producer surplus from sales that could have provided surplus but do not occur. If a tax on jackets increased the price to $61, the jacket you would otherwise have purchased might not be sold. This reduction in the quantity of jackets sold leads to a loss of both the $10 in consumer surplus and the $15 in producer surplus. Without that jacket, the producer can avoid the cost of making it and the consumer can save the price of buying it, but the surpluses that would have gone to the buyer and seller disappear as if lost at sea. That amounts to $25 in deadweight loss. Note that the taxes collected on jackets that are sold do not constitute a deadweight loss; rather, tax revenues represent a *transfer* from consumers or producers to the government. Like taxes, monopolies and cartels create deadweight loss by increasing prices and decreasing the quantity sold, thereby eliminating sales that would have provided surplus.

GIFTS AND DISAPPOINTMENTS

In a 1993 article in the *American Economic Review* titled "The Deadweight Loss of Christmas," Joel Waldfogel explained the downside of noncash gift giving. Gifts create deadweight loss when the recipient could have taken the amount spent on the gift and received more utility spending it on something else. Waldfogel estimated that between a tenth and a third of the money spent on gifts is wasted because it exceeds the value that recipients place on the goods. As a whole, he estimated that the deadweight loss from gift giving in the United States is between $5 billion and $18 billion each year.[4]

The deadweight loss is greater from less-informed givers. In Waldfogel's study, friends, significant others, siblings, and parents had a relatively good idea of what the recipients wanted and gave gifts that on average were worth 98.8, 91.7, 86.5, and 86.2 percent as much to the recipient as their price, respectively. Aunts and uncles and grandparents were not as well informed and gave gifts that were worth between 62.9 and 64.4 percent of their price, respectively.

There are a few drawbacks to giving cash as a gift. One is that the sentimental value of an item purchased with a cash gift will often fall below that of a gift given directly. Another is that there is no difference between the perceived price of the good and the true cost of providing it. Some gift givers strive to find an item that looks like it cost $50 but really cost only $25.

Like everything else, cash gifts involve trade-offs. As a compromise between the inflexibility of a bundt cake gift and the impersonal feel of a cash gift, gift certificates have grown in popularity in recent years. A gift certificate from Tiffany's shows that the gift giver put some thought into the purchase while providing the flexibility that also makes gift recipients happy.

The importance of budget flexibility is relevant in other settings as well. Government programs and community food banks sometimes provide packaged food, housing, clothes, and other in-kind assistance to the poor. Although these items are generally useful to the recipients, they are unlikely to match their needs as closely as would the items they could obtain with the more flexible provision of food stamps or cash. Another drawback of cash, unlike food stamps, is that recipients can spend it on tobacco and alcohol. Most donor organizations choose not to satisfy recipients' preferences for those particular goods.

Duke University recently extended the use of student meal plans to include local restaurants so that students could come closer to their optimal food consumption than

---

[4] Although his general point is well taken, Waldfogel's specific estimates have been questioned as a result of his reliance on a survey of Yale undergraduates. See, for example, Sara J. Solnick and David Hemenway (1996), "The Deadweight Loss of Christmas: Comment," *American Economic Review*, 86:5, 1299–1305.

on-campus eateries would allow. In a similar innovation, a growing number of travel-abroad programs are allowing students to control the food-cost component of their trips. Whereas the dinner buffet at the hotel used to be part of the package, for example, students can now allocate the $25 buffet cost to a $10 take-out meal and an extra $15 museum visit, to a $3 bowl of cereal and a $22 souvenir sombrero, or to whatever else makes them happiest.

CONCLUSION

Individuals, firms, and governments can make the most of limited budgets by spending money to equate the bang per buck across purchases. The logic behind this principle, which is called the *optimal consumption rule*, is that if one good provides more benefit per dollar than another, more should be spent on the good with the relatively high return and less should be spent on low-return goods until the discrepancy in relative benefits no longer exists. People generally prefer variety and balance in their consumption, although the combination of purchases that one person prefers is unlikely to match someone else's ideal mix. Cash provides complete spending flexibility. Gifts, in-kind government support, and packaged meal plans, in contrast, can impose unfortunate rigidities and force recipients away from their preferred levels of consumption.

The benefit from buying goods comes in the form of consumer surplus—the difference between the value of a product to the consumer and the product's price. Producers seek producer surplus—the difference between price and marginal cost. When goods that would have provided consumer or producer surplus are not bought and sold, the result is deadweight loss: The surplus is received by no one and completely disappears. Deadweight loss can result from taxation, monopolization, and even a holiday gift that gives you less joy than you would have received if you had picked your own gift. If your grandmother sends you $20 for your birthday, it isn't necessarily because she doesn't want to shop for you. If you're excited to see that her gift is cash and not another pair of slippers, you're enjoying a release from the deadweight loss of gift giving.

DISCUSSION STARTERS

1. How do you make budgetary decisions about the allocation of your funds? Does your decision making resemble the optimal consumption rule? Is there any way in which you could revise your spending habits to receive more bang per buck? What does that imply about your consumption decisions?

2. Suppose you consumed apples and oranges; each cost $1, and you received 30 utils from your last apple and 10 utils from your last orange. What should you do in order to maximize your utility? What will happen to the marginal utility you receive per orange as you make this change? Why? What will happen to the marginal utility you receive per apple as this change occurs? Why?

3. Cash provides flexibility, but sometimes complete flexibility is a concern because it permits spending on addictive substances. What compromises did the chapter suggest in the context of gift giving and aid for the poor? How might a properly conceived voucher system solve similar problems in the context of education? What drawbacks might a voucher system involve?

4. What would you receive on an ideal birthday? Would you prefer cash to spend as you desire, goods and services selected by your friends and family, or some balance between the two? Why?

5. For sentimental reasons, might you prefer a shirt selected by a loved one, even though you wouldn't pick it for yourself? Can you think of ways (other than by using gift certificates as discussed in the chapter) to benefit from both flexibility in gift choices and sentimental value when it comes time to give gifts?

CHAPTER 10

WHY SHOULD WE PAY FOR WHAT WE THROW AWAY?
Incentives for Efficiency from Pay-Per-Unit Pricing

People in the United States generate more than 236 million tons of trash each year.[1] U.S. citizens incinerate 17 percent of the trash from homes, small businesses, and municipalities, but even the resulting ash is more than landfills can handle. Among the results have been several infamous "tours de trash"—garbage barges wandering the seas in search of dumping grounds. In July 2002, one such journey ended sixteen years after it began. In 1986, operators of Philadelphia's Roxborough incinerator could find no nearby home for more than 14,000 tons of toxic ash, so they loaded it onto a ship called the *Khian Sea*. The ship was turned away from ports in the Bahamas, Bermuda, the Dominican Republic, Honduras, Guinea-Bissau, and the Netherlands Antilles. In 1988, some 4,000 tons of the ash were unloaded on the beach in Haiti, the poorest country in the Western Hemisphere; the remainder was apparently dumped overboard as the ship sailed the Atlantic and Indian Oceans. After a decade of trying, Haiti succeeded in sending its 4,000-ton ash mountain back to Florida, and that state spent $614,000 shipping the ash by rail to Maryland. From there it was trucked to the Mountain View landfill in Montgomery, Pennsylvania—only 170 miles from where it had started. The lesson: What goes around comes around.

[1] See www.epa.gov/epaoswer/non-hw/muncpl/facts.htm.

This chapter explains incentive structures that discourage people from sending so much trash around.

FOILED BUDGET CONSTRAINTS

The trouble with trash begins with a loophole in the limits that prevent us from overindulging. Chapter 9 introduced the concept of a budget constraint, which holds within it all the combinations of various goods that one can afford. A budget constraint is essentially a barrier between you and the unlimited quantities of goods and services that you might consume if money were no object. The barrier is usually impenetrable, but exceptions exist. The Jumbo Buffet restaurant in Troy, Michigan, provides an unlimited number of trips to the 100-plus-item buffet at $6.25 for lunch and $12.99 for dinner. Having paid the price, customers have no constraint on their consumption of food beyond the size of their stomachs. The financial barrier between them and mass consumption is erased, and consume they do.

There's a twist in the budget constraint story whenever consumers can enjoy more of 1 good without giving something up, and all-you-can-eat restaurants aren't the only example. If you live in a residence hall, you may pay a fixed price for water and electricity that is independent of your level of use. Disney World and other amusement parks now charge a fixed price for unlimited rides. Professors at many colleges enjoy unlimited use of copy machines. Internet access increasingly comes at a fixed monthly price for unlimited use. Traditional garbage pickup is a fixed-rate service, too. One benefit from these price plans is simplicity; there is no need to monitor the level of use.

A problem with "all-you-can" offerings is that they lead to overconsumption. After paying the fixed price, the cost of 1 more becomes 0. This encourages the rational consumer to consume until the marginal benefit equals the 0 marginal cost to the consumer. Do you ever leave the water running while you brush your teeth? Are 0-marginal-cost music downloads clogging your 0-marginal-cost Internet bandwidth? Although the marginal cost of these activities to the user may be 0, the marginal cost to others is not. Efficient consumption ends when the marginal benefit falls to the level of the marginal cost to society. By consuming right up to the point at which the marginal benefit is 0, you, as a consumer, use up goods and services that aren't worth their cost to society, and thereby impose an undue burden on others, if not yourself. That is, if you eat like a bird in the all-you-can-eat cafeteria, you're subsidizing the human food receptacle sitting next to you. The next section explains policy implications in the context of the plastic trash receptacle sitting in your garage.

TRASHING THE PLACE

Although virtually all forms of waste could be either recycled or composted (placed in a bin where it would turn back into soil), the average American creates 4.5 pounds of garbage daily.[2] Citizens of most other countries throw away less than us, but they're starting to catch up. According to the Environmental Protection Agency (EPA), 61

---

[2] See www.epa.gov/epaoswer/non-hw/muncpl/facts.htm.

percent of our garbage is paper, plastic, metal, or glass and could be recycled; 23 percent is food scraps and yard trimmings, which could be composted; and 16 percent is wood, rubber, leather, textiles, and miscellaneous other materials that are somewhat harder (though not impossible) to eliminate from the waste stream. If people unfailingly recycled and composted, 84 percent of the waste disposal issue would disappear.

In 500 B.C.E., the city of Athens, Greece, organized the first municipal dump in the Western world. Athenians were required to dispose of their waste at least 1 mile from the city's walls, and the long haul provided a distinct downside to waste creation. U.S. city dwellers of the nineteenth century invited pigs, rats, cockroaches, and disease by throwing refuse into the streets, or went through the trouble of digging pits to hold their garbage. In 1895, New York City unveiled the first system for public garbage management in the United States.[3] Modern curbside garbage pickup is a luxury that presents a lamentable incentive problem. The pricing plans for garbage collection often resemble those at all-you-can-eat restaurants but in reverse. Whereas the restaurants allow customers to take in as much food as they want for a flat price, many garbage services allow customers to set out as much garbage as they want for a flat fee. For example, residents of Brazil, Indiana, pay the city $8.50 for curbside pickup of all their trash, including heavy items and recyclables. Under this plan, a household doesn't pay more when it throws away more. Thus, there is no incentive to conserve, reuse, compost, or recycle, even when it would be easy to do so.

PAY AS YOU THROW

Per-unit pricing is the solution to the flat-fee blues. For instance, the city of Pemberville, Ohio, charges 75 cents per bag of trash left at the curb. In other communities the per-bag fees range from 50 cents to $3.25. Participants in this type of "pay-as-you-throw" (PAYT) program purchase specially marked trash bags (or stickers to place on their own bags) to indicate to the garbage collectors that they have paid for each unit of trash picked up. The more they throw away, the more they must pay. This pricing structure creates a trade-off between discarding more trash and purchasing goods and services, effectively resurrecting a budget constraint for trash. The programs also introduce an element of fairness. Whereas light users subsidize heavy users under fixed-rate systems, per-unit pricing requires participants to pay more for higher levels of use.

According to the EPA, the implementation of PAYT programs reduces community waste levels by 14 to 27 percent and increases recycling rates by 32 to 59 percent.[4] The EPA estimates that for the average PAYT participant, annual emissions of greenhouse gases are reduced by 0.085 metric tons of carbon equivalent (a standard measure of climate-changing greenhouse gases). The success of pay-as-you-throw programs relative to all-you-can-waste arrangements suggests that consumers do make choices with attention to their budget constraints and that incentives do indeed matter. Pay-

---

[3] See www.epa.gov/epaoswer/non-hw/muncpl/timeline_alt.htm.

[4] See www.epa.gov/epaoswer/non-hw/muncpl/ghg/climpayt.pdf. For related research, see http://web.utk.edu/~dfolz/payt.pdf.

as-you-throw programs have been adopted in roughly 6,000 of the 19,429 U.S. cities, as well as in Germany, Austria, Sweden, and the Netherlands. In 2005, Ireland enacted a nationwide mandate for local authorities and private waste haulers to restructure their billing to reward waste reduction by charging consumers according to the weight of their trash.

OTHER PAY-PER-UNIT APPLICATIONS

The logic behind per-unit pricing for trash is applicable to myriad situations involving insufficient constraints. For example, incentive-minded Ireland was the first country in the world to combat a glut of plastic shopping bags with a per-unit bag tax. The result was a 90 percent reduction in plastic bag use.[5] Ireland also taxes polystyrene food wrappers and cash machine receipts, with revenues earmarked to fund trash cleanup and recycling centers. Some countries, including South Africa and Bangladesh, have banned disposable plastic shopping bags altogether, but per-unit charges can be more efficient because they allow those who receive large benefits from plastic bags to keep using them.

Toll roads that charge according to the distance driven help limit congestion, and technology is making pay-as-you-go driving more feasible. The United Kingdom is considering proposals to install boxes in cars that allow satellites to track their exact location and mileage.[6] If the plan is adopted, charges will vary from $0.03 per mile in rural areas to almost $2 per mile in big cities during rush hour. Distance-based driving charges are attractive as a means of assessing larger costs on drivers who use the roads more.

Sometimes there are good reasons to overlook pay-per-unit pricing plans. Many citizens understandably dislike the prospect of having the government know when, where, and how fast they are driving at all times, as pay-as-you-go driving would allow. Unrestricted consumption is also easier to administer. With a simple entry fee, amusement parks don't need a ticket taker at every ride. And by offering all-you-can-eat buffets, many restaurants find that they can save enough money on wait staff to offset the cost of higher food consumption levels.

CONCLUSION

Households, businesses, and institutions produce about 230 million tons of garbage each year. For efficiency, people should carry out each activity until the marginal benefit no longer exceeds the marginal cost. When the marginal cost to an individual of creating waste is 0, as it is in traditional garbage pickup systems, it is rational for that individual to go on generating waste until the marginal benefit of any more waste is 0. If it takes an iota of energy to reduce, reuse, or recycle, the individual has little incentive to conserve resources because the alternative—neglect—is free. Because society pays high costs for waste disposal even when individuals do not, 0-marginal-cost garbage pickup programs encourage inefficiently high levels of waste production. A

[5] See www.epa.gov/epaoswer/non-hw/payt/tools/bulletin/spring-04.htm.
[6] See http://news.bbc.co.uk/1/hi/uk/4610755.stm.

solution is to charge for garbage disposal according to volume. If the price of discarding each bag of garbage were set to resemble the cost that dealing with that bag of garbage imposes on society, people would generate more waste only if the benefits of doing so exceeded the costs, and efficiency would result. Similar variable-cost pricing structures improve the efficiency of water, electricity, copy machine use, music downloads, and factory emissions, to mention a few examples.

DISCUSSION STARTERS

1. Do you buy things in bulk to avoid unnecessary packaging? What products do you recycle? Would you give more thought to packaging and recycling if you had to pay $3 per bag for trash disposal?

2. Does your school have an all-you-can-eat cafeteria? On the basis of your own observation, how would you say the consumption and food-waste levels compare between all-you-can-eat and à la carte eateries?

3. E-mail, local phone service, and cable television generally have fixed-rate pricing structures. Do fixed rates for these services present the same problems as fixed rates for all-you-can-eat food, photocopying, and trash pickup?

4. The demise of free music sharing on Napster was followed by the rise of new services that require a $1 payment per downloaded song. How have per-song fees affected your personal downloading practices? In what way does everyone benefit from the per-unit fees?

5. How might incentives work against the goals of society if PAYT programs charged too much? That is, what would you do with your trash if you had to pay $50 per bag to trash collectors? Can you think of other potential problems with PAYT programs that policymakers should consider?

CHAPTER 11

WHY NOT SPLIT THE CHECK?
A Briefing on Market Failure

Last Friday, somewhere near you, a group of students slurped root beers at a popular burger joint. Frosted mugs cluttered the table like miniature Manhattan skyscrapers. Gossip and wisecracks filled the air. When the check arrived, a student in blue jeans and a black concert t-shirt called out, "Let's just split it." Those with the most mugs before them greeted the motion with nods. Those with fewer mugs had blank faces. One light drinker meekly mumbled something about fairness. An equal splitting of the check seemed inevitable. Then a baseball player sitting in the corner leaned up to the table, his face illuminated by the restaurant's blinking red neon light. "My friends," he inserted into the awkward silence, "to split the check isn't only an injustice to those who had fewer drinks; it also creates a strong incentive for overindulgence." The others were perplexed. But as he leaned back, the light illuminated his economics society t-shirt and they knew that logic was on his side. This chapter explains the error of these students' ways and reveals other sources of market failure that surround us daily and confound many of our stabs at efficiency.

MARKET FAILURE
Ideal market conditions yield efficient allocations of inputs and outputs. *Market failure* is the reason why some markets do *not* bring about the best outcomes for society.

As explained in Chapter 6, perfectly competitive firms achieve market efficiency by equating marginal costs and marginal benefits. This chapter provides a constructive overview of the sources of market failure: externalities, imperfect competition, imperfect information, and public goods. Each of these sources receives further mention later in the book: Imperfect information is the focus of Chapter 12; imperfect competition is central to the issues in Chapters 13 and 14; public goods are the topic of Chapter 18; and externalities are reprised in Chapter 29. As you're about to learn, some of the solutions to market failure are as simple as paying for your own root beers.

Externalities

Externalities are costs or benefits felt beyond, or external to, the people causing them. When you get a flu shot, you create positive externalities because other people won't catch the flu from you. When you drive a car, you create the negative externalities of road congestion and air pollution. To emit toxins into the air or water during a manufacturing process, smoke in public, play loud music, catch fish that other fishers are angling for, or paint your house a dreadful shade of green is to impose external costs—negative externalities—on other people.

You may not think of root beer as a potential source of negative externalities, but when you buy a root beer with a group that is splitting the check equally, you impose a cost on everyone in that group.[1] Suppose a root beer costs $2 and you have 10 people in your group. Suppose also that diminishing marginal utility leads you to value your first 5 root beers at $3, $2.50, $1.25, $0.50, and $0.10, respectively. If you were not splitting the check, you would buy 2 root beers for $2 each—the first that's worth $3 to you and the second that's worth $2.50. You wouldn't pay $2 for a third root beer that's worth $1.25. The situation changes when you're splitting the check 10 ways. In that case each root beer raises the tab by $2, but it raises your share of the tab by only $2/10 = 20 cents. Thus, it's rational for you to purchase 4 root beers—all of those that are worth at least 20 cents to you—even though the last 2 are worth less than the $2 price that the group pays.

The problem grows because everyone in the group faces the same incentive to overconsume. If your friends share your preference for root beer, each of the 10 friends will consume 4 beverages, bringing the total bill up to $80. Each friend's share of the bill will be $8—twice what they would have paid on their own and 75 cents more than the $3 + $2.50 + $1.25 + $0.50 = $7.25 value of the root beers to them. Notice that you cannot improve on this situation by reducing your order. If you ordered 3 root beers, you would reduce your tab by $0.20 and you would receive $0.60 cents less worth of beverage. By splitting the check, your group creates externalities that thwart efficient decisions.

Externality problems can be resolved if ways can be found to have everyone internalize, or feel for themselves, the full costs or benefits of their decisions. In the root beer example, that means having everyone pay his or her own bill. The negative externalities from goods such as gasoline, cigarettes, and alcohol are internalized if *ex-*

---

[1] For more on the negative externality problem with splitting the check, and for empirical evidence of the problem, see www.gsb.uchicago.edu/fac/uri.gneezy/vita/Restaurant.pdf.

cise taxes (taxes levied on particular goods such as these) approximate the associated external costs. A solution to the underconsumption that accompanies positive externalities is for the government to subsidize purchases, as is the case for flu shots as well as education, tree planting, and clean energy.

Because goods creating positive externalities are underconsumed and goods creating negative externalities are overconsumed from a societal standpoint, another solution is to require people to purchase the efficient quantity of these goods. It is common for governments to require a particular number of childhood immunizations and education through high school while limiting the volume of power plant emissions and the number of pets that can be kept in a household. For example, in the interest of neighborhood serenity and sanitation, no resident in the city of Grand Junction, Colorado, may keep more than 3 adult pets, such as dogs or cats. Chapter 26 elaborates on the role of government and explains how the enforcement of private property rights can assist with externality problems.

Imperfect Competition

Hawaiian shirts sell for $30 and up in the gift shop of the Honolulu International Airport. In downtown Honolulu, the Daiei supermarket sells similar Hawaiian shirts for $14. Both places sell shirts that are made in Hawaii at comparable costs; most of the price differential stems from differing levels of competition. Daiei faces competition from hundreds of other shirt sellers, and if the managers were to raise their prices significantly above marginal cost, competitors would undercut their prices and steal away some of their customers and profits. That's how prices in competitive environments are brought down to approximately the marginal cost of production. When price equals marginal cost, consumers keep buying until their marginal benefit equals the price, and because price equals marginal cost, the efficiency condition of marginal cost equaling marginal benefit is satisfied. As explained in further detail in Chapter 6, competitive markets can achieve productive, allocative, and distributive efficiency.

Prices are higher at the airport because the number of sellers is limited[2] and their clientele is captive. Many of the airport customers are leaving the island and have no choice but to make any additional purchases at the airport gift shop. That gives the gift shop *market power*—the ability to influence prices—in that location. It is market power that allows a single operator of ballpark concession stands to charge relatively more for hot dogs and allows a campus bookstore to charge more for batteries than do competing stores in a distant shopping area. In the absence of competitors who would try to undercut excessive prices, the gift shop can charge prices above the marginal cost of production. Suppose for simplicity that it costs $14 to put each Hawaiian shirt on the market (that is, the $14 downtown price equals the marginal cost, as is the case in perfectly competitive markets). Different consumers place a variety of values on Hawaiian shirts, from 0 to more than $100. When the price is $30, consumers who value the shirts in the range between $14 and $30 are dissuaded from purchasing shirts, even though they value shirts at more than the $14 cost of production. For

---

[2] It is common for airports to offer exclusive "master concession" agreements to retailers. For example, HMSHost Corp. owns master concession rights for all food and beverage operations at Honolulu International Airport. See http://starbulletin.com/2002/08/29/business/story1.html.

example, when someone who values a shirt at $20 does not buy 1 because it costs $30, deadweight loss occurs because society loses the $20 − $14 = $6 net benefit that the shirt could have provided. Imperfect competition leads to market failure as a result of these lost opportunities for net gains.

Imperfect Information

McDonald's Restaurant and Doug's Restaurant are both located on North Canal Boulevard in Thibodaux, Louisiana. Why would visitors to Cajun country eat at McDonald's when they could encounter local cuisine at Doug's? One reason involves *imperfect information*, which exists when at least one buyer doesn't know the true benefit of a good or service or at least one seller doesn't know the true cost of providing a good or service. As far as visitors know, Doug's may or may not be a good place to eat. There is relatively little uncertainty about a meal at McDonald's because most visitors know exactly what's on the menu and how it will taste. The additional investment of time and money that customers must make to determine food quality at an unknown restaurant stands in the way of competition from new, no-name-brand competitors, such as Doug's, and thereby thwarts market efficiency. More broadly, although plenty of businesses charge prices above marginal cost, the difficulty and expense of acquiring anything close to perfect information stand in the way of competition from new entries, such as Bob's Bank, Carl's Cars, and Dave's Diner, which lose customers because of uncertainty about quality.

When buyers and sellers don't share the same information, the problem of *asymmetric information* arises. As explained in Chapter 5, those in the marriage market use ease of attraction as a signal of the unseen qualities of a potential mate. Employers and shoppers likewise use college degrees, grades, name brands, and prices as imperfect signals of quality among workers and products when perfect information is not available. Nobel laureate George Akerlof pointed out that there is asymmetric information between buyers and sellers of used cars: Sellers know things about the quality of their cars that potential buyers do not. Suppose that used cars are either good or bad and that good used cars are worth $20,000, whereas bad used cars are worth $10,000. Given the uncertainty about whether a car will be a "lemon" (bad), buyers are unlikely to pay $20,000 for a used car. If, in the buyer's estimation, there is a 20 percent chance that the car is a lemon and an 80 percent chance that it's worth $20,000, the expected value of the car (the sum of each probability times the outcome that occurs with that probability) is (0.2)($10,000) + (0.8)($20,000) = $18,000. Thus, sellers of good used cars won't get fair prices for their cars, but sellers of lemons will. The result is that owners of good used cars are more likely to hold on to their cars and the used car market may be made up primarily of lemons.

In response to the risk that the market for used cars might become a market for lemons, many buyers of used cars (and homes and boats) invest in a professional evaluation of their contemplated purchase to try to gain more of the information held by the seller. Car buyers are also wise to request a vehicle identification number (VIN) check on their car at a Web site such as www.carfax.com, which will reveal information on odometer readings, the number of previous owners, any major accidents in the vehicle's past, and similar potential problems that sellers know about and buyers otherwise don't.

Adverse selection occurs when it costs varying amounts of money to serve different customers but sellers cannot distinguish between high-need and low-need buyers. It would make sense for people who take more physical risks to buy more health insurance; for big eaters to patronize all-you-can-eat restaurants; for people with terminal diseases to buy more life insurance; and for employees with larger families to seek employers who provide better family health, vision, and dental benefits. In efforts to limit adverse selection, insurance companies typically require physical exams and may not cover preexisting illnesses. All-you-can-eat restaurants and employers have a harder time dodging the adverse-selection bullet because they cannot discriminate on the basis of appetite or family size.

Moral hazard is the tendency for those with insurance against a problem to take fewer precautions to avoid that problem. Knowing that a hospital stay can cost $2,000 or more per day, people with insurance may be more likely to take up skydiving than are people who have to shoulder their entire medical bill themselves. Laid-off workers covered by unemployment insurance take more time to find new jobs than do those who are ineligible or whose coverage has lapsed. And people with fire insurance may take more risks with candles in their homes because they will not have to pay the entire price of a new house if there is a fire. Insurance companies would relish the ability to better monitor the risk-taking behavior of their customers. A more practical but imperfect solution is for insurers to increase copayments and experienced-based premiums to boost the share of the burden that insured people must pay when their precautions turn out to be inadequate. People respond to incentives in rational ways, so the more they have to pay for their mistakes, the less likely they will be to make mistakes.

Clearly, the solutions to imperfect information are themselves imperfect and costly. Car and human checkups intended to level the informational playing field sometimes do not. High copayments place a financial burden on the poor. Only a 100 percent copayment would bring decision makers to internalize the full costs of their behaviors, and that would eliminate the risk-sharing benefits of insurance. When solutions are unavailable or incomplete, the information problems explained in this section obscure true marginal benefits or marginal costs and deter the efficient convergence of the two.

Public Goods

A handful of spy satellites spin 100 miles above the earth, recording a constant video stream of activities below. These billion-dollar detectives are intended to make the world safer by tracking military, drug, and terrorist activities. The U.S. National Reconnaissance Office operates satellites to intercept messages, draw maps, and gather visual information for U.S. intelligence agencies.[3] United Nations inspectors used satellites to get an advance look at possible nuclear facilities in Iraq. And satellites help the U.S. Drug Enforcement Agency peek into the hideouts of druglords in Cali, Colombia, before a raid. As useful as spy satellites are to society, it would be difficult for a spy satellite market to bring about the efficient number of them because there

---

[3] See www.spacetoday.org/Satellites/YugoWarSats.html.

are incentives for beneficiaries to receive the benefits of satellites without helping out with the costs.

A few relevant terms are useful in explaining why this is the case. A good or service is *nonrival in consumption* if 1 person's consumption of it does not affect anyone else's consumption of it. A street band is nonrival in consumption because 1 passerby's enjoyment of the music doesn't prevent others from enjoying it. In contrast, shoes are rival in consumption because if 1 person is wearing them another person cannot. A good or service is *nonexcludable* if it is impossible to prevent other people from benefiting as long as 1 person is benefiting from it. A streetlight is nonexcludable because, if it is lighting the way for 1 driver, other drivers can benefit from the same light. Dorm rooms are excludable because you can lock your door and prevent others from entering. Goods and services that are both nonrival in consumption and nonexcludable are called *public goods*.

The challenge of creating the efficient number of spy satellites, as with street bands and streetlights, is that they are public goods. Everyone can benefit from them no matter who pays for them. Thus, the temptation is to be a *free rider* and enjoy the benefits of someone else's expenditures. Some street bands appear because some people give them tips, but more would appear if everyone who enjoyed the music chipped in. If the Central Intelligence Agency (CIA) went from door to door asking everyone to pitch in to pay for the next satellite, it would be rational from an individual standpoint for many people to contribute less than their fair share of the price in hopes that others would purchase the satellites to the benefit of all. The result is that private markets for public goods generally don't bring about the efficient quantity of the goods in question.

A common solution to the free-rider problem is for the government to collect taxes from all the beneficiaries of public goods and use the revenues to fund the appropriate quantities of them. The spy satellites are indeed paid for with tax dollars, as are streetlights, police and fire departments, the Environmental Protection Agency, and the military, among other public goods. Given the unequal use of public goods by taxpayers and the difficulty of estimating the ideal quantity of public goods, private solutions can be appealing. In some cases technological advances help to turn public goods into private goods with no free-rider problem. For instance, uncongested roads are public goods (congested roads become rival in consumption). Devices called Smart Tags can be attached to car windshields or license plates to communicate electronically with computers at toll booths and deduct tolls from the accounts of drivers, who need not stop as they pass through a toll lane. For drivers on the Dulles Greenway in Virginia, for example, this system takes much of the hassle out of toll booths and increases the viability of toll roads that require everyone to pay their fair share of highway costs.

IT'S NOT ONLY ROOT BEER

Entire books have been written about each of these types of market failure. In terms of the primary example in this chapter, it is interesting to note that the local root beer stand isn't the only place where the check is split. In 2005, health-care costs amounted to 15 percent of gross domestic product, up from 5 percent in 1960. Although expensive high-tech advances, doctors, malpractice lawyers, and insurance companies may all share the blame for higher prices, remember that hospitals are another place where people typically split the check. The great benefit from insurance is that it allows them to spread risks and rising costs. The downside is that, as with root beer, people make decisions about additional health-care purchases knowing that they will personally bear only a small fraction of the price of these services. Since 1960, the share of health-care costs paid out of pocket dropped from 55 to 16 percent.[4] According to John C. Goodman, president of the National Center for Policy Analysis, "the primary reason health care costs are rising is that most spending on health care is done with someone else's money rather than the patient's."[5] If the doctor asked you whether you'd like to use an X-ray to rule out the possibility that the frozen pizza you dropped on your foot broke a toe, you might consider your copayment for the procedure rather than the full cost of an X-ray and request X-rays that are not justified by their true cost. Similarly, if your car is dented by an errant baseball, you might weigh the benefit of getting it fixed against the amount by which your premiums will go up rather than the true cost of the repair. As with the moral hazard problem of insufficient care taken by those with insurance, the problem of splitting the insurance check could be solved by charging consumers higher copayments so that they'd bear more of the cost of their decisions.

CONCLUSION

This chapter highlights situations in which market incentives and the decisions they drive run afoul of efficiency. When individuals don't bear the cost of their personal consumption choices, the incentive is to buy too much of goods and services that place burdens on others and too little of goods and services that benefit others. When barriers to competition exist, people can expect prices above marginal cost and lost opportunities to produce goods that are valued beyond their production cost. When information is imperfect, people cannot respond appropriately to true marginal costs and marginal benefits. And when goods are nonrival in consumption and nonexcludable, people have incentives to minimize expenditures on these public goods in hopes of free riding on the purchases of others. These problems prevent consumption from continuing until the benefit from another unit no longer exceeds the cost; as a result, the market fails to create all the net benefits that it otherwise could.

DISCUSSION STARTERS

1. If someone smokes cigarettes in the desert and no one else is there to smell the smoke, does the smoking create a negative externality? Why or why not?

2. To what extent do people consider only the private costs and overlook the social costs of their actions? Do you consider the burden you impose on others when you and your friends order root beers and split the check? Do

[4] See http://aspe.hhs.gov/health/MedicalExpenditures/index.shtml.
[5] See www.econlib.org/library/Enc/HealthInsurance.html.

you consider the burden you impose on others when you order new shoes, thus creating production, transportation, and disposal externalities? Do you think about the congestion and pollution you create when you decide how many car trips to take?

3. As a deterrent to burglary, you could install alarms around your home that help the police catch criminals or install a fence around your home that keeps intruders out. In terms of crime (and disregarding the attractiveness of the fence), which of these deterrents might create positive externalities? Which might create negative externalities? Which method of crime deterrence might a neighborhood association want to subsidize? Why?

4. Do you ever participate in adverse selection? How might adverse selection cause you to pay higher interest rates on your credit card balances?

5. Are you ever affected by moral hazard? How might moral hazard influence your decision to go water-skiing?

6. Why do you suppose there are 50 McDonald's restaurants within 10 miles of the tourism mecca of Orlando, Florida, but only 17 within the same distance of Oxnard, California (a town of similar size)? Hint: One would expect this difference in the number of golden arches even if the same number of restaurant meals were eaten in each city.

CHAPTER 12

HOW GULLIBLE ARE WE?

Information Problems and Their Applications to Schools of Economic Thought

In the United States the burden of proof for a criminal conviction is evidence of guilt "beyond a reasonable doubt." In death penalty cases, over and above the due process rights to fair and just proceedings, the Supreme Court calls for "super due process," a painstaking sequence of trials, appeals, and reviews. Even so, the Death Penalty Information Center reports that 119 people have been exonerated from death row since 1973. Death row inmates, such as John Thompson who served eighteen years before an investigator discovered evidence "hidden" by the prosecution, were found to be innocent under the law despite the extraordinary attention that had been paid to factual information at their trials. These mistaken verdicts are information failures of the worst type, and they occur after what are typically protracted, multimillion-dollar explorations into the truth. If society can't get things right after all that, imagine the errors that might be made with less closely scrutinized information. This chapter discusses barriers to information and rationality and examines the potential for consequent failures in markets and economic models.

INFORMATION AND EFFICIENCY

Anyone who pays $30,000 a year for college tuition or $50 a month for Internet access demonstrates that information is a cherished commodity that requires time and money to acquire. Often the cost of obtaining all the information desired is prohibitive, and the result is often ill-informed decisions based on incomplete facts. One testament to the degree of misinformation in our economy is the large volume of litigation spurred by alleged information failures. Here are a few examples:

- The Federal Trade Commission (FTC) received 431,000 complaints of consumer fraud in 2005.

- In 1999, the United States filed suit against Philip Morris and other major cigarette manufacturers for having "repeatedly and consistently" denied the disease and addiction dangers of tobacco.[1]

- An ongoing lawsuit alleges that many children have suffered obesity, diabetes, heart disease, high blood pressure, elevated cholesterol, and related health problems after being misled by fast-food restaurant chains about the health-related aspects of their food.

- McDonald's lost a legendary case alleging a failure to inform customers about their unexpectedly hot coffee, which is served at a temperature about 20 degrees higher than that of coffee served at other restaurants.[2]

- Stockholders have filed suit against companies from Audible, Inc., to AstraZeneca PLC claiming that they had received inadequate information about the value of those stocks at the time of purchase.

Uninformed consumers may consume too much of products that have hidden costs, pay more for products than their value, or purchase products that are inferior in price or quality to those available elsewhere. Uninformed sellers face the same problems when purchasing inputs; the possibility of excess costs that result from moral hazard and asymmetric information is discussed in Chapter 11. Incomplete information and irrational behavior also stab at the heart of *Homo economicus*—the fully informed and rational representative agent whose unfailing utility maximization is used by many economists to model the behavior of us all.

If perfect information and rationality are what spawn efficient decision making, how concerned should people be about errors, bias, and incomplete information as sources of inefficient behavior and inaccurate applications of traditional economic models? This chapter examines chinks in our armor of information and cognitive ability and the implications of those weaknesses for economic theory and practice.

NEOCLASSICAL ASSUMPTIONS ON THE ROPES

There are differing schools of thought about the significance of information problems and behavioral anomalies. *Neoclassical economists,* such as Milton Friedman, Arthur Pigou, and Gary Becker, place considerable reliance on *rational choice theory,* which

---

[1] See http://www.usdoj.gov/civil/cases/tobacco2/.

[2] See www.jacksonwilson.com/articles/article_mcdonaldsfacts.htm. This case is held up by some as an example of excessive litigation (see, for example, www.overlawyered.com/2003/12/mcdonalds_coffee_revisited. html). However, the failure to inform patrons regarding the especially high temperature of McDonald's coffee is seldom disputed.

holds that decision makers are able to compare all their alternatives with full information about the ramifications of their choices. *Institutional economists*, including Thorstein Veblen, John Commons, John Kenneth Galbraith, and Joseph Stiglitz, stress that decision makers may not behave according to neoclassical theory. They point out that *institutions*—rules, relationships, organizations, and systems of norms—along with cognitive ability limit our reception and retention of information and our responses to it. Governments, corporations, communities, labor unions, and markets all have rules and norms that can interfere with rational, fully informed decision making.

Researchers in the field of behavioral economics study the rationality of market participants and find that people often make decisions based on *heuristics*, or rules of thumb. For instance, many retailers flout the pricing formulas of economic theory and use the *keystone* pricing method, which means they determine their retail price by simply doubling the wholesale price they paid to their supplier.

As with anything else, it is efficient to continue to seek more information until the marginal cost of doing so equals the marginal benefit. When information comes only at a cost, it may well be rational to act on incomplete information. This does not, however, explain every questionable use of information. In defiance of rationality, individuals are often responsive to the way in which information is framed. A half-full glass is equivalent to a half-empty glass in volume but not in perception. Psychologists Daniel Kahneman and Amos Tversky found that among 4 identical outcomes presented with differing descriptions, respondents overwhelmingly preferred a disease-control program that would save 200 out of 600 people to a program that would allow 400 out of 600 people to die.[3]

Dubious about models based on the ever-rational and informed *Homo economicus*, Nobel laureate Herbert Simon explained that rationality is bounded by limitations in the ability of decision makers to formulate and solve complex problems. In his book *Models of My Life* (1991), Simon argued that even Albert Einstein could not match the mental gymnastics ascribed to the fictional "economic man." In further violation of neoclassical theory, some people do pay voluntarily for public goods that could be enjoyed on someone else's dime. Although it would be rational to free ride on clean air, sermons, and lobbying efforts paid for by others, the Sierra Club has more than 750,000 paying members, most churchgoers give to their parishes, and about 4.3 million National Rifle Association members pay dues to that organization.

Again straying from the expectations of *Homo economicus*, decision makers sometimes make biased choices among competing options. *Status quo bias* induces people to stick with what they've got despite equally attractive alternatives. The authors of *Smart Choices* (2002), John Hammond, Ralph Keeney, and Howard Raiffa, describe a natural experiment in which the state governments of New Jersey and Pennsylvania both adopted 2 options for automobile insurance. Under plan A, insurance premiums were lower but drivers had a limited right to litigate after an accident. Under plan B, the premiums were higher but litigation options were broader. In New Jersey drivers received plan A unless they specified otherwise; Pennsylvania drivers were assigned to plan B unless they opted for plan A. The result was that the majority of drivers in each state stuck with the status quo, meaning the plan they were given in the first place.

---

[3] "The Framing of Decisions and the Psychology of Choice," *Science* (January, 1981), *211*, 30.

Neoclassical theories of consumer choice rely on assumptions that the amount an individual would be willing to pay for a good and the amount he or she would accept to give up an identical good are the same. However, researchers have found *endowment effects,* meaning that people place a higher value on what they have than on what they don't have. In a famous example, Daniel Kahneman, Jack Knetsch, and Richard Thaler found that, after randomly selecting half the students in a class to receive coffee mugs, students without mugs were willing to pay less than half as much to buy one as the people with a mug had to be paid to give one up.[4] In auctions of seats in overcrowded classrooms, students with seats typically demand more to give them up than those without seats are willing to pay for them.[5]

It would also be rational for everyone to ignore *sunk costs*—costs that have already been incurred and cannot be recovered. No matter how much money one has sunk into a project, the project should be abandoned if the future benefits do not exceed the future (or recoverable) costs. For example, the makers of the ill-fated movie *Waterworld* would likely have lost less money if they had dropped the project when costs ran hopelessly out of control, but having spent tens of millions already, they felt (irrationally) compelled to complete the film at a reported cost of more than $200 million; at the time (1995), it was the most expensive movie ever made. As another example, Air France and British Airways were slow to discontinue their supersonic Concorde passenger jet service despite losses, ostensibly because they had already spent so much money to get the program off the ground. All these examples demonstrate that even when good information is available, people may not use it wisely.

WHOM CAN WE TRUST?

The information superhighway isn't always super when it comes to accuracy. As one example, the Flat Earth Society asserts that the earth is flat; that all places named Springfield are linked in hyperspace to a single, real Springfield; that gravity is a lie; and that Idaho, North Dakota, and Australia do not exist.[6] Other Web sites suggest that North Dakota and more than one Springfield may exist after all, so there may be some stretching of the truth on-line.

Consumers look to newspapers and news organizations for credible information, but even the *New York Times* and *USA Today* have admitted that certain reporters have faked news stories. Al Franken's book *Lies and the Lying Liars Who Tell Them: A Fair and Balanced Look at the Right* (2004) sparked a lawsuit from Fox News. Did Fox sue because of the many allegations of lies told by their broadcasters? No, they merely objected to Franken's use of the words *fair and balanced*, which Fox had been using as its slogan. And in 2005, four employees of CBS News were fired or resigned after an independent panel concluded that a *60 Minutes Wednesday* story criticizing President George Bush's service in the National Guard was based on evidence that might have been forged. Fears that the news media distort the truth have given rise to dozens of

---

[4] "Experimental Tests of the Endowment Effect and the Coase Theorem," *Journal of Political Economy,* (December, 1990), *98*, 1325–1348.

[5] An anonymous reviewer of early drafts of this book described this phenomenon.

[6] See www.flat-earth.org.

watchdog organizations and Web sites, including the conservative www.ChronWatch. com and the liberal www.MediaMatters.com. If what the watchdogs say is to be believed, the media will not save us from our information problems.

The information received about market goods and services can be similarly misleading. Advertisers are under the close legal scrutiny of the FTC, the Food and Drug Administration (FDA), and the Federal Communications Commission (FCC). The FTC regulates national advertising, with the goal of protecting both consumers and competitors from deceptive or unfair ads. One function of the FDA is to regulate food and drug labels to "ensure that they are truthful and that they provide usable information that helps consumers make healthy, safe decisions when using the product."[7] This includes setting strict legal definitions for terms such as *fresh*, *light*, *low fat*, and *reduced calories*. The FCC shares control with the FTC for broadcast advertising and has the authority to grant and revoke broadcast licenses for television, radio, cable, and satellite communications.

With these and other agencies in place to interpret and enforce truth-in-advertising laws, do consumers in fact get the truth? Perhaps not. The FTC finds hundreds of misinformation cases worth investigating each year, and the agency does not pursue such subjective claims as "We have the best product in the world." This type of embellishment is called *puffing*. It might also be called another dead end in the search for credible information.

But we can still trust our friends, right? I put some stories I heard from my friends to the test. According to the urban-legend-busting Web site www.snopes.com and contrary to common lore:

- The body of the late Walt Disney is not cryogenically frozen.

- John Kennedy did not injure the men's hat industry by not wearing one at his inauguration (he actually did wear a hat), although Clark Gable may have wounded the undershirt industry by not wearing one in the 1934 movie *It Happened One Night.*

- A tooth left in a glass of Coca-Cola will not dissolve overnight; Coke is not a reliable spermicide; the combination of Coke and aspirin will not get you high; and the fiasco that ensued when the original Coca-Cola was replaced by New Coke in 1985 was not a marketing ploy.

- The use of a preprinted IRS label to mail in your tax return does not increase your chances of being audited.

- Subliminal advertising spliced into theater movies does not increase the demand for popcorn and soda.

All these myths persist in the information age, in which mass-communication networks bring news and information rapidly even to remote areas. This is not to say that technology has failed to make market participants better informed. Fishers on the southern coast of India now use cell phones to discover where they can command the highest prices for their lobsters. To improve the fishers' gains from information, a com-

---

[7] See www.fda.gov.

pany called Bharti Tele-Ventures plans to offer them wireless Internet service that will "significantly increase their earnings" by providing real-time catch prices and allow them to book orders from their boats.[8] Of course, these opportunities for efficiency improvements indicate that the currently available information is incomplete and in violation of neoclassical assumptions.

"HE HIT ME FIRST!" AND OTHER MISINFORMATION INVOLVING LIFE AND LIMB

Our information is imperfect even in those decisions that matter the most. The cost–benefit analysis that in 2003 led to the war in Iraq included the assumption that Saddam Hussein held weapons of mass destruction. However, in 2004, the Deuffler Report indicated that Iraq had unilaterally destroyed its undeclared chemical weapons stockpile in 1991. The investigators found "no credible indications that Baghdad resumed production of chemical munitions" after the Gulf War and no evidence of concerted efforts to restart the nuclear program after 1991.

Controversial foundations for war are nothing new. Other military offensives initially have been justified as defensive maneuvers. On August 4, 1964, in the Gulf of Tonkin between Vietnam and China, two U.S. warships reported attacks by North Vietnamese torpedo boats. U.S. Secretary of Defense Robert McNamara informed Congress that these and previous attacks were genuine and unprovoked. On August 7, 1964, Congress passed the Gulf of Tonkin Resolution, empowering the president to "take all necessary measures to repel any armed attack against the forces of the United States and to prevent further aggression" and to use armed force to assist allies that had signed the Southeast Asia Collective Defense Treaty of 1954. This resolution was used to justify repeated escalations of U.S. involvement in the Vietnam War under Presidents Johnson and Nixon. However, pilots flying over the area, ship captains, and leaked Pentagon documents suggest that the earlier North Vietnamese attacks had been provoked by covert U.S. assistance to the South Vietnamese and that the August 4 battle had been fabricated.[9]

Although World War II may have been touched off in 1937 with battles between Japan and China, alleged deception in 1939 allowed Germany to justify its critical offensive into Poland. On August 31, Hitler's operatives used murdered German prisoners dressed in Polish uniforms to stage a Polish attack on a German radio station. The next day Hitler declared war on Poland, stating among his reasons this and other alleged Polish attacks. On September 3, Britain and France both declared war on Germany, and World War II had begun in earnest.[10]

CONCLUSION

Market failure and efficiency loss can result when buyers don't have full information about available products and prices and when sellers don't have full information about inputs, manufacturing processes, and buyers. The information that neoclassical the-

---

[8] See http://meaindia.nic.in/bestoftheweb/2005/02/23bw01.htm.

[9] See, for example, www.thehistorynet.com/mhq/bltonkin/index.html.

[10] See www.nationmaster.com/encyclopedia/Attack-on-Sender-Gleiwitz.

ory treats as fully and freely available is often costly, incomplete, and asymmetric. And well informed or not, market participants do not always use the information they have in rational ways. The question is whether problems with information justify an abandonment of neoclassical precepts, some revisions and expansions in rational choice theory, or none of the above. Most contemporary economists stake out middle ground, leaning toward the neoclassical side. Indeed, in the past century, neoclassical theory overcame institutional theory as the predominant school of economic thought.

Despite their flaws, neoclassical models provide useful guidance and predictive power. Experiments find that people—not to mention rats, dolphins, and other decision makers broadly defined—generally respond to incentives in rational ways: They all tend to follow the cheese and sardines. As models predict, competition decreases the prices of goods and services. For example, my research suggests that every additional athletic shoe retailer in a small-to-mid-size town causes the average price of running shoes to decrease by about 5 percent. And decision makers tend to weigh benefits and costs, including opportunity costs, as do teen rock stars and athletes who decide to put off college to pursue their careers.

"On the other hand" (as economists infamously say), compelling evidence of problems with information and their effects on behavior has led to critical revisions and expansions of accepted economic analysis. Institutional economists point out that lousy information leads to lousy decisions—"garbage in, garbage out"—and that sometimes decisions aren't very rational even when the incoming information is far from garbage. In the prediction and interpretation of human behavior, it is beneficial to account for possible errors, biases, information failures, and responses to uncertainty. New forays into behavioral economics and the economics of information do just that. We must also acknowledge our low standards for truth and seek improvements in our information whenever the benefits of better knowledge exceed the costs. Ignorance may be bliss, but it doesn't necessarily lead to the best allocation of resources.

DISCUSSION STARTERS

1. How gullible are you? Do you tend to believe what you hear from your friends and what you read on the Internet? Have you ever learned that these or other information sources had fooled you?

2. Do you agree with the institutional economists' claim that our information is far from complete? Is the dearth of information an important consideration? Why do you suppose that institutional economics receives less attention than neoclassical economics?

3. Would a product's effects on global warming or acid rain influence your decision to buy it? Can you name the greenhouse gases that cause global warming and the chemicals that cause acid rain? In what sense is this information too costly for most people to obtain?

4. Why do you suppose so many stores list prices ending with 99 cents, such as $19.99 rather than $20.00? To what type of error or bias in the use of information might they be appealing? Does this approach ever work on you?

5. With the purpose of determining whether he had molested a 13-year-old boy, the 2005 trial of singer Michael Jackson cost more than $2.5 million. In what ways might human decision making differ if all information were truly free rather than taking so much time and money to obtain?

6. What evidence have you seen of the failure or success of neoclassical models? Have you noticed changes in the quality, quantity, or prices of goods and services as the number of competitors changed? Could anything that you do be considered irrational?

CHAPTER 13

WHAT'S BEHIND THE MUSIC INDUSTRY'S WOES?
The Sound of Market Power

Secrets can make or break market power. Sometimes the critical secrets are held by sellers. In 1925, the Coca-Cola Company deposited the formula for its market-dominating soft drink in an Atlanta bank and set a policy that only two company officials would be privy to the formula at any given time. Stashed in a vault in Louisville, Kentucky, is Colonel Sanders's secret recipe for the eleven herbs and spices that make Kentucky Fried Chicken (KFC) finger-lickin' good. For greater security, incomplete sets of KFC's ingredients are mixed in two separate locations and then combined in a third location so that no one at any single location can identify all the seasonings.[1] Such trade secrets create informational barriers that prevent competitors from entering a market and pilfering profits.

In the case of the music industry, the consumers hold the most influential secrets, and they work to break down the barriers to competition. Music fans, perhaps even you, secretly duplicate CDs and cassettes and try to hide their true identities while swapping music files on-line. The songs are copyrighted, but relative secrecy and advancing technology allow the practice to compete with retail music venues. Is this development the death knell for the $32 billion global music industry? And how did the

[1] For more on the Coke and KFC stories, see www.snopes.com/cokelore/formula.asp.

industry become so lucrative in the first place? The answers play to the tune of market power.

POWER IN THE MARKETPLACE

When a single producer enjoys a *monopoly* on a product as its only seller and some sort of barrier prevents the entry of competitors, that producer can restrict the quantity sold and raise the price in pursuit of profits. For instance, glass artist Stephen Rolfe Powell can make a fair number of remarkable "vessels" in a month, but by selling fewer than he is able to make, he keeps his artwork relatively scarce and can charge more than $20,000 for a vessel.[2] This would not be the case if he flooded the market with his unique works of art.

The typical monopoly is inefficient from the standpoint of society because it holds output below the level at which the marginal cost of production equals the price consumers are willing to pay. The failure to produce additional units that could be made for less than the benefit to consumers represents a deadweight loss[3] equal to the difference between the missed benefits and the avoided costs. For example, if Powell could produce another glass vessel using $5,000 worth of materials, equipment, fuel, and labor time and sell it for $20,000, that vessel would create $15,000 worth of net benefits. It might not be in Powell's best interest to create that net gain if he charges a standard price for each vessel (that is, if he can't *price discriminate* by charging different customers different prices). Suppose Powell can either sell 8 vessels per month for $22,000 each or drop the price to $20,000 and sell 9. At the lower price he gains $20,000 − $5,000 = $15,000 in profit from the ninth unit but loses $2,000 on each of the 8 units he could otherwise sell for $22,000, for a net loss of ($2,000 × 8) − ($15,000) = $1,000. Powell is better off selling fewer units at the higher price. More generally, firms with market power often produce less than the quantity that is efficient for society and charge more than the price that would exist in a competitive market.

An *oligopoly* exists when a small number of firms dominate the market. As in a monopoly, firms in an oligopoly can influence prices and quantities to their advantage, although the ability to earn profits typically falls as the number of firms in the market increases. To remedy that problem, producers of similar products sometimes organize into *cartels*, which are groups of firms working together to restrict production quantity and charge prices as a monopoly would. Cartels are prohibited in most countries; the U.S. Department of Justice has recently taken legal action against international cartels in the citric acid, vitamin, lysine, and graphite electrode industries.[4]

Market power can be measured by the market share held by the biggest competing firms. A *four-firm concentration ratio*, for example, is the sum of the market shares of the four largest firms in a market. Safeway, Kroger, Wal-Mart, and Albertson's hold 34 percent of the retail food market in the United States. The market structure is considered an oligopoly if the four-firm concentration ratio is 40 percent or more. The

---

[2] See, for example, www.bluespiral1.com/Master-HTML/artist/powell_stephe_10115/home.htm.
[3] As explained in Chapter 9, a deadweight loss is a loss that is not balanced by any resulting gain.
[4] See www.usdoj.gov/atr/public/criminal/8279.pdf.

United States clearly has oligopolies in tobacco, soft drinks, computer software, and long-distance telephone service, all of which have a four-firm concentration ratio higher than 90 percent. There are four major groups in the music industry—Universal, Sony/BMG, Warner, and EMI—and together they hold about 85 percent of the market.

BARRIERS TO ENTRY IN THE MUSIC INDUSTRY

In previous chapters, it was explained how profits can draw competition, increase supply, and bring price down to equal average cost. Profits continue for firms that erect barriers to the entry of competitors. These barriers may include legal barriers, such as patents and licenses; information barriers, such as secret recipes; the control of resources, such as diamonds; and economies of scale, as with a small town that cannot support a second cineplex. Chapter 20 focuses on the struggle between the chief pros and cons of barriers to entry: incentives for innovation (pros) and high prices (cons). Here, how firms make use of market power and how some consumer vigilantes work against it are examined.

At its peak, the music industry enjoyed $40 billion in annual sales, thanks to barriers to competition. Particular songs are copyrighted so that 1 firm controls their sale. Media giants have the incentive to develop relationships with radio stations and concert venues that enable the corporations to promote their own artists over those of smaller, independent record companies and to influence the amount of airtime granted to particular songs. Competing firms that crop up and pose threats are often acquired through mergers. The history of the music industry resembles a feeding frenzy, with big fish, such as Sony and Universal, eating former threats, such as CBS Records and PolyGram, and merging with others, such as BMG and Geffen.[5]

From the perspective of Eagles singer and drummer Don Henley, "The industry, which was once composed of hundreds of big and small record labels, is now controlled by just a handful of unregulated, multinational corporations determined to continue their mad rush toward further consolidation and merger."[6] According to economic theory, the market power held by music companies is not simply a reason for high prices but also a source of diminished quality. Henley writes that since the days of greater competition ended, the variety of music has eroded, as have the meaningful relationships between artists and music company executives and the "unique and personal way" in which music once touched listeners.

With their "say yes to creativity and say no to concentration" campaign, members of the Independent Music Publishers and Labels Association (IMPALA) are fighting the consolidation of major firms. They say that "to flourish, creativity requires diversity, plurality, fair competition and an open society."[7] IMPALA successfully fought the proposed merger of Time Warner and EMI in 2000. IMPALA is also litigating against the European Commission for allowing Sony and BMG to merge in 2004, and the association is vigilant against new merger proposals, threatening similar legal actions to prevent them.[8]

[5] For a description of this history, see www.tangentsunset.com/recordindustry.htm.
[6] Don Henley, "Killing the Music," *Washington Post,* February 17, 2004, p. A-19.
[7] See www.forculturaldiversity.org/intro.html.
[8] See www.impalasite.org.

MUSIC PIRACY AND PATCHWORK IN THE BARRIERS TO ENTRY

Music piracy can involve duplicating a music recording; *counterfeiting* of products and packaging to mislead consumers into thinking they're buying a legal product; and *bootlegging,* which involves the unauthorized recording and sale of live or broadcast performances. The International Federation of the Phonographic Industry estimates that 1.1 billion CDs are pirated each year, representing 35 percent of all music CDs sold worldwide.[9] The Recording Industry Association of America (RIAA) blames illegal file sharing for slumping CD sales, which decreased by 22 percent between 1999 and 2004. In the view of Steve Marks, general counsel for the RIAA, "Millions and millions of people now download billions of songs for free that they used to buy. Simply stated, an industry cannot survive when its content can be acquired for free with no more effort than the click of a mouse."[10]

Pernicious symptoms of market power may have contributed to the decline in CD sales. *Rolling Stone* magazine's ranking of the top 500 albums reveals that the perceived quality of music has gone downhill since the early 1970s. As suggested by Don Henley, the lack of competition may have led to reluctance among the consolidated music groups to take risks with new artists and unconventional approaches. Conservative tactics and complacency may have opened the door for competitors such as purevolume.com, which offers free music by unsigned groups. Regardless of whether you're a fan of independent bands, such as Fat Kid Running, the ability to find alternative music on-line has an appeal similar to that of used bookstores, where one can finally find an array of titles beyond those on the best-seller list.

The big firms are also losing control of bricks-and-mortar sales outlets. Historically, record stores, such as Virgin Records, which was purchased by EMI Music in 1992, have allowed the music industry greater influence on the marketing, product mix, and prices of the albums they issue. Although Internet sales constitute less than 5 percent of the legal market, Wal-Mart makes one-fifth of all retail CD sales in the United States.[11] Superstores, such as Kmart and Wal-Mart, are pricing specialty stores, big and small, out of existence and stocking only a narrow list of music titles. Adding to all these woes—competition from Internet piracy, physical CD piracy, independent record labels, and megaretailers that control and limit music offerings—other forms of entertainment, including DVDs and videogames, are vying for consumers' CD dollars. These alternatives offer retailers higher profit margins, thereby garnering increasing shares of available shelf space.

The music industry has responded with efforts to maintain and rebuild barriers. The RIAA initiated several thousand lawsuits for alleged copyright violations using peer-to-peer (P2P) file-sharing systems, such as Napster, Grokster, and Kazaa. Legal competitors in the music-downloading business have also created barriers against the use of music sold by their legitimate rivals. For example, Apple's iPod digital music players can receive music purchased from the associated iTunes Web site but not from

---

[9] See www.ifpi.org.
[10] See www.riaa.com/news/newsletter/041504.asp.
[11] See "Music's Brighter Future," *The Economist,* October 28, 2004, available at http://www.economist.com/displaystory.cfm?story_id=E1_PPNJTGJ.

Sony Connect or Microsoft's MSN Music Store. Because these barriers generally apply to proprietary music files and not to the more general MP3 files shared illegally, these restrictions on the usability of purchased files may, in fact, encourage the use of illegal files.

MUSIC LESSONS

Historically, the music industry has weathered many a technology-based storm. Along the way, eight-track tapes lost a war over media formats,[12] cassette tapes allowed illegal copying that records did not, and CD burners dramatically improved the quality of copied music. After some casualties, the industry has always adapted with new strategies and business models, a recent example being on-line stores' practice of selling low-priced music downloads.

Firms in *contestable markets,* into which competitors could enter, can be enticed to approximate the prices, quantities, and qualities of a competitive industry to forestall the entry of new competitors. Rampant music piracy in the oligopolistic music industry provides a persistent, if illegal, threat of competition. No sooner did a court dismember the original Napster than myriad alternatives made the scene. As lawsuits against second-generation P2P systems, such as Grokster, come to a head, "censorship-resistant" substitutes, such as Freenet, are waiting in the wings with improved opportunities for anonymous file sharing. Given the unlikely prospects of reining in the expanding universe of P2P technology, the music industry may need to act more like a competitive firm, taking risks with innovative acts, lowering prices, and providing more variety. Along these lines, Universal and Warner are investing in independent labels, such as Canada's Maple Music, to help them identify promising new artists.

When something is cheap or free, it is sometimes said that it can be bought "for a song," but saying that an illegal music download can be had for a song is both misleading and a bad pun. As firms in the contestable market for music address their clandestine competition, it is important for them to assess the true costs inherent in file sharing. Beyond the negligible "click of a mouse" cost mentioned by Steve Marks, P2P music downloads impose several other types of costs. The expected legal cost is the probability of detection multiplied by the fine if detected. *Risk-averse* people are uncomfortable with uncertain prospects, and the *risk burden* is the amount above the expected legal cost that a risk-averse individual would pay to avoid uncertainty about being caught. The *guilt burden* is the amount an individual would pay to avoid feeling guilty about breaking the law and depriving workers in the music industry of compensation. Music downloads also take time and thus impose an opportunity cost equal to the value of the next-best alternative use of the time spent downloading.

When similar music variety and quality are available from both legal and illegal sources, consumers must compare the price of legal music with the sum of the expected legal cost, risk burden, guilt burden, and opportunity cost of time required for illegal downloads. The common 99-cent price of legal downloads may be the indus-

---

[12] See www.8trackheaven.com/8THistory.html.

try's closest approximation of that sum (in this case, minus the opportunity cost of time spent downloading the music, which is paid by the consumer for either type of download). More than 300 million 99-cent downloads were purchased from the iTunes music store during its first two years,[13] so apparently that price hits the mark for many consumers. The continuing popularity of P2P file sharing indicates that, for many, either that price is too high or the limited legal offerings are inadequate.

The lessons from the music industry are relevant to a broad set of related industries. Movies, photos, and audio books are all among the items that can be accessed at file-sharing sites, such as Kazaa. Piracy and Internet sales are a growing problem for textbook publishers in an industry dominated by a similarly small number of giants. And the power of the large media companies, such as News Corp. (parent company to Fox News), Time Warner, and GE (parent company to NBC), may become diluted by a growing number of free, on-line news and entertainment services and new entries, such as satellite radio, that are made available by advancing technology.

CONCLUSION

About 1900, seashells inscribed with ancient Chinese characters turned up in Xiaotun, China, and commanded handsome profits from scholars and collectors. Dealers kept the source a secret to maintain their monopoly. Villagers caught up in the trade of these "dragon bones" subsequently engaged in fights and lawsuits.[14] In the music industry the dragon bones are songs and the secrets are held by clandestine copiers of music, but the fierce fight for market power is the same. Market power confers profits that cannot be maintained in a competitive industry, and that power comes from barriers to entry. When the walls come tumbling down, competitors enter the market and bring profits down as well. Competition is good for consumers in terms of price, quantity, and quality, but it's bad for business.

Firms have long fought to establish and maintain what barriers they could. For example, in the fifteenth and sixteenth centuries, spices such as nutmeg, cinnamon, and myrrh garnered high profits in Europe. In hopes of preventing competitors from entering the market, spice merchants claimed that their source was Africa, although the goods really came from the Far East. Today, pharmaceutical companies create barriers with patents and update products when old patents run out. Movie theaters, convention centers, and school food-service providers typically forbid consumers to bring food in from elsewhere in order to maintain a monopoly. And the recording industry fights to uphold the copyrights to songs for the same reason. New technology makes P2P file sharing an available-yet-illegal competitor to the big music-recording firms. As consumers grapple with their consciences and firms weigh the wisdom of litigating against young perpetrators, artists and fans alike argue that the temptation to steal music and to patronize P2P sites would be eased if the music industry would offer prices and variety that more closely resemble the competitive ideal.

---

[13] See www.answers.com/topic/itunes-music-store.
[14] See Peter Hessler, "The New Story of China's Ancient Past," *National Geographic*, July 2003, p. 65.

DISCUSSION STARTERS

1. What would you guess is the four-firm concentration ratio for pizza in your town? What is the four-firm concentration ratio for submarine sandwiches? How is the market power in these markets reflected in the relative price and quality of pizzas and subs available in your town?

2. How has the retail music scene evolved in the town where you have lived for the longest period of time? Are there more or fewer music stores than there were 10 years ago? In what ways do trends in the price, variety, and quality of retail music offerings in your town fit with economic theory?

3. What barriers to entry exist in the following industries?
   a. electric power utilities
   b. word processing software
   c. cold remedies
   d. textbooks
   e. family medicine

4. Who are the three highest-paid people of whom you can think? Is there market power in their industries? What barriers to entry exist for labor market participants who might want to compete for the positions of those three people? Are the lowest-paying jobs those with the fewest barriers to entry?

5. To what do you attribute declining sales in the music industry? Where do you obtain your music? What strategies would you adopt in regard to P2P file sharing if you were a music-industry CEO?

6. Suppose that by providing more exposure to new groups, P2P systems increased the demand for legal music. Would that justify the illegal act of file sharing?

CHAPTER 14

WAL-MART: FRIEND OR FOE?
Economies of Scale, Low Prices, Low Wages, and Thinking outside the Box

The products that Wal-Mart sells are not known for being particularly durable or high fashion. The checkout lines are long, the stores are short on décor, and the service leaves something to be desired. Wal-Mart allegedly prices quaint competitors into oblivion, exploits workers, hires illegal immigrants to do their cleaning, and discriminates against women. Most of the corporation's own products are outsourced, and its record for community service is less than stellar. There are Web sites, documentaries, and books brimming with Wal-Mart criticism. Oh, and—last but not least—Wal-Mart is the world's most popular retailer. Why? Because the stores are open when shoppers need them, they sell almost everything they want, and their efficiency reduces the dollar cost of weekly groceries. Are they efficient to a fault? Can consumers shop there in good conscience? And what are the ramifications of their market power? This chapter examines the economics of the world's biggest big-box retailer.

INSIDE THE BIG BOX

Tiffany and Company operates 55 U.S. stores, each with an average of 8,109 square feet of retail space—about the size of a baseball diamond—and each store has more than a few diamonds inside. Every Tiffany's store is different. Some are triangular, some are square, some have ornate metal doors, and others greet customers with entryways of glass or carved wood. Customers are pampered with complimentary shopping consultants, fragrance samples, and a lovely, big box in which to nestle plenty of padding around crystal and glass purchases that seldom cost less than $100.

Although they sell diamonds too, the "big-box" retailers are in most respects the antithesis of Tiffany's. California Assembly Bill 178 defines a *big-box retailer* as a store with more than 75,000 square feet of floor space. Wal-Mart, Home Depot, Target, Kmart, Lowe's, and Best Buy stores typically fit both the legal definition and the image the title conjures up—they're big, largely indistinguishable concrete boxes filled with lots of things to buy at low prices with few amenities. Big-box retailers lack the elegance of a Tiffany's and they sell a lot more plastic than crystal or glass, but the shoppers of the world love them. In this chapter, the focus is on the ultimate big box: Wal-Mart, the world's largest retailer and the biggest corporation on earth. The story is similar for many other large discount retailers as well.

At the inception of Wal-Mart in the early 1960s, founder Sam Walton targeted towns of 5,000 to 25,000 residents, where his stores could enjoy a virtual monopoly as a discounter. Recently, Wal-Mart has raised its sights to include some of the world's biggest cities, but it still enjoys a dominant share of the retail market. Wal-Mart operates more than 5,300 discount stores, Supercenters, Sam's Clubs, and Neighborhood Markets in 10 countries. The 1,343 Wal-Mart discount stores in the United States cover about 98,000 square feet each—as much as two football fields—and sell 62,500 general merchandise items. Each of the 1,730 Wal-Mart Supercenters offers about 187,000 square feet (more than three football fields) of general merchandise, groceries, and pharmaceuticals, with 116,000 items in all. Each of the 552 Sam's Clubs offers about 127,000 square feet of general merchandise and bulk items, and the 86 Neighborhood Markets average about 43,000 square feet and 38,000 items each. Net sales for all these operations total about $319 billion annually.[1]

ALWAYS LOW PRICES

Wal-Mart is the most popular store in the world because consumers appreciate the convenience of one-stop shopping; the long hours; the vast selection; the ample parking; and, of course, the "every day low prices." Large retailers such as Wal-Mart benefit from *economies of scale*, which exist when the average cost of providing goods decreases as the quantity increases. As stores get bigger, some costs don't grow in proportion to the size of the operation. A store with 2,000 square feet might require only 1 manager, just like a store with 1,000 square feet, but the management cost per dollar of sales is lower in the larger store, where the cost can be spread across a larger volume of sales. A store with 100,000 square feet might need a team of 4 managers, but the fourfold increase in management is small compared with the 100-fold increase in floor space.

In these examples, it is evident that the cost of management grows proportionately less than the size of stores. If the salary of each manager is $50,000 per year and stores average $250 in sales per square foot, the cost of management is $50,000/$250,000 = 20 percent of sales in a 1,000-square-foot store, $50,000/$500,000 = 10 percent of sales in a 2,000-square-foot store, and $200,000/$25,000,000 = 0.8 percent of sales

[1] See www.wal-mart.com and www.standardandpoors.com.

in a 100,000-square-foot store. Similar economies of scale are realized in terms of cash registers, loading docks, security arrangements, distribution systems, warehouses, and most types of staffing. A 2001 report by the McKinsey Global Institute credited Wal-Mart's aggressive use of economies of scale, direct purchasing to eliminate wholesalers, management innovations that increased "competition intensity," and high-tech product distribution systems with causing "the bulk of the productivity acceleration" in the retail sector between 1995 and 2000.

Low prices boost consumer surplus, but not everything about low prices is good. Like other big-box retailers, Wal-Mart is often accused of predatory pricing, which entails toppling competitors with below-cost prices and then charging higher prices on gaining market power. Some people boycott Wal-Mart because the company's aggressive discounting is a death knell for smaller shops that provide more services. Wal-Mart is blamed for closing locally owned pharmacies, groceries, and specialty shops, and for bankrupting bigger foes, such as toy seller FAO Schwarz Inc. To some people, the aesthetics of the shopping experience are meaningful, and there are irreplaceable elements of charm associated with traditional retailers that are lost in the big boxes. On the Doll Collecting page of About.com,[2] Denise Van Patten lamented FAO's struggles to stay afloat and sell favorites, such as Breakfast at Tiffany's dolls, while under increased pressure from major discounters: "You might be able to buy your fine dolls and toys cheaper at Wal-Mart than FAO Schwarz, but trust me, you aren't going to feel the magic of toys and dolls at Wal-Mart, or make Wal-Mart part of your treasured Christmas tradition, the way you could at FAO."

In terms of its lauded efficiency, one problem with Wal-Mart is that the prices may be *too* low; they may lead us to buy too much. Given the externalities of resource depletion, pollution, and postconsumption levels of municipal solid waste, Wal-Mart's artificially low prices foil the moderating effect of higher prices that better reflect true societal costs.[3] Consider the question of how many small kitchen appliances to buy. For about $50 apiece at Wal-Mart, a consumer can buy the Presto Pizzazz Pizza Oven; the George Foreman Lean Mean Grilling Machine; and more fryers, toasters, poppers, and food processors than you can shake a stick at. Suppose the Dough family would pay up to $65 for a fryer, up to $55 for a food processor, and no more than $45 for any of the other items. They can be expected to buy only the 2 appliances that are worth more to them than the $50 price.

Here's the rub: The price doesn't reflect the full cost of an appliance. It doesn't include, for starters, the pollution costs imposed by the production, packaging, transportation, use, and disposal of these products. Taxpayers cover some of the health costs via Medicare and Medicaid; pollution victims bear some of the medical and insurance costs; and the global climate, wildlife species, and future generations all bear some of the burden. Then there are the external costs of resource extraction, involving, for example, strip mines, mountaintop removal, oil drilling, and deforestation.

[2] This story is no longer available at About.com.
[3] When other retailers charge higher prices, it is not for the purpose of including externalities. Nonetheless, quantity demanded and external costs go down when price goes up for any reason. It is also important to note that higher prices aren't always better. It is quite possible that prices at Tiffany's are too high in the sense that they exceed the marginal cost of goods to society and result in inefficiently low consumption levels.

Add to that the loss of nonrenewable resources and the burden of waste disposal. All of these costs are hidden but real. The World Conservation Union lists resource extraction and pollution among the primary dangers to 16,119 species currently threatened with extinction.[4] The consumption habits of the average U.S. citizen require 25 tons of raw materials annually. More than one-third of our citizens live in counties where pollution levels exceed the National Ambient Air Quality Standards. Only 29 states have more than 10 years of landfill capacity left.[5]

Wal-Mart prices may be artificially low for reasons beyond external costs. Some Wal-Mart stores have allegedly been cleaned by poorly paid illegal aliens, and others stand accused of not paying overtime and forcing employees to work "off the clock." If health, environmental, and other hidden costs raise the kitchen appliances' true prices from $50 to $60, only the one worth more than $60—the $65 fryer—should be purchased. The $60 social marginal cost (meaning the full cost to society of one more) exceeds the $55 and $45 benefits from the other gadgets. Because the appliances were priced below social marginal cost, our representative Dough family purchased twice the quantity that would best serve society. That becomes a real problem if the other 137,999,999 Wal-Mart shoppers behave the same way.

ALWAYS LOW WAGES?

The Wal-Mart Corporation employs more than 1.5 million people. In 2005, Wal-Mart president and chief executive officer H. Lee Scott boasted that the company paid an average hourly wage of about $10.[6] Critics point out that averages are skewed by the much higher pay executives receive (for example, Mr. Scott earned $23 million in 2004) and that the average pay for associates (as Wal-Mart calls its sales clerks) is closer to $8.50 per hour.[7] A study by Arindrajit Dube and Ken Jacobs found that Wal-Mart employees in California earn 31 percent less in wages than workers at other large retailers.[8] In part, this difference may reflect Wal-Mart's vigilance against labor unions, which use collective bargaining to improve compensation packages and secure the fair treatment of workers. In 2004, a store in Jonquiere, Canada, became the first unionized Wal-Mart in North America, but in 2005 the company announced that it would close the store. In 2000, a week after meat cutters organized a union at a Texas Wal-Mart store, Wal-Mart announced that it would be completely phasing out its meat-cutting departments. These antiunion practices have raised the ire of the American Federation of Labor and Congress of Industrial Organizations (AFL-CIO), a voluntary federation of labor unions, which has its own Web site devoted to Wal-Mart problems: http://aflcio.org/corporateamerica/walmart/main.cfm.

Low wages can be a burden even to the broader population that enjoys the associated low prices: They can necessitate higher taxes because recipients of low wages must rely more heavily on public assistance. The Democratic staff of the congressional

---

[4] See www.iucn.org/themes/SSC/redlist2006/threatened_species_facts.htm.

[5] See www.epa.gov/ncea/ROEIndicators/pdfs/MSWGENMNG_FINAL.pdf.

[6] See http://slate.msn.com/id/2113954/.

[7] Steven Greenhouse, "Wal-Mart, Driving Workers and Supermarkets Crazy," *New York Times*, October 19, 2003, sec. 4, p. 3.

[8] See www.wakeupwalmart.com/facts/berkeley-report.pdf.

Committee on Education and the Workforce estimates that a Wal-Mart with 200 employees costs federal taxpayers $420,750 annually in public assistance for benefits such as health care, subsidized meals, energy, and housing.[9] The problem of low wages is intensified by the fact that wages and prices at Wal-Mart influence wages and prices elsewhere. In order to compete with Wal-Mart prices, other retailers must cut their wages. For example, after striking for 5 months, unionized grocery workers in southern California agreed to cuts in pay and benefits in hopes of saving their jobs against a growing threat from Wal-Mart. In order to be Wal-Mart suppliers, producers face pressure to cut prices and, therefore, wages as well. Wal-Mart suppliers Huffy and Levi's closed their last U.S. plants in 1999 and 2004, respectively, to reduce costs, enacting the ultimate wage cut for their workers by laying them off. Cutthroat practices at 1 retailer thus have a cascading effect on prices and wages at a whole line of suppliers and producers.

The general issue of compensation at Wal-Mart is magnified for women. In *Selling Women Short: The Landmark Battle for Workers' Rights at Wal-Mart* (2005), author Liza Featherstone claims that a history of gender discrimination at Wal-Mart has led to what may become the largest class-action lawsuit in history: *Dukes* vs. *Wal-Mart Stores Inc.* The plaintiffs in the case note that, although two-thirds of Wal-Mart's hourly workers are women, only one-third of managerial positions are held by women and fewer than 15 percent of store managers are women. They also assert that, since 1997, despite having higher average performance levels and lower turnover rates than men, women have earned less than men with the same seniority in every major job category.[10]

THE FREE RIDE

Supporters point out that although the demise of beloved local businesses is a problem, Wal-Mart merely offers consumers another choice. Each week more than 138 million customers worldwide choose to support Wal-Mart by shopping there, and 80 percent of Americans shop there at least once each year. If consumers cared more about the mom-and-pop bakery than the buck they save buying cake at Wal-Mart, they'd support mom and pop, right?

Well, not necessarily. The actions of shoppers may reflect the temptation to free ride on public goods, as discussed in Chapter 11. Charming downtowns and undeveloped wilderness areas, or *green space,* on the periphery of towns are public goods because 1 person's enjoyment of them doesn't interfere with other people's enjoyment and because it is not possible to exclude people from enjoying these amenities when they exist. The temptation, then, is to free ride on other people's efforts to preserve green space and, if the discount stores are built, to shop at them and hope that others will spend the extra money it takes to support a vibrant downtown. Just as you can't have your cake and eat it too, you can't have your lovely downtown cake shop and eat at Wal-Mart prices too!

[9] See www.nea.org/topics/walmart-fact.html.
[10] See www.walmartclass.com.

THINKING OUTSIDE THE BOX

Some communities have decided that the costs of a Wal-Mart exceed the benefits. Boxboro, Massachusetts, is among 248 communities listed on www.Sprawl-Busters.com as having successfully opposed new or bigger big-box stores. When Wal-Mart proposed a superstore for part of a Stafford County, Virginia, farm where George Washington lived as a boy and reportedly could not tell a lie about chopping down his father's cherry tree, local opposition killed the idea. Consultants, such as Jon Schallert and Al Norman, travel to towns with new or proposed Wal-Marts to help smaller businesses consider how to stand their ground. Anti-Wal-Mart Web sites include www. AgainstTheWal.com, www.WalMartSurvivor.com, and www.WalmartWatch.com.

Wal-Mart, too, is thinking outside the box. After losing battles over the development of green space, in 2005 Wal-Mart pledged $35 million over 10 years toward its largest environmental endeavor: Acres for America. This program aims to offset the development of land for corporate use with the conservation of 138,000 acres of wilderness. In addition, each Wal-Mart location provides a $500 grant for an environmental cleanup project. The company is also a supporter of the Children's Miracle Network, the United Way, National Public Radio, and numerous scholarship programs, among other charitable organizations. These are some of the ways in which Wal-Mart gives back to the communities that accept its stores.[11]

CONCLUSION

How are priorities established among vibrant downtowns, one-stop shopping, customer service, low prices, and the environment? The developed world faces these dilemmas as strip malls and superstores invade the turf of local merchants. With city centers on the endangered list, shoppers might be expected to vote with their pocketbooks, in which case megastores would not and could not stay on the scene because they wouldn't have the monetary "vote" of the public. The very existence of big-box retailers would seem to demonstrate their desirability.

Alas, the acceptance criteria for large chain stores are not that straightforward. Countervailing forces in the retail market may prevent a fair "election." For example, pocketbook voters may be tempted into free riding on the efforts and expenditures of others. Higher rent, lower volume, and more services for customers lead to higher prices in smaller stores. Although citizens might value the prosperity of their downtown enough to absorb the cost differential, they may consider their individual support to be inconsequential; as a result, they may rely on others to support the downtown shops while they seek lower prices elsewhere.

Wal-Mart has cut costs and shipping delays with innovations in the areas of satellite communications, computerization, product tracking, and streamlined distribution. The company also uses its influence to help suppliers cut costs and pass the savings on to Wal-Mart and its customers. Further efficiencies come from economies of scale, resistance against unions, and relatively low compensation levels for employees. All this leads to low prices that provide low-income shoppers with a higher standard of

[11] More information on Wal-Mart's charitable giving is available at www.wal-mart.com.

living. These benefits weigh against the associated costs, including the environmental costs of increased development, manufacturing, product transportation, and waste disposal; low wages and the tax burden of public services for low-wage workers; the alleged use of sweatshops, child labor, and undocumented workers; and the loss of historic downtowns and smaller stores. Our challenge, then, is to find ways to have consumers factor the full costs and benefits of discount shopping into their purchasing decisions or to purchase as if they did. Otherwise, consumers may collectively but unwittingly lose more than always low prices.

DISCUSSION STARTERS

1. In what ways does Wal-Mart help poor people? In what ways does it hurt them? Can you think of ways of providing benefits to the poor without harm? (Remember: Higher wages would necessitate higher prices.)

2. How do you discriminate between "fair" and "unfair" compensation for workers? Does the fact that employment at Wal-Mart is strictly voluntary (nobody is forced to take a job there) imply that Wal-Mart's level of compensation is adequate? Why or why not?

3. In what specific ways do large retailers exemplify the sources of market failure: imperfect competition, externalities, imperfect information, and public goods?

4. The chapter gave examples of economies of scale in terms of managing stores. Given this, why do you suppose some small stores still exist? In contrast to the big-box stores, how do you explain the success of small, high-priced retailers, such as Starbucks?

5. Do you appreciate a charming, vibrant downtown with small shops and local offerings? Do you ever shop at Wal-Mart? In what ways is it rational for people to value a nice Main Street over the low prices at discount retailers? What solutions might resolve the inherent free-rider problem?

6. Bargains are a boon to all shoppers. What are three potential downsides to low prices? Which, if any, of these downsides do you typically consider when making purchasing decisions? If you do not think about all the repercussions of your consumption decisions, what are possible remedies for such oversights?

7. In the December 16, 2004, issue of *The New York Review of Books*,[12] Simon Head wrote, "To keep the growth of productivity and real wages far apart, Wal-Mart has reached back beyond the New Deal to the harsh, abrasive capitalism of the 1920s." How do you interpret this statement? Is it fair? What obligations, if any, do corporations have to employees and to society?

---

[12] See www.nybooks.com/articles/17647.

CHAPTER 15

WHAT IS THE VALUE OF HUMAN LIFE?

Reasons and Methods for Placing Finite Values on Unidentified Human Lives

Imagine if we placed an infinite value on human life. It would then be rational for us to protect it at all costs. Every health-care expenditure that would save a life would be infinitely more valuable than expenditures on, say, entertainment, so we wouldn't start spending on movies, sports, or amusement parks until every beneficial health-care measure had been adopted. We would spend no money on nonessential goods, such as holiday gifts, furniture, and artwork, until all research with a positive probability of yielding cures for deadly diseases had been performed. Products would become far more expensive because product and workplace safety standards would be set high enough to eliminate risks to life. For instance, no amount would be too much to spend on safety measures in automobiles because the extra money it takes to build cars stronger than tanks would be well worth the priceless lives saved. Activities such as smoking, drinking alcohol, eating red meat, and crossing streets are preventable causes of death, threatening the loss of infinite value and trumping any finite value for the benefits of those activities. We exchange risks of death for money whenever we decline options for side-impact airbags and antilock brakes on cars and whenever we accept money for increasing our risk of death by leaving the safety of our home to go to work. Trade-offs between lives and dollars imply a finite value of life, but is it necessary to specify that value? And, if so, who's got the number?

MUST WE QUANTIFY THE VALUE OF LIFE?

As much as anyone hates to place values on human lives, there are several important reasons why this is done. When making policy decisions, legislators must decide where to draw the line when they require manufacturers to spend money to comply with regulations that will save lives. Fire safety standards for aircraft cabins that save lives for $148,000 each and requirements that children's sleepwear be nonflammable at an added cost of $1.2 million per life saved may be no-brainers. How about asbestos regulations that cost $163 million per life saved? Should we stick with legal limits on occupational exposure to formaldehyde that costs $127 billion per life saved? We could always spend more money to avoid increasingly remote chances of death, but, as a practical matter, we must draw the line somewhere.

When contemplating unidentified lives that we can predict will be lost on the basis of statistics, we want to identify the value of a *statistical life*. For example, we know that every year in the United States there are about 22 traffic fatalities for every 100,000 licensed drivers. We don't know who the victims will be, but everyone who drives faces a risk, and with 200 million licensed drivers we have reasonable certainty that about 44,000 unidentified lives will be lost each year. As we look into the future and make decisions about appropriate speed limits, automobile safety standards, and drunk driving policies, we are discussing not specific lives but statistical lives. A nationwide speed limit of 10 miles per hour would save many statistical lives but at a tremendous cost. The fact that we allow cars to go 70 mph on many highways indicates that we have accepted a trade-off between the statistical lives that will be lost in accidents at such speeds and the benefits of getting places quickly. Naturally, the value we place on a particular life, especially our own, is in another ballpark.

In a wrongful-death lawsuit, one person's death is attributable to the willful or negligent act of another. Jurors must decide how much the victim's family should receive from the defendant. If the goal is to elicit efficient decisions about dangerous behavior and safety precautions that might affect lives, then a *deterrence value* for a life equal to the full value of a statistical life is needed. If decision makers know they must pay the full value of a statistical life in the event that their actions kill someone, they will not take those actions unless the benefits exceed the expected loss. Automobile manufacturers, for example, are often faced with the dilemma of whether to spend more money on safety features that will save lives in accidents. In the 1970s, the Ford Motor Company estimated that 180 deaths and 180 serious burn injuries would be prevented if it installed an $11 part to avoid fuel fires on each new Pinto (a line of small cars). With the expectation of being required to pay $200,000 per lost life and $67,000 for each serious injury, Ford calculated that the benefit of installing the parts would be $49.5 million, whereas the cost would be $137 million.[1] On that basis, the company made the unfortunate and inefficient decision to forgo the safety measure. If Ford had anticipated court-imposed penalties similar to the actual value of a statistical life, the company would have installed the part.

In some wrongful-death cases the goal is to compensate the family of the victim for the financial burden of losing a wage earner, in which case an award equal to the

---

[1] See www.fordpinto.com/blowup.htm. These estimates of the payment per lost life and per serious injury are from the National Highway Safety Administration.

value of lost earnings will suffice. When we purchase life insurance, it is our own task to decide how much money our families should receive if we die. This value—the *insurance value* of a life—is generally less than the deterrence value of a life. The insurance value is really a bequest to others that the victim will not enjoy directly, and when deciding how much to leave for others, people typically choose an amount that is less than the full value of their lost earnings. W. Kip Viscusi and William Evans estimate that the insurance value of a life is about 85 percent of the value of lost earnings.[2]

HOW ARE VALUES FOR LIFE CALCULATED?

The dilemma of how to value lives does not lend itself well to surveys. The task of assigning a value to life on the spot is daunting, and responses tend to be at one extreme or the other. In wrongful-death cases the basis is often the value of lost earnings over the expected lifetime of the victim, sometimes with adjustments including family members' losses of love, affection, and companionship from the victim (termed *consortium* in legalese). After the September 11, 2001, terrorist attacks, Congress set up the September 11 Victim Compensation Fund for the families of people who had been killed or injured. To compensate for nonmonetary damages, including pain and suffering, lost consortium, and emotional distress, the families of victims received $250,000 plus $100,000 for the spouse (if any) and for each dependent of the victim. Each family also received an award to compensate for the victim's lost earnings less the amount of any "collateral sources of compensation," such as life insurance, Social Security benefits, and pension funds. On average, the total Victim Compensation Fund award per family was $2,082,035.[3]

Although they are popular in lawsuits, values of life based on earnings involve a critical flaw: We are not what we earn. The value of retired people, homemakers, and chronically unemployed people is clearly not 0, even though their earnings are 0. Lost-earnings values provide guidance for the compensation of families, but they are much smaller than the values society places on statistical lives. To make a better value-of-life estimate, we need to know the number of dollars people would accept in exchange for a certain statistical probability of death. Suppose you would accept $800 in exchange for taking a 1 in 10,000 risk of death (roughly the annual fatality risk for U.S. manufacturing workers). You are effectively valuing 1/10,000 of your life at $800, indicating an implicit statistical value of life of $8 million (10,000 × $800). The following sections describe assessments of the true value people place on statistical lives, calculated on the basis of real-world trade-offs between money and risks rather than on surveys or lost earnings.

Labor Market Values

During the past 30 years, economists have favored estimates of the value of human life that are based on trade-offs made in labor markets. Other things being equal, jobs that

[2] "Utility Functions That Depend on Health Status: Estimates and Economic Implications," *American Economic Review* (1990), *80*:3, 353–374.
[3] See www.usdoj.gov/final_report.pdf.

entail greater risk of death pay more than safer jobs. Compared to jobs with similar prerequisites, for example, miners, firefighters, contractors in war zones, and construction workers receive wage premiums in exchange for their higher risks of death. More subtle variations in risks and wages appear throughout the workforce. Using *econometric analysis*, economists can input data on hundreds of thousands of workers and have computers adjust for differences in worker age, experience, education, and other determinants of wages to calculate the trade-off between wages and risk of death apart from other influences. Extrapolating as we did with the $800 figure in the preceding example, the amount the typical worker is willing to accept for a small risk of death can be used to estimate the value of a statistical life. In similar ways, 27 labor market–based studies determined an average value for a statistical life of $8.76 million. These estimates can be adjusted to fit individuals who are, for example, younger or older than the average worker. Discomfort with suggestions that some people are worth more than others makes applying the average figure to everyone an attractive alternative.

Trade-Offs outside the Labor Market

Orley Ashenfelter and Michael Greenstone used the choice of speed limits to assess the implicit value of a statistical life.[4] They examined the choices of 21 states to raise their speed limits from 55 mph to 65 mph when the federal government permitted that change in 1987. The increase in the speed limit increased highway fatality rates by 35 percent and saved about 125,000 hours of driving time per life lost. By valuing time at the average hourly wage rate, Ashenfelter and Greenstone estimated that the speed limit increase saved $1.89 million worth of time per life lost, suggesting that amount as the upper bound for the implicit value of statistical lives in those states. (States that did not raise the speed limit indicated a higher value for life.) Other value-of-life studies have considered dollar-risk trade-offs involving property values and the mortality effects of air pollution, expenditures on smoke detectors, and expenditures on automobiles with varying accident risks. The results were all in the range of $1 million to $6 million.

When Safety Measures Make Things Worse

Although we can save lives with regulations, if regulations go too far in requiring spending on certain safety measures, they actually cause more deaths than they prevent. The problem is that expenditures on compliance with regulations divert money away from other expenditures, some of which influence our risk of death. Each dollar spent to comply with regulations can't be spent on organic food, a health club membership, or a car with side airbags. Of course, many of the dollars spent on regulations would otherwise go toward goods and services that have no bearing on the length of one's life, but health and safety items are among those normal goods that consumers purchase less of when incomes fall.

Consider the Food and Drug Administration's ban on a cattle-fattening hormone called diethylstilbestrol (DES), which has been linked to cancer. The Office of Management and Budget estimates that the ban on DES in cattle feed costs $185

[4] "Using Mandated Speed Limits to Measure the Value of a Statistical Life," *Journal of Political Economy* (2004), *112*:S1, S226–S267.

million per premature death avoided. This cost, which is reflected in the incomes of workers in the cattle industry and is shared by beef consumers via higher prices, competes with expenditures on everything else, including safer vehicles, healthy food, medical care, exercise equipment, and so on. Randall Lutter, John F. Morrall III, and W. Kip Viscusi examined how the demand for lifesaving and life-endangering goods is influenced by income levels and estimated that each expenditure of $17 million on regulations diverts enough money away from life-affecting goods to cause the loss of a statistical life.[5] Thus, regulations that save lives at a cost of more than $17 million each may also cause the loss of more lives than they save. In fact, each life saved by the DES ban corresponds with the loss of about 11 other lives.

CONCLUSION

A popular 1970s television show had the telling title *The Six Million Dollar Man*. Who knew that each of us is worth approximately that amount? It's a touchy subject, given our respect for humanity, but we must place values on human lives for the purposes of drawing the line on regulations, compensating the families of victims, and establishing appropriate incentives for those whose decisions affect lives. Even if we chose to devote the entire value of the U.S. gross domestic product to avoiding fatal accidents, we would be able to spend less than $100 million per fatality. In our everyday decisions we express even more modest valuations of statistical lives by accepting risks that earn or save measurable amounts of money. The alternative would be to save lives at all costs and to live in a world with many lives and few freedoms or luxuries. Before you let anyone convince you that it's cold to place a dollar value on human lives, ask them if they've ever taken money that could have been spent on health care and used it to buy a television set instead, or if they've ever crossed the street to receive a paycheck.

DISCUSSION STARTERS

1. If we built a pedestrian bridge at every street corner, we could prevent most street-crossing deaths. What does it mean in terms of the value of human life that few street corners have pedestrian bridges?

2. During the Iraq war, U.S. decision makers were criticized by those on the front lines for not purchasing life-saving armor for all the military vehicles. It costs about $75,000 to outfit a vehicle with armor. If you were in charge of making decisions about military vehicles, how would you determine the optimal expenditure on armor? How would you respond to those who say that more vehicles should be armored?

3. Suppose the average American were willing to accept $100 for a 1 in 100,000 risk of death. What implicit value for human life does this decision reflect?

[5] "The Cost-per-Life-Saved Cutoff for Safety-Enhancing Regulations," *Economic Inquiry* (1999), 37:4, 599–608.

4. What is the least amount you would accept in exchange for a 1 in 10,000 chance of death? What is the least you would accept in exchange for a 1 in 10 risk of death (a risk 1,000 times higher)? What is the least you would accept for a 1 in 2 risk of death (a risk 5,000 times higher)? Do the amounts you are willing to accept increase in proportion to the risk of death? Why or why not?

CHAPTER 16

DO POTENTIAL CRIMINALS CONTEMPLATE THEIR FATES?
Making Incentives Matter in the Face
of Risk and Uncertainty

Early in the nineteenth century, England had more than 220 crimes, from picking pockets to murder, that would earn perpetrators one-way trips to the gallows. Thousands of criminals were executed before crowds of onlookers. Strangely enough, undeterred by the fates of their colleagues, pickpockets routinely worked the crowds at public hangings. The irony of this situation raises several questions of importance to modern policymaking: In what ways do punishments matter? To what extent can society address today's crime problems with more severe punishments? And can we confidently assume that criminals are rational and informed? This chapter discusses crime, punishment, and approaches to uncertainty that are relevant to everyday decision making as well as to the choice to pick pockets at a pickpocket's hanging.

RATIONAL CRIME

They say crime never pays, but if that's true, why do as many as 40 percent of automobile riders break mandatory seatbelt laws, 51 percent of drivers exceed the legal speed limit, and 79 percent of employees steal from their employers?[1] Classical economic theorists going back to Jeremy Bentham have argued that human behavior, including crime, is the result of rational calculations of the pleasure and pain that would

[1] See www.investigation.com/articles/library/1999articles/articles22.htm.

result from various contemplated acts. In other words, even transgressions against society may be rooted in cost–benefit analysis.

Efficiency dictates that the optimal amount of lawbreaking is not 0. If you're late for a career-launching interview on the *Today Show*, it might be wise to double park. If you can see lava from an erupting volcano in your rearview mirror, you might well exceed the speed limit. And if the only way to feed your family is to steal a loaf of bread, the benefits of that crime exceed the costs. Rational, informed criminals commit crimes until the marginal benefit from 1 more criminal act no longer exceeds the marginal cost. Unfortunately, criminals consider their own costs and benefits rather than those of society as a whole, so they commit more than the socially optimal quantity of crimes. Deadbolt locks, fences, and alarm systems that decrease the benefits of time spent committing crimes can sometimes forestall misdeeds, as can increased punishments or enforcement measures that raise the cost.

Are lawbreakers really that responsive to costs and benefits? Consider the example of speeding. If this infraction is rational, we should expect the frequency to increase among those who receive greater benefits from it. If there is no accident or ticket, the benefit from speeding is a saving of time. The opportunity cost of time spent driving is higher for those who earn more per hour, so economic theory would predict more speeding among those with higher incomes. Indeed, the 2005 Northwest Insurance Poll by PEMCO Insurance found that two-thirds of drivers with annual incomes exceeding $75,000 speed often or sometimes, compared to 55 percent of drivers who earn between $35,000 and $74,999, and only 43 percent of those who make less than $35,000.

On the cost side, other things being equal, we would expect larger fines to result in fewer infractions. The relationship between fines and infractions is more complex than that, however, because the value of fines may not be known and because the rational driver must also consider the probability of being caught and the large effect that speeding tickets may have on insurance costs. Concerned citizens argue that differing risks of being caught make it rational to drive more aggressively in Oregon, which has 241 state troopers, than in Washington state, which has 658 troopers, or in Florida, which has 1,360.[2] Even if people respond rationally to what they know well, such as the opportunity cost of our time, issues of uncertainty become important to decision making and policy. Most people do not know the number of troopers in their states or the fines for driving 20 mph over the speed limit. The influence of uncertain aspects of law enforcement depends on whether a person is blissfully ignorant of strict laws or paralyzed by the fear of potentially high punishments. The remainder of this chapter explains some rational ways to approach the uncertainties in our lives, the extent of exceptions to rationality, and the implications for public policy.

DEALING WITH UNCERTAINTY

Criminals are not the only ones grappling with uncertainty. When developer Donald Trump contemplated building the Trump World Tower in New York City, the world's largest residential tower, he did so not knowing the future of housing prices. Students

2 See www.blueoregon.com/2005/04/oregon_the_stat.html.

face uncertainty about their employment prospects after graduation. Consumers are uncertain about the quality and safety of many of the products available for purchase. Business owners face uncertainty about their future levels of sales. The insurance industry exists to reduce uncertainty about the costs of health care, car and home ownership, and a host of misfortunes. As Benjamin Franklin put it, "In this world nothing is certain but death and taxes," and there are even insurance markets to deal with the uncertainties of death (euphemistically called life insurance) and tax audits.

Expected-value calculations offer a rational way to deal with risk. The *expected value* of an outcome is calculated by multiplying the probability of that outcome by its value. Consider the outlook for a rational and informed potential auto thief in Minnesota who would weigh the benefit he or she receives from a stolen car against the expected punishment. About 21 percent of car thieves in Minnesota are arrested, 91 percent of offenders are incarcerated, and the average prison sentence is 27 months.[3] The average income in Minnesota is close to $3,000 per month, so the 27 months of incarceration would amount to an income loss of 27 × $3,000 = $81,000. If this were the only loss associated with incarceration, the expected value of punishment for stealing a car would be 0.21 × 0.91 × $81,000 = $15,479, and a car worth $20,000 would be enticing. That helps to explain why more than 15,000 cars are stolen in Minnesota in a typical year. Many people would lose far more than $81,000, considering the difficulty of finding a job after serving time, separation from family, a tarnished reputation, and extreme embarrassment.[4] Conversely, other people have little to lose in terms of employment, family, or reputation. As a result, some people are avid car thieves and most people wouldn't even consider committing the crime.

Risky decisions are influenced by your attitude toward risk. Even if the theft of a car would net you more than the expected value of punishment, the downside risk of a heavy fine or imprisonment might be too great for you to accept. A person who cares only about the expected value of an outcome is described as *risk neutral*. Risk-averse people care about variation in possible outcomes in addition to the expected value and would pay extra to avoid uncertainty. For example, a risk-averse person would be willing to pay more than the expected value of a tax evasion fine for insurance that would pay any fines resulting from a tax audit. *Risk-loving* people prefer variation in possible outcomes. These are the folks who go to Las Vegas and pay more than the expected outcome (as is generally the case in gambling situations) for the possibility of winning big. Economists often simplify analysis by assuming that decision makers are risk neutral, which is likely for larger firms and wealthy individuals who can handle most downside risks and close to the truth for the average individual, although most people lean toward risk aversion.

When contemplating infractions of the law, potential criminals face uncertainty about being caught, being convicted if caught, and receiving various sentences if convicted. The U.S. Department of Justice reports that the probability of being arrested

---

[3] See www.msgc.state.mn.us/Data%20Reports/mv1998.pdf.
[4] Economist John R. Lott has studied the importance of these aspects. See "The Optimal Level of Criminal Fines in the Presence of Reputation," *Managerial and Decision Economics* (July–August 1996), 363–380; and "An Attempt at Measuring the Total Monetary Penalty from Drug Convictions: The Importance of an Individual's Reputation," *Journal of Legal Studies* (January 1992), 159–187.

is 67 percent for murder and nonnegligent manslaughter, 58 percent for aggravated assault, 52 percent for forcible rape, 47 percent for all violent crime, and 18 percent for all property crime. Felony conviction rates are 73 percent for drug trafficking; 67 percent for murder, burglary, and weapons offenses; and, at the low end, 41 percent for assault. Seventy-one percent of all convicted felons are sentenced to periods of confinement, and 41 percent are ordered to pay fines or victim restitution, receive treatment, perform community service, or comply with some other additional penalty.

The next section discusses punishment and the likelihood that various types of criminals are cogent enough to be deterred by changes in the penal code.

PUNISHMENT AND DETERRENCE

There are four primary reasons for punishing criminals:

- **General deterrence:** Other criminals may be deterred by the punishment of one.

- **Specific deterrence:** The criminal being punished may be deterred from committing additional crimes.

- **Rehabilitation:** The criminal may be reformed by the experience.

- **Restitution:** The victims and other members of society may appreciate knowing that justice has been served.

According to the *deterrence hypothesis,* an increase in the punishment for a crime—effectively, a rise in the price of committing the crime—will decrease the quantity of crimes committed. The validity of the deterrence hypothesis depends on people being sufficiently informed and rational to make the necessary calculations. In order to respond appropriately to harsher punishments, such as the death penalty or mandatory sentencing, people must have some idea of the punishments for contemplated crimes and of the likelihood of being caught, and they must consider those possibilities when deciding whether to act.

A research team and I interviewed 278 male inmates at two medium-security state prisons and one county jail to determine how many of them possessed the information and the mindset needed to respond to punishments at the times of their offenses.[5] Sixty-three percent of the criminals either did not think they would be apprehended or did not think about the possibility. Fifty-three percent either did not know what the punishment would be if they were convicted or did not think about it. And a combined 76 percent of the inmates did not contemplate their fates, had no meaningful information with which to do so, or both. Still others had inhibited responses to known punishments as a result of rage, drugs, psychosis, or heat-of-the-moment impulses.

Current threats of punishment deter countless would-be criminals; the relevant question here is whether harsher punishments would deter many of those who are active criminals despite existing disincentives. The ability to respond to punishments differed among perpetrators of various types of crimes. Whereas 89 percent of those in-

---

[5] See David A. Anderson, "The Deterrence Hypothesis and Picking Pockets at the Pick-Pocket's Hanging," *American Law and Economics Review* (Fall 2002), 4:2, 295–313.

carcerated for escape, parole violations, nonpayment of child support, and forgery had thought about the punishments they might receive, only 45 percent of murderers had contemplated likely punishments. Between 21 and 47 percent of nonviolent offenders knew exactly what their punishments would be, but only 4 to 16 percent of the violent criminals could predict their sentences. As for the possibility of thwarting existing criminals with stricter laws and increased detection rates, almost half the people who committed minor offenses were calculating and informed enough to be deterred by a change in law enforcement. Unfortunately, 89 percent of deadly criminals, 91 percent of sex offenders, and 88 percent of robbers lacked the requirements for making informed, rational judgments and for responding to harsher punishments. Given these criminals' mindsets and the information available to them, simply ratcheting up punishments is unlikely to have the intended effect, and supplemental approaches are advisable to better address the worst types of crimes.

POLICY IMPLICATIONS

When criminals are lucid and well informed, as is more often the case in property crimes than in violent crimes, deterrence can result from an increase in the expected cost of crime. For efficiency, we want the expected cost of each crime to equal its cost to society. That way people will commit the crime only if their benefit exceeds the burden to society. For instance, if the illegal dumping of old tires causes $500 worth of ugliness and cleanup costs for a community, a cost (including the expected value of the fine and any costs associated with guilt or risk taking) of $500 will prevent tire dumping except in those few cases in which the benefit is greater than the $500 cost to society. When the benefit truly exceeds the cost, from an efficiency standpoint, it makes sense for the dumping to occur.

Because the expected value of a fine is the product of the likelihood of arrest and conviction multiplied by the actual fine, it's noteworthy that any desired increase in the expected fine can be achieved by increasing any of these three elements. In light of the large expenditures on policing and trials needed to increase arrest and conviction rates, the cost-minimizing law enforcement strategy is to maximize the punishment and thereby minimize the arrest and conviction rates necessary to achieve a particular expected cost. Suppose an expected fine of $500 yields the efficient amount of tire dumping. This could be achieved with a 50 percent probability of arrest and conviction and a $1,000 fine ($0.50 \times \$1,000 = \$500$) or a 1 percent probability of paying a $50,000 fine ($0.01 \times \$50,000 = \$500$), but the policing cost of catching 1 percent of perpetrators would be far lower than that of catching 50 percent.

Of course, the cost-minimizing enforcement plan comes down hard on the few who do get punished. Chapter 13 introduced risk aversion and related risk and guilt burdens. The possibility of having to pay $50,000 creates a burden for risk-averse people, who prefer as little variation in the potential outcomes as possible. If the risk burden (the amount that risk-averse people would pay to avoid uncertainty about the possible outcome) is $100 and there is no guilt burden, an expected fine of $400 will yield efficient behavior because the total cost of dumping, $100 + $400 = $500, equals the social cost. If the expected fine is $500, then the total cost of $100 +

$500 = $600 will deter people from dumping even when their benefit is, say, $550, which exceeds the social cost and makes the dumping efficient. It may seem strange to hear that it could be efficient to dump tires, but remember that the precondition is that the combination of every related cost falls below the benefit received.

For those potential criminals who are less informed or perhaps less rational, including the most violent offenders, effective deterrence requires policies beyond adjustments in the expected punishment cost. One approach is to increase the level of information and prudence among potential criminals. Educational programs could foster better methods of decision making. For those who feel invincible, billboards touting "There are a million people in prison who didn't think they'd be caught" might be a start. For those who don't know the punishments for crimes they consider, a campaign advertising specific consequences would help. And for those who might snap emotionally, teachings on how to handle strong emotions could make a difference in a way that ratcheting up punishments cannot.

There is also a more general deterrent founded on economic theory and proven in the real world: education. Remember the importance of opportunity costs, which include the next-best alternative value of time spent on crime or in prison. Those with more education have more to lose by committing crimes because they are more likely to be gainfully employed and to earn higher incomes than those with less education. The frequency of most types of crime dropped steadily in the 1990s as employment prospects improved and rose in the early 2000s when more people were out of work and had a lower opportunity cost of time spent on crime and punishment.

CONCLUSION

Although some crimes create a net gain for society, most are inefficient, either because of the criminals' neglect of the costs imposed on others or because of poor information, powerful emotions, or perceived invincibility on the part of the criminals. A perfunctory application of economic principles to fight crime may fail to place effective incentives in the right places. The deterrence hypothesis that harsher penalties will deter crimes is valid only when potential criminals have some idea of the penalties for contemplated crimes and think they might be caught. Most criminals know neither the penalty for laws they break nor the risk of being caught, so increases in fines or enforcement lack the desired punch. Alarmingly, the information and mindset required to respond to typical crime prevention efforts, such as mandatory sentencing and "three-strikes" laws with strict penalties for third offenses, is particularly lacking among the most violent offenders. Effective policies against the worst types of crime must address the information costs that prevent criminals from making appropriate decisions about risks of detection, conviction, and punishment. Opportunity costs are relatively well known, which points to remedies such as job creation, drug rehabilitation, and education—services that elevate careers and reputations among more certain and influential opportunity costs of a life of crime.

[6] For example, see David Anderson, *Sometimes I Get So Angry! Anger Management for Everyone* (Danville, KY: Pensive Press, 2007).

DISCUSSION STARTERS

1. Are you risk averse, risk neutral, or risk loving? What are some of the determinants of your attitude toward risk? What is an example of behavior that demonstrates this attitude?

2. Daily weather reports include the probability of rain. Did you take an umbrella to your last class meeting? Why or why not? In what way did your decision resemble an expected-value calculation?

3. Should leaders of study-abroad programs be more or less concerned about students engaging in promiscuous activities in areas where AIDS is a big problem? What does your answer imply in terms of people making rational, calculated decisions under uncertainty? When people do get AIDS, do you suppose that it's most often a problem of information, irrationality, improper approaches to uncertainty, or something else? Explain your answer.

4. Do you ever jaywalk? How would it influence your behavior if you heard that the penalty for jaywalking had been doubled? Do you know the specific punishment for any legal infraction?

5. What solutions to the problem of violent crime do you favor? Why?

CHAPTER 17

SHOULD DAMAGE AWARDS IN LAWSUITS BE CAPPED?
Benefits and Costs of Limiting the Burden of Litigation

A doctor in Kentucky who stands accused of negligence in what he calls a frivolous malpractice lawsuit described his ordeal this way: As he struggles through the prolonged litigation, he works for several months each year simply to cover his six-figure legal and insurance costs. He sees each new patient as a potential litigant. He doesn't enjoy his work the way he used to. What with the stress of the lawsuit, the expense, the lost sleep, and the loss of faith in humanity, the quality of his life has gone downhill.

The husband of a woman in Michigan who died as a result of what he calls a missed diagnosis described his ordeal this way: As his sons struggle with the absence of their mother, he works through the loss of his life partner. He sees malpractice litigation as a needed inducement for attentive medical care. He doesn't enjoy his time at home the way he used to. What with the stress of single parenthood, the expense, the lost sleep, and the loss of faith in humanity, the quality of his life has gone downhill.

This doctor and this widower represent two valid sides of a debate that affects thousands of Americans who are involved in negligence lawsuits. The consequences of litigation are grave, as are the repercussions of human error. Is uncapped litigation a prudent and effective inducement to minimize error? We can invoke the economic way of thinking to guide public policy and foster virtuous litigation with checks on its emotional burden, frequency, and expense.

LAW AND ECONOMICS

Since the 1960s, a fruitful collaboration between legal scholars and economists has fashioned the new subfield of law and economics. To the analysis of law, economists lend tools with which to seek the optimal level of litigation, create incentive structures for swift and fair resolution of disputes, and evaluate schemes for punishment. The growing discipline of law and economics now boasts national and international professional associations and prominent journals as testaments to the popularity of applying economic reasoning to legal issues.

Consider disputes over liability for product failures. The challenge is to decide whether the manufacturer of a product that has caused harm, such as a soda bottle that exploded, an oil tanker that spilled oil, or an airplane that crashed, should be held responsible for the injuries. Courts now embrace "risk–utility" tests that essentially perform cost–benefit analyses on products that involve risk. This procedure for assessing liability, developed by legal scholar Dean Wade, evaluates the following seven factors:

1. the usefulness of the product to the user and society as a whole
2. the likelihood and degree of injury involved
3. the availability of safer products that serve the same purpose
4. the manufacturer's ability to make the product safer without making it prohibitively expensive
5. the user's ability to avoid harm by exercising care
6. the user's likely awareness of the inherent dangers
7. the manufacturer's ability to spread the burden of liability by charging higher prices or carrying liability insurance

The court adopted this procedure in the case of a helicopter pilot who noticed a loss of oil pressure and attempted an emergency landing. Fog in the area caused the landing to go awry: The helicopter crashed, and the passengers and crew were seriously injured. It turned out that the loss of oil pressure resulted from a loose oil-supply line that had been inadequately secured by a "lock tab" washer. Other helicopter engine manufacturers use safety wire, threaded through holes in the nut and bolt head, instead of lock tab washers to secure the nut against the constant vibration of a helicopter's engine. At trial, an expert witness demonstrated how easy it would have been for the manufacturer to use safety wire to prevent the nut from unscrewing. The safety wire cost little more than the lock tab washer. The jury decided that the lock tab washer did not pass the risk–utility test: The washer served an important purpose, but the likelihood and degree of injury were high and safer products were available at little additional cost.[1]

---

[1] See www.avweb.com/news/avlaw/181885-1.html.

Economic reasoning can be applied to legal issues in countless ways; the remainder of this chapter focuses on the economics of damage awards in tort litigation. A *tort* is a private wrong, or a wrongful act that—intentionally or not—causes injury to another person. Examples include injuring another person by driving recklessly, failing to warn consumers about product dangers, and taking insufficient care when practicing medicine. Tort law provides remedies for such injuries, allowing victims to seek compensation for harm. There is some overlap between torts and crimes, as, for example, when the crime of burglary involves the tort of trespassing. Torts differ from crimes in that (1) the victims of torts initiate litigation, whereas representatives of public bodies, such as the United States or the state of Maine, initiate criminal actions and (2) tort litigation cannot result in incarceration.

THE BENEFITS OF DAMAGE AWARDS

It would be grand if we could do away with lawsuits—if everyone would show due respect and take all appropriate care not to harm others—but that is unlikely given the opportunity costs involved. One problem is that incentives often work against humanitarian interests. Manufacturers can save money by skimping on safety mechanisms. It takes time and money to remove tree limbs that dangle precariously above roadways and to fix dangerous cracks in sidewalks. And it often is financially rewarding for safety inspectors and health-care providers, like just about everyone else, to work quickly so that they can increase the volume of their work.

Financial *damage awards* in legal cases provide a countervailing incentive to manufacture safer products, to make streets and sidewalks safe, and to spend more time examining and treating each patient. Although most tort claims do not reach trial, it is the threat of damage awards at trial that motivates out-of-court settlements, which are the more common resolution. *Punitive damages* are awarded to punish the wrongdoer for his or her mistakes and to deter such behavior in the future. *Compensatory damages* are intended to compensate, or repay, the victim for the extent of the injury, pain and suffering, lost earnings, medical expenses, and lost consortium (love, care, affection, companionship, and other benefits from a relationship).

The existence of damage awards can encourage safety precautions, and when that fails, such awards can help victims recoup their losses. Court cases involving accidental shootings offer a dramatic example. As of 1995, no major gun manufacturer included an internal lock in its guns to prevent accidental or unauthorized use. In that year, victims of accidental shootings began filing lawsuits against gun manufacturers to challenge the inadequacy of safety features on guns. Today, although no federal statute requires internal locks, more than a dozen gun makers offer guns with internal locks. The entire line of handguns made by Taurus Firearms, for example, features internal locks. The Brady Campaign to Prevent Gun Violence[2] describes this trend as "the most significant safety advance in firearm design in decades," and its members worry that legislation limiting the liability of gun manufacturers would eliminate the incentive for manufacturers to implement such safety-related innovations.

---

[2] See www.bradycampaign.org.

In the 2002 case of *Grunow* vs. *Valor Corp. of Florida*, a West Palm Beach jury awarded $24 million to the widow of a teacher who had been shot and killed by a middle school student. The jury placed 45 percent of the blame on the school board because the student was able to enter campus with a gun; 50 percent on the owner of the gun, who kept it in an unlocked drawer; and 5 percent on the gun distributor, who was found negligent for supplying the gun without appropriate safety measures.

We'd like to think that people would never place time, money, or other interests ahead of risks to health and life. Consider, however, the number of deaths that could be avoided with adequate care. In a typical year in the United States, about 43,000 people die in motor vehicle crashes, 29,000 die in incidents involving firearms, and 20,000 die as the result of illnesses associated with sexual behavior (primarily HIV, hepatitis B and C, and cervical cancer).[3] It takes time to label medicines legibly and to check labels carefully, and an Institute of Medicine study estimates that 7,000 U.S. deaths are caused by medication errors each year. The United States Pharmacopoeia, the official public standards-setting authority for all medicines sold in the United States, tracked medication errors from 1999 through 2003 and recorded a total of 235,139 errors. Given the number of fatalities that occur despite high damage awards, any reduction in the incentives for safety should be applied with great care.

THE COSTS OF DAMAGE AWARDS

In previous chapters, it was explained that the burden of even a small risk of large losses is intolerable. For instance, despite the roughly 1-in-300 chance that your home will catch fire this year, your family probably purchases fire insurance because, tiny though the risk may be, the remote chance of losing the value of a home must be eliminated. Litigation poses similarly small risks of tremendous losses for everyone who could be sued. The top 100 U.S. verdicts in 2005, as compiled by www.verdict search.com, all exceeded $17 million, and the highest verdict was $1.4 billion.

Most businesses, doctors, governments, and schools can't afford the small-but-conceivable risk of a devastating lawsuit, and so they make large expenditures on insurance, limit their services, or reduce innovation. Litigation costs can drive firms out of business or out of the country and can drive doctors out of states with high insurance premiums or a record of large jury awards. According to the American College of Obstetricians and Gynecologists, the average ob-gyn is sued 2.5 times during his or her career and the average claim takes 4 years to resolve.[4] As of 2004, the median award in medical liability cases was $3.5 million.[5]

Don't think that doctors, institutions, and firms are the only ones paying the cost of litigation. Even if you stay far afield from litigation, you pay a share of the costs. The litigation burden is woven into the prices paid for health care, education, and almost every product or service. An organization called Citizens against Lawsuit Abuse

---

[3] See Ali H. Mokdad et al., "Actual Causes of Death in the United States, 2000," *Journal of the American Medical Association* (2004), *291*, 1238–1245.

[4] See www.acog.org.

[5] See www.msms.org/grpa/federalgov/MedicalLiability.html.

in Orange County, California, claims that every year nearly $1,200 in litigation costs is passed on to each U.S. consumer.[6] Before the closing of the Clark forklift manufacturing plant in Danville, Kentucky, company executives explained that $1,000 of the price of each forklift went to cover litigation expenses.

As important as the tort system is to decisions that promote safety and health, there may be too much of a good thing. The potential for large damage awards provides incentives for frivolous lawsuits as well as meritorious ones, and some steps taken to avoid litigation have unfortunate results. We can live with the sporadic loss of homecoming parades, Junior Achievement birdhouse projects, and diving boards at hotel pools for fear of litigation; it is of greater concern when doctors shy away from high-risk services, such as delivering babies, and pharmaceutical companies hesitate to introduce new medications.

Opponents to legal reform correctly argue that most lawsuits are settled out of court, plaintiffs often lose, and many exorbitant damage awards are reduced on appeal. For example, when a jury awarded an Alabama couple $581 million in punitive damages and $975,000 for mental anguish because they were overcharged $1,200 for the installation of two satellite dishes, the trial court reduced the award to $300 million and the case was settled. Even when settlement occurs or plaintiffs get nothing at trial, however, the legal wrangling can take many years, cause many tears, and cost fortunes.

LEGAL REFORM EFFORTS

A large body of economic literature suggests that people respond to incentives in rational ways. The trick is to find the best ways to deliver incentives that reduce frivolous lawsuits and bring disputing parties to swift and fair resolutions. England is among many countries with *loser-pays* policies that require losing parties to assist with winners' legal fees. This effectively reduces the number of frivolous lawsuits because plaintiffs whose cases lack merit must foot the hefty bill for the defense team. The trade-off (there's always a trade-off!) is that the threat of being held liable for the legal fees of the other side can also deter meritorious plaintiffs who are uncertain of a win. In the United States, losing parties generally pay the relatively negligible court costs, but not the legal fees, of the winning party. Stronger versions of loser-pays rules have appeared in legislative proposals but have not been adopted.[7]

President George W. Bush and many state legislators have endorsed a $250,000 cap on damage awards. By limiting awards for pain and suffering, caps can rein in the limitless uncertainty of litigation. States with such caps have experienced relatively slow growth in medical malpractice insurance premiums. The problem with a cap at that level is that it erodes desired incentives for safety and prevents adequate compensation for victims of the worst harms. A $250,000 award might be acceptable for a lost limb but not for a lost life. Or as Senator Edward M. Kennedy (D-MA) puts

[6] See www.occala.org/facts.html.
[7] See Thomas D. Rowe, Jr., and David A. Anderson, "One-Way Fee Shifting Statutes and Offer of Judgment Rules: An Empirical Experiment," *Jurimetrics Journal of Law, Science, and Technology* (1996), 36, 255–273.

it, "It is absurd to suggest that $250,000 is fair compensation for a person paralyzed for life."[8] A cap that applies to all injuries must be high enough to compensate all victims and to motivate an efficient level of precaution. If applied only to noneconomic damages, such as pain and suffering, as is often proposed, caps could coincide with full coverage for medical care and lost earnings; this means that no victim would have to struggle to pay bills or put food on the table as the result of caps. In May 2006, the U.S. Senate blocked two separate bills that would have capped awards for pain and suffering damages in most cases to $250,000.

GRADUATED CAPS AS A COMPROMISE

Damage caps reduce uncertainty but threaten unfair treatment of those who receive the worst injuries. An attractive solution is to set relatively high caps that differ according to the type of injury received. For example, caps on noneconomic damages for each type of injury could be set at the 95th percentile of awards granted over the past 10 years. That means that, if the future resembled the past, only the highest 5 percent of awards for even the worst injuries would be affected by the caps. The cap might be $50,000 for a lost finger and $5 million for a lost life. These caps would allow courts the latitude to grant more compensation to those who suffer more but would eliminate awards in the hundreds of millions or billions of dollars.

High, graduated caps would permit the incentives and justice of most awards. They would allow potential defendants, including drivers, home and business owners, coaches, and teachers, to sleep easier knowing that a mind-numbing jury award wouldn't ruin their lives. The incentives for lawyers to sponsor billboards and advertisements that encourage litigation would be reduced. Fewer doctors would curtail their services, and fewer producers would think twice about innovating. High caps are a compromise between the extremes of unconstrained litigation and unchecked capitalism. Some will complain that even these caps are too low because the only cap should be infinity. Others will say that they're too high to solve all the existing problems. The real question is whether there's a better set of incentives among the viable alternatives. The fact is that high, graduated caps aren't without risk, but they may well pass the risk–utility test.

CONCLUSION

Spurred by the importance of economic incentives in our litigious society, the new subfield of law and economics is changing the way people think about legal policy. Lawsuits create tremendous benefits and tragic costs; the optimal level of litigation would include only those cases from which the benefit exceeds the cost. There is widespread belief that current caseloads include frivolous lawsuits, meaning that the optimal level has been exceeded, but a moderate volume of litigation would promote safety and justice well worth the cost. If that's true, public policy should focus on reducing the burden of lawsuits and dispensing with baseless cases, without undermining the incentives, restitution, and accountability that protect society from selfishness run amok.

[8] See www.latimes.com/news/nationworld/nation/la-na-medmal9may09,1,2717190.story?coll=la-headlines-nation.

Caps on damages would reduce the risk burden of litigation by eliminating the possibility of awards that eclipse common expectations. Graduated caps could achieve these goals without limiting severely injured individuals to the same maximum award as those whose injuries are less serious. Reduced awards would also decrease the incentives to litigate and, therefore, the volume of litigation, as would loser-pays rules, among other proposed legal reform measures.[9]

There is no consensus among economists about whether caps on damages are warranted, but the economic way of thinking helps narrow the advisable options. Graduated caps provide a viable compromise between the weighty risk burden of uncapped awards and the inefficient incentives and unjust compensation provided by a single modest cap.

DISCUSSION STARTERS

1. Has anyone you know been involved in a lawsuit? With respect to that case or to any other lawsuit with which you are familiar, discuss the incentives that existed for the claim to be filed, for the case to be settled out of court, and for avoidance of the type of behavior that allegedly caused the harm.

2. Do you think it is common for people to place selfish interests ahead of safety precautions? How often do you hear of people drinking and driving? Creating secondhand smoke? Selling drugs?

3. As we consider public policy to promote responsible behavior, are there any particular professions that deserve attention? Do physicians, educators, and religious leaders have adequate incentives to uphold appropriate standards of conduct? If not, provide examples that support your belief that people in these positions might act selfishly and need outside incentives to behave virtuously.

4. Are there particular professions in which the incentives for proper conduct are excessive? What examples can you provide?

5. Explain your own stance on the prudence of placing caps on legal damages. What specific plan would you implement if you had the authority?

[9] See, for example, www.whitehouse.gov/news/releases/2005/01/20050105-2.html.

CHAPTER 18

WHAT'S TO LOVE ABOUT TAXES?
Free Riding on Public Goods, Deadweight Loss,
and the Lesser of Two Evils

The Stamp Act of 1765 required American colonists to pay taxes to Great Britain for all newspapers, legal documents, commercial contracts, licenses, pamphlets, and playing cards. What rubbed colonists the wrong way was not taxation as such but the fact that they were taxed without having direct representation in the British Parliament. American colonists' tax dollars were going toward things that they cared little about, such as paying down Britain's debt after the French and Indian War and supporting British troops who were posted to "protect" the colonies. The Tea Act of 1773 was the last straw, spurring the Boston Tea Party and helping to spark the Revolutionary War. The Tea Act actually reduced taxes and trade barriers for tea imported from the British East India Company, lowering tea prices for colonists. The taxes had been beneficial, however, to colonial tea merchants who sold tea smuggled from Holland. Lower taxes on British tea left little room for competition and gave the East India Company a virtual monopoly on tea sales.

After winning the Revolutionary War, the Americans passed tax legislation as one of the first steps in forming the United States, and taxation is now a favored means of providing public goods throughout the world. We all love to hate taxes, but in our zeal to get the tax man off our backs, we might make missteps if we don't step back and consider the wisdom as well as the woes of this exercise in pooling money. This chapter examines some of the pros and cons of taxation.

WHY TAXES?

Chapter 11 introduced the concept of *public goods*—those goods that anyone can use without paying for them and which rational wealth maximizers would not voluntarily purchase because they can free ride on the purchases of other people. Taxes are the ticket to adequate funding for public goods, such as police, parks, firefighters, national forests, national defense, public transportation, public schools, prisons, courts, environmental protection, and disaster relief. People tend to take public goods for granted, but they form the foundation for civilization as we know it, and taxes are simply the way of paying for them.

Taxes are about cooperation to achieve a greater good. The incentive is for individuals to evade taxes and free ride, but the Internal Revenue Service is in the business of balancing that incentive with the prospects of fines and imprisonment. There are many calls for lower tax rates as a route to fatter wallets without the risk of punishment. The bad news is that tax cuts can necessitate erosion in the provision of public goods, and public goods can be a tremendous bargain. When a neighborhood of 100 homes pools funds for a playground and tennis courts, each family has these services at 1/100th of the cost of building its own playground and courts. When 100 million taxpayers pitch in to pay for the U.S. Centers for Disease Control and Prevention,[1] for a tiny fraction of the cost of a noncooperative approach, the country receives better disease prevention services than individual efforts could provide.

Virtually every society on earth has grappled with the concept of taxation and decided it's a keeper. In ancient times, scribes collected taxes for the Egyptian pharaohs. The ancient Athenians imposed a monthly tax, called a *metoikion*, on immigrants. Caesar Augustus provided retirement funds for protectors of the Roman Empire by levying an inheritance tax. After Rome fell, the Saxon kings imposed custom duties and property taxes.

As useful as taxes appear to be, voters gobble up promises of lower taxes. The cliché is that, if elected, new politician X will lower taxes without reducing services by cleaning house and eliminating the wasteful inefficiencies of government bureaucracy. Greater frugality is a virtuous goal, but after the election, politician X generally has a much harder time finding and eliminating waste than was suggested in campaign rhetoric. Soon after taking office in 2004, California governor Arnold Schwarzenegger kept his promises to revoke the car tax, freeze state spending, and audit the state budget. Rather than finding enough painless ways to tighten up the budget, the trade-offs necessitated by these measures included cuts in spending for education and transportation, higher tuition fees at state colleges, and $15 billion worth of debt from the sale of bonds. A similar scenario unfolded in Virginia when the 1997 gubernatorial election hinged on promises to revoke a car tax. At the Web site www.virginiaplaces. org/taxes/, the problem is summed up this way: "Cutting government costs without reducing services that are appreciated by the voters is like trying to find the fat marbled through a piece of steak."

---

[1] See www.cdc.gov.

TAX TROUBLE

Taxes can achieve great things, but that doesn't mean that all taxes are good, that higher taxes would be better, or that any taxes come without their own troubles. As a student of the economic way of thinking, you know that each particular tax should be evaluated in terms of its costs and benefits, and taxes should be raised or lowered until an additional dollar collected will cause more harm than good. Among many potential pitfalls, taxes can be misused, too high or low, unfair, or inefficient.

Equity: What's Fair?

When contemplating new taxes during the Civil War, Senator Garrett Davis pronounced that the guiding principles of taxation should include "the idea that taxes shall be paid according to the abilities of a person to pay." If it is proper for people who earn more to pay more, how much more should they pay?

A *progressive tax* obligates people with low incomes to pay smaller proportions of their incomes in taxes than people with high incomes do. For example, the Tax Act of 1862, signed by President Abraham Lincoln to help pay for the Civil War, collected 3 percent of income more than $600 and 5 percent of income more than $10,000.[2] Like the current U.S. income tax, the 1862 tax collected a relatively large share of large incomes and was, therefore, progressive.

A *proportional tax* represents the same proportion of every person's income. At the end of the Civil War the tax laws were changed to require a flat 5 percent of income from all taxpayers. A flat tax is proportional because each person pays the same proportion (in this case 5 percent) of his or her income in taxes. A flat tax can be transformed into a progressive tax by making an initial amount of earnings tax free. The post–Civil War tax code allowed an exemption of up to $1,000 for rent payments or the rental value of one's home. In the simplified case in which everyone received the full $1,000 exemption, a person earning $5,000 would pay 5 percent of $5,000 − $1,000, or $200, in taxes, and a person earning $10,000 would pay 5 percent of $10,000 − $1,000, or $450, in taxes. Because $200 is 4 percent of $5,000 and $450 is 4.5 percent of $10,000, the tax is progressive.

A *regressive tax* obligates people with low incomes to pay a larger proportion of their income in taxes than people with high incomes do. For example, in 1643 the British Parliament imposed taxes on essential commodities, such as grain and meat, to pay for the army commanded by Oliver Cromwell. This excise tax was regressive because the poor devote a larger share of their income to essential commodities than the rich do. That is, a person who earns $4,000 per year might spend 75 percent of that income ($3,000) on food, whereas a person who earns $40,000 might spend only 15 percent ($6,000) on food. If there were a 5 percent tax rate on food purchases, the lower-income person would pay $150 of his or her income in taxes, which amounts to 3.75 percent, and the higher-income person would pay $300, or 0.75 percent. The resulting tax burden on the poor led to the Smithfield riots of 1647.

---

[2] See www.taxworld.org/History/TaxHistory.htm.

Efficiency: Dealing with Deadweight Loss

Chapter 9 explained that *deadweight loss* is loss that, unlike any sort of transfer from one person to another, does not become anyone else's gain. Taxation is a potential source of deadweight loss. Tax revenues themselves represent transfers from taxpayers to the government. However, when goods and services are taxed, fewer of them are bought and sold, the result being a loss of the net gains that would otherwise be received from units not sold because of the tax. Consider the example of airline tickets. Suppose that, in the absence of taxes, the equilibrium price for a round-trip flight from Reno to Atlanta would be $350. In reality, the tax on this flight is $65. The airlines can't simply raise the price by $65 and keep filling the same number of flights because fewer people are willing to pay $350 + $65 = $415 for a flight than are willing to pay $350. With any sizable increase in the ticket price, fewer flights will be demanded and the marginal cost of providing flights will fall.[3] The airlines will raise the price until an even higher price would deter enough customers to decrease revenues by more than the decrease in costs.

Regardless of who actually sends the tax payment to the government, the tax burden is typically shared between customers who pay more than the no-tax price and producers (in this case, airlines) who receive less than the no-tax price. Indeed, the actual airfare for a flight from Reno to Atlanta is $380—$30 more than the supposed no-tax price. After the tax amount of $65 goes to the government, American Airlines receives the remaining $315—$35 less than the no-tax price. The tax revenue is money that would have been part of consumer or producer surplus, but it does not represent a net loss because the government gains what the consumer and producer lose. The deadweight loss results from the decrease in the number of flights. Those flights created consumer and producer surplus—benefits beyond the price for consumers and revenues beyond the cost for airlines—and the surplus from those flights is completely lost.

The Joint Economic Committee of the U.S. Congress reports that each additional dollar of income taxes collected creates a deadweight loss of 25 cents.[4] The deadweight loss created by a tax is often unavoidable, but policymakers decide that the loss is outweighed by the benefit of the tax. There are also ways to craft tax plans that minimize or eliminate deadweight loss. When consumers will purchase the same quantity of a good at any price, as might be expected for a lifesaving medication that has no substitutes, the demand is described as *perfectly inelastic* and the demand curve is vertical. If a $10 tax on heart medicine did not change the quantity purchased because of inelastic demand, no deadweight loss would result because there is no reduction in consumption and, therefore, no loss of surplus. The manufacturer would not need to absorb any of the tax burden because the consumers would pay any price for the product, and the $10 tax revenue would come entirely from patients and would exactly offset the lost consumer surplus. A tax on heart medicine may be unpopular, but the same logic applies to taxes on, say, cigarettes, whose addictive qualities create demand that is inelastic, though not perfectly inelastic.

---

[3] The law of diminishing marginal returns implies that marginal cost decreases as quantity decreases.

[4] See www.house.gov/jec/tax/taxrates/taxrates.pdf.

A *lump-sum tax* is a predetermined amount that is collected from firms or individuals regardless of their behavior. Lump-sum taxes create no deadweight loss because they do not distort incentives to produce or consume. Firms produce until the marginal revenue no longer exceeds the marginal cost. If each airline paid a $200,000 lump-sum tax, the marginal revenue or the marginal cost of flights would not be affected, so the behavior of the airlines would not change unless the tax put them out of business. A sizable lump-sum tax on consumers might induce them to purchase fewer goods as a result of the decrease in their disposable (after-tax) income, but there would be no distortion in the incentives to buy some goods rather than others, as is created by taxes on particular goods, and lump-sum taxes are the most efficient way to collect a given amount of tax revenue.

Fans of efficiency praise lump-sum taxes for keeping deadweight loss at bay; fans of equity dislike them because they are regressive. Choosing among the equity of proportional taxes, the arguable fairness of progressive taxes, and the efficiency of lump-sum taxes is a tough call. Jean Baptiste Colbert (1619–1683), French economist and minister of finance under King Louis XIV, summed up his view of the dilemma this way: "The art of taxation consists of so plucking the goose as to get the most feathers with the least hissing." Given the morals, politics, and emotions involved, there is no easy answer, and the next section explains that in practice we see a mixed bag of taxes.

A SAMPLING OF TAXES IN PRACTICE

Income taxes, collected as a percentage of earnings, generate more than $1 trillion in annual revenue for the U. S. government. For single taxpayers, the Internal Revenue Service collects 10 percent of the first $6,000 of taxable income, 15 percent of the next $20,500, 25 percent of the next $37,250, 28 percent of the next $70,000, 33 percent of the next $156,000, and 35 percent of all additional income (these dollar values are approximate). The rising marginal tax rates make this tax progressive. In practice, the progressivity of the tax depends not only on the tax rates but also on the abilities of taxpayers at various income levels to shelter their earnings from taxation by taking advantage of legal exemptions and deductions. Billionaire Leona Helmsley is infamous for saying, "Only the little people pay taxes." But then, Helmsley went to prison for tax evasion, so the little people got the last laugh.

A *sales tax* is collected as a percentage of payments for purchases. The United States currently has no national sales tax; state sales tax rates range from 7.25 percent in California to 0 in Alaska, Delaware, Montana, New Hampshire, and Oregon. Sales taxes are regressive because relatively rich people devote more of their wealth to saving and investment and spend a smaller share of their income. Most states exempt food from sales taxes, a policy that reduces the regressivity of the tax. A fixed sales-tax credit to low-income families based on the number of residents in a household is used in Canada, and has been considered in the United States,[5] to mitigate the regressivity of sales taxes.

An *excise tax* differs from a sales tax in that it is imposed on particular goods and services. Excise taxes are usually *unit taxes,* meaning that a certain amount is collected per unit, but they can also be *ad valorem taxes,* meaning that the tax is a percentage

[5] See www.willamette.edu/centers/publicpolicy/projects/oregonsfuture/PDFvol2no3/2_3mcbri.pdf.

of the sales price. The state excise taxes on cigarettes (ranging from 5 cents to $2.46 per pack) and liquor (ranging from $1.50 to $12.80 per gallon)[6] are unit taxes. These taxes are sometimes called "sin taxes" because they are usually imposed on goods that some consider immoral or unhealthy. The reasons behind these taxes may also have to do with the desire to minimize the hissing to which Colbert referred: It's harder for the "goose" to complain about taxes on products that can be deadly, and the relatively inelastic demands for addictive substances result in a smaller consumer response to the taxes. Sin taxes are often regressive because relatively poor people spend a larger proportion of their incomes (not to be confused with spending more in absolute terms) on consumer goods, including cigarettes and alcohol. Conversely, some excise taxes are applied to the indulgences of the rich, such as yachts and large homes, and these "luxury taxes" are clearly progressive.

Value-added taxes (VAT), known as *goods and services taxes* in Australia and Canada, are imposed at every step along the path to market. Producers of raw materials, manufacturers, wholesalers, and retailers pay the tax on the difference between what they paid for their input and what they received for their output. On selling sugar to Cadbury, Inc., a sugar beet farmer in England is charged a VAT of 17.5 percent of the price she receives for her product. When Cadbury sells its chocolate to a wholesaler, the company pays 17.5 percent of the difference between what it paid for its ingredients and what it received for its chocolate. The wholesaler then pays the VAT on the difference between what it paid Cadbury and what it received from the retail store, and the retail store pays the tax on its markup.

A *poll tax* is a type of lump-sum tax that requires a specific payment from each adult. Poll taxes are regressive because they require the same payment from each individual regardless of income. A poll tax of a half-shekel (about 31 cents) per adult is mentioned in the Bible (Exodus 30:12–16), and poll taxes were common in the United States until the early twentieth century. In 1964, the 24th Amendment to the U.S. Constitution disallowed poll taxes as prerequisites for voting in federal elections, and in 1966 the U.S. Supreme Court extended that prohibition to all elections. The political demise of British prime minister Margaret Thatcher is widely attributed to her unpopular attempt to impose a poll tax in England in 1990.

A *property tax* is levied on some measure of the value of property, such as a home, an automobile, land, or an inheritance. For simplicity, the value of homes has previously been measured according to the number of windows, and, as one would expect, people responded by bricking up windows in old homes and installing fewer windows in new ones. Property taxes are generally progressive because people with high incomes are more likely than lower-income people to own homes, cars, and land.

A *capital gains tax* is levied on profits from the sale of an asset, such as a home or shares of a stock. Capital gains on assets held for less than a year (for example, that Coca-Cola stock you bought yesterday and sold today) are taxed at the same rate as ordinary income. Capital gains on assets held for more than a year are taxed at a lower rate, which depends on your income and the length of time that you held the asset. Because capital gains go disproportionately to wealthy investors, the favorable treatment of income from capital gains makes the tax code less progressive.

---

[6] See http://www.taxadmin.org/fta/rate/liquor.html.

CONCLUSION

Participation in the popular sport of tax bashing is good fun, but when it comes time to fine-tune tax policies, it is important to understand both sides of the tax dilemma. As a solution to the inadequate provision of public goods because of free riding, taxes can be the lesser of two evils. When people complain that the roads are full of potholes, that the public schools should have more resources, that the police should stop more crimes, and that more should be done to fight disease, they're calling for benefits that more tax dollars could provide. Taxes are like medicine: It's terrible to have the wrong medicine and bad to have too much, but you'll be glad tomorrow if you take the right dose today. The provision of public goods is central to our quality of life; the challenge for policymakers is to develop a tax system that does as little as possible to distort the incentives to produce and consume and that reflects a proper balance between equity and efficiency.

DISCUSSION STARTERS

1. From your perspective, what are the best and worst aspects of taxation?

2. What would life be like in the absence of taxes to pool funds for group purchases? What would you drive on after leaving your driveway? Would everyone pay to have household trash hauled to an appropriate place? Who would police toxic emissions from factories and motor vehicles? What else would be different?

3. If you controlled the budget in your state and had to reduce tax revenues by $10 million, what specific expenditures would you eliminate to keep the budget in balance?

4. Characterize the following types of taxes as progressive, regressive, or proportional:
   a. taxes in ancient China that required 20 percent of each farmer's crops
   b. a roughly $130 per car tax similar to the one Governor Schwarzenegger eliminated in California (assuming for simplicity that the same amount was collected for each car)
   c. a 10 percent tax on all income, with an exemption for the first $1,000 earned

5. Draw a diagram with an upward-sloping supply curve and a downward-sloping demand curve to represent the supply of and demand for cellular phones. Suppose a unit tax of $10 per phone is collected from suppliers. Shift the entire supply curve up by $10 to reflect the added cost of supplying each phone. Label the new equilibrium price P_c to indicate the price that consumers will pay. Label the equilibrium quantity Q_t. Label the new price that cell phone sellers will receive after paying the tax as P_s. Shade in the resulting tax revenue, which is the rectangle whose width extends from the vertical axis to Q_t and whose height extends from P_s to P_c. Review the definition of *deadweight loss* and then identify the area on the graph that represents this loss.

6. Repeat question 5 for open-heart surgery, which has a perfectly inelastic (vertical) demand.

CHAPTER 19

WILL TECHNOLOGY PUT US ALL OUT OF WORK?

Unemployment, Creative Destruction, and Quality of Life

Robots are making our cars these days. They're stamping metal, screwing in bolts, welding, and painting. Robots also make furniture, hamburgers, and Oreo cookies. ATMs do the work of bank tellers. Travelocity.com and Orbitz.com take the place of travel agents. Grocery stores now have self-checkout lines, gas pumps now accept payment, and self-service kiosks are cropping up like weeds. Some McDonald's restaurants have kiosks in their play areas so that customers don't need to visit the friendly human at the counter. McDonald's is also experimenting with kiosks that sell DVDs—who needs that sales clerk at Blockbuster? Airlines now allow travelers to bypass the check-in desk and obtain their boarding passes from a machine—if they haven't printed them beforehand via the Internet. According to Marshall Brain, "The problem is that these systems will also eliminate jobs in massive numbers. In fact, we are about to see a seismic shift in the American workforce. As a nation, we have no way to understand or handle the level of unemployment that we will see in our economy over the next several decades."[1] This chapter describes the sources of unemployment and the counterpoints to the argument that robots will soon eat our lunch.

---

[1] http://marshallbrain.com/robotic-nation.htm.

THERE'S NO DISCOUNTING THE VALUE OF A GOOD JOB

In movies, such as *After the Sunset* (2004) and *Office Space* (1999), the happy ending finds the lead characters living the good life in a tropical paradise. Tropical islands are a great place to visit, but there's more to utility maximization than sun and sand. If you've been to Haiti, the Philippines, Jamaica, or St. Lucia, you've seen poverty and populations with many needs. However, Aruba and Hawaii enjoy high standards of health and education, low crime rates, and nary a dirt-floored shack. The ingredient that makes these islands blissful even for those who haven't succeeded in a Hollywood-style heist is an abundance of jobs. Hawaii has the triple bonus of flourishing agriculture, thriving tourism, and seven active military installations, among other fruitful industries. Aruba has ample jobs from tourism, retail trade, and oil refining. Good jobs are central to human satisfaction on the mainland as well. We travel far from the otherwise idyllic bliss of islands and Alps to land good jobs, and it is understandable that emotions run high when it comes to technology, outsourcing, immigration, and other perceived threats to employment.

Outsourcing and immigration are covered in Chapters 23 and 30, respectively. This chapter focuses on the threat from technology, which can cause three broad categories of unemployment. Workers who have the skills to work but are between jobs in the process of improving their work situations are experiencing *frictional unemployment*. This definition applies, for example, to the 5 to 10 percent of new college graduates who quit their first jobs within 1 year.[2] Frictional unemployment exists because there are "frictions" in the labor market that prevent an instantaneous, flawless pairing of workers and employers even when the workers have useful skills. After losing or leaving a job, completing education, or finishing a seasonal job, it takes time for workers to discover, acquire, and begin new work. This makes frictional unemployment necessary and ever present in our economy.

Workers who are forced out of their jobs by a downturn in the cycle of business peaks and troughs are experiencing *cyclical unemployment*. Thus, the recession of the early 2000s caused large-scale layoffs. The job losses included 5,000 at AT&T, 22,000 at Ford, 15,000 at Merrill Lynch, and 15,000 at the U.S. Postal Service. Many laid-off workers can expect to regain employment when the economy recovers and begins to climb toward a new peak.

Through most of the twentieth century, elevators were guided not by the push of a button, but by human operators who flipped levers to send the elevator cars up and down. With self-guided elevators came the loss of jobs for people who had developed the skill of safe and accurate elevator maneuvering. This is an example of *structural unemployment*, which occurs when a worker lacks the skills necessary for available jobs. Technology and innovation have a long history of creating structural unemployment. The invention of the light bulb put many a candle maker out of work. The automobile was a bane to people in the horse and buggy industries. Automatic telephone exchanges have eliminated the jobs of half a million switchboard operators since the 1970s. Until the personal computer became practical in the 1980s, résumés were professionally typeset, and writers without a lot of time, patience, and correction tape

---

[2] See www.collegejournal.com/successwork/changingcareers/20041202-stevens.html.

would hire typists to convert their handwritten notes into typed letters, reports, and book manuscripts.

Even with all these job losses, the unemployment rate has always recovered. The average unemployment rate since World War II has been about 6 percent. In 2000, the rate dipped to below 4 percent, and in 2005, the rate was about 5 percent. The next section explains why the U.S. workforce's history of successful adaptation to technological change is likely to be its future as well.

TECHNOLOGY: FRIEND OR FOE?

> *Over the long sweep of American generations and waves of economic change, we simply have not experienced a net drain of jobs to advancing technology.*

> —Alan Greenspan, Boston College Finance Conference, March 12, 2004[3]

Necessity may be the mother of invention, but unemployment need not be its off-spring. Former Federal Reserve chairman Alan Greenspan's words suggest that technology creates at least as many jobs as it eliminates. The fear that technological advances will cause widespread unemployment can be countered in a number of ways. To begin with, mature industries do little for job creation; innovation is the real engine for growth in that area. Technology is the source of new industries that employ large numbers of people. In the United States, the computer and electronic product manufacturing industry employs 1,162,971 workers, chemical manufacturing employs 829,499, and plastic product manufacturing employs 762,721. Among older industries, apparel manufacturing employs 296,076, textile mills employ 247,474, and beverage and tobacco product manufacturing employs 151,253. Despite its extensive use of robots, the transportation equipment manufacturing industry employs 1,580,898 workers, making it the largest employer in the manufacturing sector.[4]

Technology can increase the productivity of workers and thus the usefulness of these workers to employers and customers. An eye doctor who uses surgical lasers accomplishes more than colleagues who don't. The same applies to a drug enforcement officer with night-vision glasses, a librarian with a bar code scanner, and a secretary with a computer. Some types of technology will increase the demand for the workers who use them. As an example, robot-assisted surgery that is less invasive and more precise than traditional surgery (watch a video of this at www.or-live.com) is likely to increase the demand for doctors.

In other cases, the increased productivity of some workers will lead to the layoff of others. A chiropractor with a robotic massage table can treat more patients in a day because she can adjust one patient's spine while another patient is receiving a massage. Likewise, a pizza chef with an automatic mixer can make more pizza. As explained in Chapter 7, the demand for labor depends on the price of output and the additional output gained from another worker. If pizza prices remained constant, any increase in productivity would increase the demand for pizza chefs because each would

---

[3] www.federalreserve.gov/boarddocs/speeches/2004/20040312/default.htm.

[4] U.S. Census Bureau, *Statistics for Industry Groups and Industries: 2003*, April 2005. See www.census.gov/prod/ec02/am0331gs1.pdf.

make more pizzas and, therefore, contribute more to pizzeria revenues. However, the following chain of events can undermine that possibility: The increased productivity of chefs can decrease the marginal cost of producing pizzas, increase the market supply of pizzas, and lower the equilibrium price. If the price falls by more than the marginal product of labor rises, each chef's contribution to revenues will decrease, and thus fewer will be hired. In the case of pizza, the productivity gains from automatic mixers and ovens were outpaced by increases in the demand for pizzas—from 0 to 3 billion per year since 1905, according to the Wheat Foods Council[5]—and the number of pizza chefs is still growing.

The potential loss of jobs, as in the chiropractor and pizza chef examples, is not the end of the story. New jobs are simultaneously created in the industries that produce the technology—those new engines of job growth—for example, robotics, consumer electronics, and solar voltaic cells. And then there are the industries that technology creates. For example, two centuries ago the tourism industry was virtually nonexistent in North America, and people who traveled long distances were called explorers. In 1804, it took explorers Meriwether Lewis and William Clark 18 months to travel from St. Louis to the Pacific Ocean. Thanks to modern transportation technology that can whisk people from St. Louis to the Pacific in less than 5 hours, tourism is now among the largest industries in the United States and the world. The usual trade-offs exist; the arrival of the airplane and the family car resulted in lost jobs in the passenger rail industry; however, far more jobs were created in the airline and automobile industries than were ever lost on the railroads. Sometimes the trade-offs have minimal impact: The industries that produce spacecraft and launchers, satellites, paging devices, air conditioners, computer software, and semiconductors have displaced few, if any, workers.

Technology has enabled some industries to exist by placing within the financial reach of the masses products that otherwise would be prohibitively expensive. A handmade watch would cost a pretty penny, and a handmade car would cost a fortune. Both items are now made with the extensive use of robots. Even handmade paper costs about $2 per sheet.[6] One can only imagine how much a textbook like this would cost if hand printed.

Technological improvements also bolster the demand for products. The addition of motors made small-boat ownership appealing to a new breed of consumer. Mechanical puppets called animatronics, such as the 289 children and 264 animals in Disney World's "It's a Small World" exhibit, heighten the allure of theme parks. High-tech special effects and animation make many a movie watchable. And even the self-service kiosks at McDonald's may reduce the lines and attract more customers.

Of course, robots and other machines don't make money; only people do. Thus, if technology creates efficiency and reduced costs, all the benefits will be passed on to humans in the form of lower prices and higher profits. If too many of the benefits go to a minority of the population, taxes and transfer payments can be used to distribute income as desired, although not without some deadweight loss, as discussed in Chapter 18. Alternatively, a dismissive stance toward technology—a prohibition of the

---

[5] www.wheatfoods.org.
[6] http://handmade-paper.us.

robots that fit cookie sandwiches together, seal packages, and turn screws—would be truly detrimental to society. Such a stance would yield a large number of undesirable, low-paying jobs, far less output to go around, and painfully high prices.

The structural unemployment problem is one of too few skills, not of too many workers. Given the shortage of skilled workers in the United States, each year the H-1B nonimmigration visa program welcomes between 65,000 and 195,000 guest workers from other countries for up to 6 years to do work that no available American citizens are qualified to perform. These individuals include teachers, occupational therapists, engineers, speech pathologists, lawyers, pharmacists, registered nurses, financial consultants, and accountants. Several related immigration programs fill similar needs.

Technology and innovation revitalize the economy and minimize cyclical unemployment. The challenge is to help the structurally unemployed gain new skills and share in the benefits. For this the U.S. Department of Labor has embraced programs such as the High Growth Job Training Initiative,[7] which identifies needed skill sets and helps community colleges convey those skills to unemployed workers. Unemployment insurance provides a safety net of roughly two-thirds of a worker's weekly income, up to a state-determined maximum, for at least 26 weeks. More generally, a focus on education and training would mend these problems, whereas an antitechnology focus would be counterproductive in terms of employment and the quality of life.

TECHNOLOGY, JOBS, AND THE QUALITY OF LIFE

> *Industrial mutation . . . incessantly revolutionizes the economic structure from within, incessantly destroying the old one, incessantly creating a new one. This process of creative destruction is the essential fact about capitalism.*
>
> —*Joseph Schumpeter*[8]

Innovation and what Schumpeter calls "creative destruction" are critical to the American way of life. With high-tech machinery and fertilizers, food is produced at a rate that, contrary to the expectations of doomsayers such as Thomas Malthus, has kept pace with population growth. Medical advances have doubled the life expectancy of humans since the Middle Ages. Computers inform us, entertain us, and race through computations so that we need not. The destruction that accompanies creation becomes evident when such new products and processes make some skills obsolete. In 1800, 80 percent of the U.S. workforce was engaged in agriculture. In 1900, the figure was 38 percent. Now it is about 2 percent. Without technological advances such as the mechanical cotton pickers that made handpicking skills obsolete by around 1950, there would be more jobs in the fields. However, by accepting innovation, we have relegated many of the dirty, difficult, and dangerous jobs to machines and enjoyed a steadily improving average level of real income at the same time.

The number of jobs has grown at least as fast as the workforce so far, but what if robots ran the whole manufacturing show, including the new industries? We already

---

[7] See www.doleta.gov/BRG/JobTrainInitiative/.

[8] *Capitalism, Socialism and Democracy.* New York: Harper & Row, (1975), p. 83.

see expansion in the service sector, which creates jobs and increases our standard of living by putting humans at the service of other humans. Technical efficiency in manufacturing could free up money and workers to expand the benefits received from service industries, such as health care, education, entertainment, environmental cleanup, and tourism. Just as the Schwan Food Company[9] employs 22,000 people and simplifies customers' lives by delivering prepared food to their doors, consumers could increase their use of cleaning services, personal trainers, musicians, artists, marriage counselors, massage therapists, beauty consultants, and innumerable other service workers.

Robots can also grant us more leisure time. Technology has helped to increase the productivity per labor hour at an average rate of 2.5 percent per year during the past half-century,[10] meaning higher incomes with less work. After a long history of workweeks in excess of 50 hours, the Fair Labor Standards Act of 1938 shortened the workweek to 40 hours in 1940, with mandated overtime pay of 1.5 times the standard wage rate for hourly workers who exceed 40 hours. With continued advancements in technology, we may enjoy income growth along with workweeks of 35 hours or less, as is common in France and Germany already.

A steady flow of innovation since *Homo sapiens* first appeared has done much for our standard of living without a net loss of jobs. What's next? The pattern is likely to continue. The high-tech horizon offers more new industries, a sampling of which involves alternative energy sources, commercial space travel, and nanotechnology—a form of molecular engineering that might allow circuits and devices to be built up from single atoms and molecules. In keeping with the themes of this chapter, Josh Wolfe writes in the *Forbes/Wolfe Nanotech Weekly Insider*[11] that "nanotech will definitively increase productivity. And it will create new jobs. And for better (or worse) it will also destroy old ones. . . . Innovation yields productivity. Productivity improves our lives." As improvements occur, the challenge for society is to assist the hardest-hit with appropriate retraining, to reassure everyone that the sky is not falling, and to make good use of the advances that ensue.

CONCLUSION

The understandable importance that people attach to their jobs translates into strong emotions and exaggerated fears when potential threats to careers are identified. On a more practical level, that same importance should prompt us to examine real and imagined reasons for job loss carefully. Structural employment as a result of changes in technology is a real, short-term phenomenon in some industries, as it has been for centuries. However, by encouraging technological innovation, we enrich the economy with new industries and jobs, improve the productivity of human workers, advance the quality of life, and promote growth in real wages—none of which are earned by robots. In adapting to technological change, policymakers should focus on helping those with limited job skills train for the many jobs that remain unfilled. As robots

---

[9] See www.schwans.com.
[10] See www.bls.gov/mfp/prod3.pdf.
[11] See www.forbesinc.com/newsletters/nanotech/public/insider/fwnwi_03262004.htm.

save us money and time by screwing in bolts and cleaning out test tubes, perhaps more attention can be granted to the solvable social, environmental, and health problems to which society could devote a nearly endless amount of work effort.

DISCUSSION STARTERS

1. Americans eat almost 10 billion donuts each year. How sensitive do you think the demand for donuts is to their price (that is, how "price elastic" is the demand for donuts)? How much higher do you think the price of donuts would be in the absence of mechanical wheat harvesters, dough mixers, and fryers? What can you conclude about the relationship between technology and employment in the donut industry on the basis of your thoughts about elasticity and price?

2. Suppose technology replaced every single job, and robots did everything from managing stores and designing bridges to finding cancer cures and creating artwork.
   a. Out of all the jobs that exist, which ones do you think would be the last handed over to robots? Explain your answer.
   b. Once robots were doing it all, what would happen to our standard of living? Would humans become penniless? Why or why not?

3. Describe one type of technology not mentioned in the chapter that
   a. caused an increase in the demand for workers in existing industries.
   b. caused a decrease in the demand for workers in existing industries.
   c. created a new industry with a large number of employees.

4. *Optional graphing question:* As explained in Chapter 7, the demand for labor is determined by the marginal revenue product, which is the marginal product of labor multiplied by the marginal revenue gained from an additional unit of output. Consider a plaque-engraving firm in a perfectly competitive industry, meaning that every unit is sold at the market price and the marginal revenue equals that price.
   a. Draw the marginal revenue product curve for the engraving company as a line that slopes up initially, peaks, and then turns into a downward-sloping line, resembling a traditional demand curve.
   b. Draw the marginal revenue product curve as you think it would look after laser-engraving technology improved the productivity of workers. Assume for now that the price of plaques would be unchanged.
   c. Draw the marginal revenue product curve as you think it would exist if lasers improved productivity a little bit and the price of plaques dropped by a lot.
   d. For a fixed wage rate, what would happen to the number of workers hired under scenarios (b) and (c)?

CHAPTER 20

DO PHARMACEUTICAL PATENTS COST LIVES OR SAVE THEM?
Balancing Incentives for Innovation with Prices More Disease Victims Can Afford

There's nothing better than a little pill that will end your pain, kill your infection, lift your depression, keep cancer at bay, prevent unwanted pregnancy, or reduce the risk of heart attack, as if by magic. Although Americans spend more than $150 billion on their magic pills each year, most of the world's population won't find the pill they need. No pill has been developed to cure many of the diseases prevalent in developing countries, and some existing pills are far too expensive for most people. For better or worse, patents provide monopoly power to the pharmaceutical companies that hold them, conveying the ability to charge high prices as an incentive to invest in research and development (R&D). Pending alternative solutions, trade-offs exist between strong patent protection that motivates new drug discoveries and weak patent laws that promote price competition and give more people access to lifesaving cures that already exist. As the debate rages on, it is prudent to examine both sides of the story, given that millions of lives are at stake.

INCENTIVES FOR INNOVATION

At the core of drug firms' decision to develop new therapies is their expected monetary return, which depends in large part on the willingness of the federal government to provide them with the monopoly power of patents.

—*Michael J. Gluck,* Federal Policies Affecting the Cost
and Availability of New Pharmaceuticals[1]

A pharmaceutical patent grants the exclusive right to produce a drug for 20 years. An extension of up to 5 years can be requested to compensate for the time it takes the Food and Drug Administration (FDA) to approve a drug, as long as the period between approval and patent expiration doesn't exceed 14 years. Copyright laws perform a similar function for books and other writings, protecting against competitive duplication for the lifetime of the author plus 70 years. The intent of patents and copyrights is to provide a financial incentive for substantial efforts. The incentives seem to work. Jacob Schmookler demonstrated that expected profits drive the pace and direction of innovation in many industries.[2] And Edwin Mansfield estimated that 65 percent of pharmaceutical products were introduced as a result of patent protection.[3]

Further evidence of the power of patents comes from the influx of R&D funds that occurs when a country starts protecting pharmaceutical patents. The U.S. Department of State reports that after Japan and Italy instituted strong patent protection in 1978, investments in pharmaceutical R&D quadrupled over a 10-year period.[4] Brazil gained about $2 billion worth of investment in new high-tech industries after the country enacted effective patent legislation in 1996. Mexico strengthened its pharmaceutical patent protection in 1990 and during the next 3 years saw related investments increase from $41 million to $103 million annually.

There is more than greed at the root of the pharmaceutical industry's interest in revenues. According to the Pharmaceutical Research and Manufacturers of America, the average new drug costs in the neighborhood of $500 million to research and develop. Along the way, each new drug carries with it the risks of failure; dangerous side effects; and expensive lawsuits, such as those filed recently against the makers of many widely used medications (both prescription and over the counter), including Vioxx, Bextra, Zyprexa, Crestor, Prempro, Baycol, Accutane, Oxycontin, Rezulin, Paxil, Celebrex, Neurontin, and Fen-Phen. Food and Drug Administration approval of a new drug requires the completion of three stages of clinical trials: safety tests, efficacy tests, and expanded randomized trials to again check both safety and efficacy. As much as 40 percent of all R&D expenditures go toward these trials. Once the risks have been taken and the firm that develops a new medicine has incurred the costs, it takes

[1] See www.kff.org/rxdrugs/3254-index.cfm.
[2] *Patents, Innovations and Economic Change: Data and Selected Essays.* Edited by Zvi Griliches and Leonid Hurwicz. (Cambridge, MA, 1972: Harvard University Press, 1972).
[3] "Patents and Innovation: An Empirical Study," *Management Science,* February 1986.
[4] http://usinfo.state.gov/products/pubs/intelprp/progress.htm. (This link is no longer active.)

little money to replicate the drug. If it were legal to do so, competitors could enter the market with relative ease and seize valuable market share.

Patent protections are in place, however, and have fostered the development of products that significantly improve health and extend life. These include chemotherapy medicines, clot busters, antibiotics, blood pressure medications, pain relievers, cholesterol-lowering drugs, AIDS cocktails, drugs that slow the progress of breast and prostate cancer and Parkinson's disease, sleeping pills, and antidepressants.

PROBLEMS WITH THE INCENTIVE STRUCTURE

Money's pull on the pharmaceutical industry doesn't always lead to ideal decision making. The major producers, known collectively as "Big Pharma," set their priorities knowing that rich people with impotence or hair loss can pay more for remedies than can poor people with deadly diseases. As in other industries, drug companies have the incentive to cater to the wealthy and maximize the length of patents and the extent of profits. Between 1997 and 2002 Big Pharma hired 675 lobbyists and spent $544 million lobbying Congress, federal agencies, and the White House.[5] The efforts of the drug lobby have not gone unrewarded. In 1995, the Uruguay Rounds Agreements Act extended the length of patents from 17 years to 20. In 2003, the Medicare Prescription Drug Improvement and Modernization Act subsidized drug purchases for seniors while it removed provisions of the act that would have allowed the reimportation of cheaper drugs from Canada.

In the opposite corner of the pharmaceutical boxing ring are special-interest groups fighting for a different set of priorities. For example, the Drugs for Neglected Diseases (DND) Working Group, Doctors without Borders, the Global Alliance for TB Drug Development, and the Medicines for Malaria Venture represent the interests of developing countries (in which 80 percent of the world's population lives), but funding for these groups is relatively small and their ability to reach legislators is limited.

The pharmaceutical industry's efforts to maintain barriers to entry and high prices go beyond lobbying. When the patent on a popular drug lapses, the manufacturer may tweak the product, obtain a new patent, and then convince consumers that the "new" product is a must. When the primary patent for the heartburn medicine Prilosec expired in 2001, drug maker AstraZeneca came out with Nexium. To understand the difference between these two drugs, you should know that chemicals often come in two versions, called left and right isomers, that are mirror images of each other. Prilosec contains both isomers, whereas Nexium contains only the left isomer of the same chemical. In other words, there isn't a whole lot of difference between the two drugs. In another example, Schering-Plough introduced the antihistamine Clarinex (desloradadine) when the patent for Claritin (loradadine) expired in 2002, although loradadine turns into desloradadine after it is swallowed.[6] Overall, the FDA classified 75 percent of the 119 drugs it approved in 2004 as similar to existing drugs in chemical makeup or therapeutic value.

---

[5] See www.pcactionfund.org/buyingalaw/.
[6] See www.drugawareness.org/pdf/tnrdrugpiece.pdf.

Related controversies involve Big Pharma's massive expenditures on advertising and drug companies' aggressive sales forces. In fact, however, advertising and marketing campaigns can provide valuable information, depending on their nature. The remainder of this chapter focuses on the greater problem of how to address illness in the developing world, where deadly diseases are common and most patients are poor. The high cost of patented pharmaceuticals is also a problem in the United States, where 45 million people do not have health insurance and 10 percent of health-care expenditures are for drugs.[7]

NEGLECTED POPULATIONS AND DISEASES

Pharmaceutical companies simply have no financial incentive to invest in the development of new treatments for diseases that affect people who can't afford the medicines.

—Els Torreele, Co-chair of the Drugs for Neglected Diseases (DND) Working Group[8]

The Global Forum for Health Research[9] is focused on remedying the *10/90 gap,* a term signifying that only 10 percent of global health research is devoted to 90 percent of the global disease burden. A survey by the DND Working Group completed in 2001 by 11 pharmaceutical companies in the United States, Europe, and Japan revealed that, in the previous year, none of the 11 had devoted R&D money to cures for sleeping sickness; 1 or 2 had spent money on treatments for leishmaniasis, Chagas disease, or malaria; and 5 of the 11 had spent money on tuberculosis (TB) cures. Out of the roughly $106 billion of annual spending on health research worldwide,[10] slightly more than $100 million, or 0.1 percent, is spent on drug R&D for the four most neglected diseases.[11]

Price is an inhibiting factor for the cures that already exist. The cost of treating a case of multidrug-resistant TB is between $1,500 and $4,000. A year of treatment with an antiretroviral drug cocktail for one HIV/AIDS victim in the United States costs $10,000 to $15,000. To put those prices into perspective, in Swaziland, where the incidence of HIV/AIDS is 42.6 percent, the average annual income is $1,350 and the unemployment rate is 34 percent. U.S. customers spend more than $150 billion annually on prescription drugs, but most global citizens simply cannot afford medicines with prices in the thousands of dollars. The World Health Organization (WHO) estimates that 14 million people die each year from communicable diseases, such as malaria, TB, sleeping sickness,[12] Chagas disease,[13] and kala azar.[14] Almost all deaths

---

[7] See www.buckeyeinstitute.org/article.php?id=223.
[8] See http://multinationalmonitor.org/mm2002/02june/june02corp1.html.
[9] See www.globalforumhealth.org.
[10] See http://www.globalforumhealth.org/filesupld/press%20releases/Financialflows%20final.pdf.
[11] See www.doctorswithoutborders.org/publications/reports/2001/fatal_imbalance_short.pdf.
[12] Human African trypanosomiasis.
[13] South American trypanosomiasis.
[14] Visceral leishmaniasis.

from communicable diseases occur among the poorest citizens of developing countries. With the neglect of the developing world's problems has come the reappearance of old diseases, the use of old medicines that are highly toxic, and a growing number of diseases that are resistant to existing drugs.

The story of sleeping sickness provides a good example with a hopeful ending. Sleeping sickness is a parasitic disease that is 100 percent fatal if not treated, and it kills more than 65,000 people each year. Until recently, sleeping sickness was treated with melarsoprol, a toxic derivative of arsenic that killed 1 out of 20 of the patients who took it. Manufacture of a relatively new, safe, and effective drug called eflornithine was discontinued in 1995 because not enough people in the affected countries could pay a price (about $20 per dose) that would make it profitable. Eflornithine production resumed in 2001 after Bristol-Myers Squibb started using it in Vaniqa ointment to prevent growth of facial hair in women. With the encouragement of Doctors without Borders and the WHO, Aventis has also agreed to resume production of eflornithine and to donate enough of the drug to treat sleeping sickness worldwide for 5 years. Aventis will also work with the WHO to find a long-term solution for the manufacture of the drug and to develop oral formulations that are cheaper and easier to administer than the current, injected version. The next section discusses a host of other approaches to the issue of missing or expensive medicines.

STRATEGIES FOR REFORMING BIG PHARMA

The only way to solve this chronic health crisis is to change the way we think about medicines for neglected diseases. They must be considered public goods, not simply consumer products.

—*Dr. James Orbinski, Co-chair of the DND Working Group*

Louis Daguerre invented an early version of photography in 1837. After granting Daguerre a patent, the French government purchased it from him and announced that rights to this invention would be a gift "free to the world." Harvard economist Michael Kremer suggests a similar procedure for pharmaceutical patents.[15] The government could purchase patents in order to place them in the public domain; however, the dilemma of appropriate payment would arise. Kremer proposes an auction mechanism that causes bidders to reveal their valuations of a patent. The purpose of the auction is for the government to learn what a patent is worth, rather than for the high bidder to actually purchase the patent; however, to elicit realistic bids, the bidders must have some chance of actually receiving the patent. After the auction, a coin flip could determine whether the government or the bidder has the opportunity to purchase the patent for the amount of the high bid, and the inventor would have the right to refuse the high bid and retain the patent. Using this method, many patents could be obtained by the government at fair prices and made available to all interested competitors, thus eliminating monopoly prices without removing incentives for private R&D.

---

[15] See http://papers.nber.org/papers/w6304.

Under other reform proposals, the trademark name for a drug would expire when the drug patent expires. For example, the drug company Pfizer sells sildenafil citrate as Viagra. When the patent runs out, generic versions of sildenafil citrate can be sold, but monopoly effects will linger if people are more familiar with the trademark name or if they mistakenly believe that the generic versions are somehow inferior to Viagra. Jennifer Haas and her colleagues estimate that, if available, identical generic drugs were consistently used, the annual cost of prescription drugs in the United States would be reduced by $9 billion.[16] In some cases a trademark inadvertently becomes the generic name for a product and loses its legal status. This has happened with the names aspirin, cellophane, nylon, escalator, yo-yo, and milk of magnesia, among others.

Another ray of hope for treatment of neglected diseases comes from public–private partnerships, such as the Global Alliance for TB Drug Development and the Medicines for Malaria Venture, that might promote public- and private-sector research into less profitable drugs. Private foundations, including the Bill and Melinda Gates Foundation, have also become increasingly involved in developing cures for neglected diseases. The Gates Foundation,[17] with an endowment of $28.8 billion, has already committed more than $750 million to the Vaccine Fund and $126.5 million to the International AIDS Vaccine Initiative.

A *price discrimination* strategy of charging higher prices in wealthier countries to create incentives for innovation and lower prices in poorer countries to increase access to crucial remedies has been tried with limited success. Such price discrimination is difficult to maintain because the products can be purchased where prices are low and resold where prices are high. Nonetheless, the FDA reports that a large volume of drugs arrives in the United States from Mexico, India, Thailand, and the Philippines, where the products are sold for less or where cheaper counterfeit versions are available.[18]

As for high drug prices in the United States, some observers suggest that the solution is to reduce the length of patent protection. Others want to allow imports from Canada, where the government controls drug prices. Of course, the U.S. government could impose price controls to achieve the same result. However, a large shift to purchasing price-controlled drugs from another country has the same effect as a decrease in patent protection: It lowers the incentives to create new products. To the extent that profits motivate critical R&D, lower prices alone, without compensatory reasons to innovate, are an incomplete solution.[19]

Tax revenues are spent on research in government laboratories, government-supported institutes, and public universities. Perhaps such publicly funded research could fill more of the gaps in the treatment of disease. It might also be appropriate for policymakers to require more price concessions from the drug industry, in light of the benefits it receives from taxpayer dollars. Pharmaceutical patent applications include extensive citations of publicly funded research. A 2002 report by Michael Gluck cites a string of evidence that public dollars contribute to many patented discoveries, in-

[16] See www.annals.org/cgi/content/full/142/11/891.
[17] See www.gatesfoundation.org.
[18] See www.fda.gov/ola/2004/importeddrugs0714.html.
[19] For further discussion of pricing issues, see Frederic M. Scherer, "The Pharmaceutical Industry: Prices and Progress," *New England Journal of Medicine*, August 26, 2004, pp. 927–932.

cluding a statement by an official of the National Cancer Institute that his institution played an important role in the R&D of 52 out of 77 FDA-approved cancer drugs and a finding that funds from the National Institute of Health or the FDA were used in the R&D of 45 out of 50 top-selling drugs approved by the FDA between 1992 and 1997.[20] Moreover, if research activities in public institutions could provide critical discoveries, then patent protection might become less necessary as a motivating force.

Governments in developed countries could make commitments to work on cures for deadly diseases elsewhere. Such commitments would test the value Americans place on benevolence. The United States currently spends a smaller percentage of its gross domestic product (GDP) on foreign aid than any other wealthy nation—about 0.1 percent—but this tightfistedness may not reflect Americans' true ideals. A 2005 study conducted by the University of Maryland's Program on International Policy Attitudes found that 65 percent of Americans would favor a commitment by the wealthiest nations to spend 0.7 percent of GDP on world poverty.[21]

As a final reform suggestion, Gary Becker has proposed that the FDA approve drugs without requiring the second and third stages of trials,[22] as was the policy until 1962. With an estimated 40 percent of R&D costs going to the trial stages, Becker argues that the sizable reduction in costs would justify a shorter patent life while offering increased incentives for companies to seek new drugs. The trade-off here is that, although the FDA would continue to judge drug safety, the burden of determining drug efficacy would be shifted to the public. This streamlined policy would bring new drugs to market quickly and at lower expense. It might also bring out "snake-oil salespeople," selling so-called remedies that are cures for nothing except fat wallets, in numbers not seen since 1962.

CONCLUSION

The current patent system does well at creating effective, though expensive, cures for many maladies of the wealthiest nations. In the eyes of critics, the failures of the pharmaceutical industry include misplaced priorities and inaccessible drugs. In 2000, Fred Hassan, chief executive officer of Pharmacia Corporation, told the World Conference on Clinical Pharmacology and Therapeutics, "The United States has become the must-win market for every pharmaceutical company. This does not mean ignoring other markets, but it does mean strategically concentrating resources and top management attention on success in the key market." The puzzle of how best to allocate resources within the pharmaceutical industry has no easy solution, but it is important to consider because solutions would save or improve the lives of millions of people every year.

There is little doubt that many lives would be saved by improved access to drugs if patent protection suddenly ceased. The question is whether patent protection today will motivate drug innovations that will save even more lives in the future. Perhaps your generation will adopt alternative incentives or sources of funding for pharmaceutical R&D, so that the trade-off between affordability and discovery will end.

[20] See www.kff.org/rxdrugs/3254-index.cfm.
[21] See www.pipa.org.
[22] See http://home.uchicago.edu/~gbecker/Businessweek/BW/2002/09_16_2002.pdf.

DISCUSSION STARTERS

1. How do you think the following policies would affect the R&D efforts made by pharmaceutical companies? How do they rate in terms of fairness and desirability?
   a. the cessation of patent rights after revenues of $700 million have been earned from sales of a particular drug
   b. an award of $700 million for cures for any of the 25 most deadly diseases, with no award of patent rights
   c. a government mandate that no patent will be awarded for cosmetic solutions, such as hair-loss remedies, until remedies for the 5 most deadly diseases are found

2. If you could rewrite any or all of the patent laws, for how many years would you offer patent rights, and what other policies would you adopt to strike the appropriate balance between drug prices and R&D incentives?

3. What are the best and worst aspects of the drug companies' practice of sending representatives to doctors' offices with brochures, baskets of food, and gifts emblazoned with the trademarks of their products?

4. Malaria, caused by the plasmodium parasite and transmitted by *Anopheline* mosquitoes in more than 100 developing countries, affects about 7 out of every 100 people worldwide and kills between 1 million and 2 million people each year. There is widespread resistance to older medicines, and many people in poor countries don't have access to new medicines. Fewer than 10 cases of malaria are contracted within the United States each year, and U.S. tourists who return from overseas with malaria have ready access to remedies. Male- and female-pattern baldness affects 35 million men and 20 million women in the United States[23] and roughly 23 percent of men and 21 percent of women worldwide.[24] If a total of $500 million in U.S. government funds were to be divided between research to develop new, public-domain cures for pattern baldness and for malaria, and the likelihood of success for each research project increased in proportion to the amount spent, how would you divide the funds between the projects? Defend your answer.

---

[23] See www.cfsan.fda.gov/~dms/cos-817.html.
[24] See http://nuhair.net/female-hair-loss.htm.

CHAPTER 21

WHY DO WE NEGLECT LEISURE AND CHEER FOR DIVORCE?

The Divergence of Gross Domestic Product and Measures of Well-Being

Gross domestic product (GDP) is the market value of all final goods and services produced in a country within a given period. Policymakers target GDP growth as if it embodied everything that is good, but as a measure of well-being, GDP represents a mixed bag at best. GDP figures can mislead because some goods and services are purchased in response to problems, such as pollution and terrorism, and many of the true joys of life, such as time spent with friends and family, are left out of GDP. Consider a typical worker, a blissful retiree, and an unemployed worker who got divorced and had heart bypass surgery in the same year. The typical worker contributes about $85,000 worth of output to GDP each year. The litigation costs for a "lightly conflicted" divorce run about $45,000, as do the health-care costs for heart bypass surgery.[1] Although the retiree may be the happiest member of this bunch, she added nothing to GDP, whereas the victim of bad luck is responsible for the largest contribution. A country beset with bad luck—wars, hurricanes, disease, crime—runs up a large GDP, too. This chapter explains the methods of calculating gross domestic product, the weakness of GDP as a measure of contentment, and alternative measures that give more accurate indications of both burdens and bliss.

---

[1] See, for example, www.raisinghappykids.com/Mediation.html and www.gsdl.com/home/assessments/cardio/appguide/.

MEASURING GDP

GDP may not be the root of happiness, but it is a valuable measure of output, with implications for employment and economic growth. In 1991, GDP replaced gross national product (GNP) as the primary measure of production used by U.S. economists. The difference is that GDP measures the value of goods and services produced by anyone on U.S. soil, whereas GNP measures the value of production by U.S. citizens anywhere in the world. Thus, Venus Williams's winnings at Wimbledon are part of U.S. GNP because she is a U.S. citizen and part of British GDP because she earned them on British soil. Government agencies and private corporations use GDP figures widely to get a read on the direction of the economy. For example, the Central Intelligence Agency (CIA) uses GDP per capita (GDP divided by the number of citizens) as a benchmark for the standard of living in nations around the world,[2] and the board of governors of the Federal Reserve System and the president's Council of Economic Advisers use GDP as a gauge of the economy's performance and a basis for policy decisions.

GDP is calculated by the Bureau of Economic Analysis (BEA), an agency of the U.S. Department of Commerce. There are three primary ways of compiling the GDP figure:

First, the *expenditure approach* adds up the following to obtain the total expenditure on goods and services:[3]

- consumption spending by households
- investment spending by businesses
- government spending
- net exports (exports minus imports)

In order to avoid double counting, only spending on "final" goods and services is included. This means that expenditures on raw materials (such as iron ore) and on intermediate goods (such as car engines) are not counted until such inputs become part of a completed product (such as a car), and spending on goods purchased for resale isn't counted until the goods are sold to the ultimate consumer. The investment component of GDP includes business spending on machinery and other capital goods, new construction of both businesses and homes, and goods that are produced and held as net additions to inventories. The purchase of stocks and bonds and the deposit of money into banks do not represent production and are not counted as investment. By adding up all these expenditures, the BEA can determine the value of final goods and services produced within a particular year.

Second, the *value-added approach,* similar to the expenditure approach, examines output values, but the method of avoiding double counting is different. Rather than considering only final goods and services, the value-added approach examines raw and intermediate goods and services as well, and it counts only the incremental change in value from one step in the production process to the next. If $1 worth of cotton becomes $5 worth of fabric, which becomes a $30 dress, the value-added approach

---

[2] For a ranking of nations according to GDP per capita, see http://www.cia.gov/cia/publications/factbook/rankorder/2004rank.html.

[3] More formally, denoting consumption as C, investment as I, government spending as G, exports as X, and imports as M, this is written as GDP $= C + I + G + (X - M)$.

is to add together the $1 value of the cotton, the $4 increase in value when the cotton becomes fabric, and the $25 increase in value when the fabric becomes a dress to get the same $30 figure that the expenditure approach takes from the final sale of the dress: $30 = $1 + ($5 − $1) + ($30 − $5).

Third, the *income approach* is based on the logic that workers receive the market value of goods and services as income. *National income* is the sum of the following:

- employee compensation
- interest payments, as on bank deposits and bonds
- rental income received by landlords
- corporate profits
- proprietors' (that is, businesses owners') income

To find GDP, national income must be adjusted by adding items that are part of the value of production but not part of income and by removing items that count toward income but not toward production.[4] Specifically, this entails doing the following:

1. subtracting government subsidies, which are part of income but don't constitute payment for a good

2. adding the value of new capital purchased to replace old capital, called *capital consumption,* or *depreciation,* because those purchases are made with depreciation reserves that don't count toward income

3. adding *net foreign factor income,* which is the difference between what foreign investors earn on assets in the United States and what U.S. investors earn from their assets elsewhere

In theory, all three of these approaches lead to the same estimate of GDP. In practice, they are similar. After the first quarter of 2006, the BEA estimated GDP to be $13.037 trillion and national income to be $11.492 trillion.[5] After making the adjustments as previously explained to estimate GDP using national income, the difference between the two GDP estimates was a "statistical discrepancy" of $33.3 billion, or about one-quarter of 1 percent. As they say, that's not bad for government work.

OUT WITH THE BADS AND IN WITH THE GOODS

Empirical economic research has established that nations that trade more enjoy higher rates of economic growth and hence higher living standards, measured in per capita gross domestic product.

—*Pete du Pont, National Center for Policy Analysis*[6]

---

[4] It used to be that *indirect business taxes,* such as excise taxes, sales taxes, and property taxes, were among the items added to national income to find GDP. However, the 2003 Comprehensive Revision of the National Income and Product Accounts (see page 15 of www.bea.gov/bea/ARTICLES/2003/06June/0603NIPArevs.pdf) redefines national income to include indirect business taxes among other "nonfactor charges."
[5] See Table 1.7.5 at www.bea.gov/bea/dn/dpga.txt.
[6] See http://waysandmeans.house.gov/hearings.asp?formmode=view&id=2835.

Our third-quarter economic growth was vibrant, and that's good.

—*President George W. Bush*[7]

Policymakers and the media often herald GDP growth as a uniformly splendid event. In fact, increases in GDP may or may not be desirable. GDP increases when money is spent to deal with social failures, such as excessive pollution and crime; when burdens are placed on future generations by the use of farming techniques that cause soil erosion and by manufacturing that depletes nonrenewable resources; and when activities shift from nonmarket to market sectors, as when nannies substitute for unpaid family members, televisions substitute for interpersonal contact, and KFC takes the place of home-cooked meals. A better measure of progress would exclude expenditures that signal bad situations and include the value of beneficial nonmarket activities. This section identifies the categories of expenditure that should and should not be parts of an accurate indicator of social welfare.

The Bads

Defensive goods and services are those necessitated by problems that make society worse off, as with corruption; natural disasters; disease; and such perils of economic growth as pollution, congestion, and work-related stress. For example, in a typical year $478.6 billion of the U.S. GDP is spent on police, prisons, security systems, and other purchases to help deal with the problem of crime.[8] If the crime rate worsens, this component of GDP will increase, but society will be worse off. As another example, $100 billion is spent each year to treat chronic back pain, which is often caused by injury, depression, or the stress and strain of fast-paced jobs.[9] Between 1996 and 2001, use of the most expensive back treatment, spinal-fusion surgery, increased 77 percent at $34,000 a pop.[10] Back pain has become a leading reason to visit a doctor, but increased expenditures on this or any other burgeoning malady do not reflect a better life. Ditto for expenditures on counterterrorism, drug treatment, oil spills, malignancies, psychologists, funerals, and so on. Increased expenditures on defensive goods and services indicate that the quality of life has diminished, and these expenditures should be subtracted from GDP to obtain a more accurate measure of social welfare.

As step 2 of the adjustment from national income to GDP in the previous section indicates, capital consumption (depreciation) is part of GDP. This erosion in the value of capital during the production process is not an indication of better living. Suppose that $5,000 worth of silk-screening equipment must be replaced because of wear and tear after the production of $100,000 worth of Hard Rock Café t-shirts. GDP would increase by $105,000 because it includes capital consumption, whereas the net gain for society would be $100,000 worth of new products because $5,000 worth of new capital would be required to replace the worn-out machinery. The U.S. government publishes net national product (NNP) figures that adjust GDP to account for the de-

---

[7] See http://transcripts.cnn.com/TRANSCRIPTS/0311/03/se.02.html.
[8] David A. Anderson, "The Aggregate Burden of Crime," *Journal of Law and Economics* (1999), *42*:2, 611–642.
[9] See, for example, www.back-pain-management.com/.
[10] See www.msnbc.msn.com/id/4767268/.

preciation of traditional (human-made) capital. NNP does not adjust for losses of forests, oil reserves, and other natural capital associated with increases in GDP. A true measure of social welfare would reflect the losses of all types of capital.

The Goods

Nonmarket production provides benefits to society in the absence of explicit prices and purchases. Work performed for the benefit of the worker and the worker's family—child care, gardening, housework, do-it-yourself home improvements—is not included in GDP, although the same duties *are* counted in GDP when performed by a paid professional. Production in the *underground economy,* also known as the *cash economy,* that is not reported to the government also is not part of GDP, despite available estimates that its value approaches $1 trillion per year in the United States.[11] And the volunteer work performed at churches, charities, nursing homes, schools, and elsewhere goes uncounted in GDP. For those with the option to work more for pay, the fact that they spend more time on these nonmarket activities indicates that they perceive larger marginal benefits from volunteering than they would receive from additional market work. It is important to include these goods and services, to the extent possible, in a true measure of social welfare.

Improvements in GDP and national income don't necessarily correspond with improvements in income distribution or guarantee that most people are earning higher incomes. It may be that a small percentage of people are earning more, whereas most incomes are stagnating or even declining. If a gauge of income distribution is desired within a measure of social welfare, the *Gini coefficient* could serve that purpose. The Gini coefficient ranges from 0 to 1, increasing with the gap between perfect equality and complete inequality in income distribution. A coefficient of 0 means that everyone receives the same income, and a coefficient of 1 means that the richest person receives all the income. In 2004, the Gini coefficient was 0.33 in Canada, 0.41 in the United States, and 0.55 in Mexico.

Finally, as elated as people might be about weekends, days off, and the prospect of early retirement, the quality and quantity of leisure time don't find their way into GDP calculations. GDP would be higher if everyone worked incessantly, but then people would have no time in which to enjoy the bumper crop of output. An ideal measure of social welfare would reflect the opportunities for leisure time.

ALTERNATIVE MEASURES

Economists have proposed several indicators of welfare and progress as alternatives to GDP. Examples include the following:

- the Measure of Economic Welfare (MEW)
- Net National Welfare (NNW)
- the Index of Leading Cultural Indicators (ILCI)

---

[11] See www.ncpa.org/ba/ba273.html.

- the Index of Social Health (ISH)
- Economic Aspects of Welfare (EAW)
- the Green GDP
- the Genuine Progress Indicator (GPI)
- the Index of Sustainable Economic Welfare (ISEW)

Most of these measures adjust GDP by adding categories that promote social welfare and subtracting categories that don't, as described previously. Some of the measures start from scratch. For instance, the ISEW is calculated as follows:

ISEW = personal consumption / distribution inequality[12]
+ household labor + value of services from consumer durables
+ streets and highways + public expenditures on health and education
− consumer durables − defensive private expenditures on health and
education
− national advertising − commuting costs − cost of urbanization
− cost of auto accidents − cost of water, air, and noise pollution
− loss of wetlands and farmlands − depletion of nonrenewable resources
− long-term environmental damage + net capital growth
+ change in net intergenerational position

Net National Welfare is an example of a measure that begins with GDP and makes adjustments:

NNW = GDP + nonmarket output − externality costs
− pollution abatement and cleanup costs − depreciation of created capital
− depreciation of natural capital

Visit http://www.foe.co.uk/campaigns/sustainable_development/progress/make-own.html for an opportunity to design your own welfare index based on the things you deem important.

Most of the alternative indexes have diverged from GDP during the past three decades. For example, the Genuine Progress Indicator suggests that GDP is out of line with true progress by $7 trillion, and GPI per capita has followed a mostly downward trend since 1977, even as GDP per capita has increased.[13] GDP calculations are relevant to employment and productivity, but a measure of social welfare would serve as a better guide for decisions that aim to improve our quality of life. Of course, politicians have a tendency to prefer the relatively high GDP values, and they have largely dismissed arguments by economists, such as Nobel laureate James Tobin, about the need to seek alternative indexes. Lobbying efforts by economists and groups, such as Redefining Progress,[14] continue, so one or more of these many available alternatives may eventually replace GDP as the focus of media attention and policymaking.

---

[12] An index similar to the Gini coefficient.
[13] See www.redefiningprogress.org/publications/gpi_march2004update.pdf.
[14] See www.redefiningprogress.org.

CONCLUSION

Gross national product does not allow for the health of our children, the quality of their education, or the joy of their play. It does not include the beauty of our poetry or the strength of our marriages; the intelligence of our public debate or the integrity of our public officials. It measures neither our wit nor our courage; neither our wisdom nor our learning; neither our compassion nor our devotion to our country; it measures everything, in short, except that which makes life worthwhile.

—Robert F. Kennedy, 1968[15]

Gross domestic product and national income are valid and useful measures of output and economic activity. However, despite their central roles as gauges for success, they do not accurately reflect well-being. Consider the median income in Shenandoah, a section of East Baton Rouge parish in Louisiana: $73,536. This figure surpasses the $43,527 median income for the United States as a whole by a generous $30,009 and indicates a high volume of output in nearby chemical, plastics, oil, and gas industries. In fact, Louisiana workers are rated among the most productive workers in the nation.[16] Even so, the high levels of income and output and the correspondingly low unemployment rate in Shenandoah may not fully explain the overall quality of life there. Shenandoah borders an industrial corridor between Baton Rouge and New Orleans that has been dubbed Cancer Alley. The environmental watchdog Web site Scorecard.org ranks East Baton Rouge first among Louisiana parishes (land areas similar to counties) in the release of lead compounds into the air. The fact that East Baton Rouge is among the worst 10 percent of U.S. counties in terms of emissions of carbon monoxide, nitrogen oxides, particulate matter, sulfur dioxide, and volatile organic compounds may influence the well-being of residents in ways that cannot be captured in income and output figures. In any location, GDP rises with smoke-blackened skies, broken homes that force both parents to work full time, disease, and disaster, and wise policymakers will consult alternative measures of progress.

DISCUSSION STARTERS

1. The CIA uses GDP as an indicator of economic activity in countries around the world. How would you explain to a noneconomist CIA director what GDP can and cannot tell the CIA about those countries?

2. Prostitution, gambling, and some types of drug use are legal in some countries and illegal in others. What implication does this have for international GDP comparisons? What other issues might cloud such comparisons?

3. In 1996, champion bicycle racer Lance Armstrong was diagnosed with cancer and spent, perhaps, $60,000 on surgery and chemotherapy. Each year

---

[15] See www.rfkmemorial.org/lifevision/rfkquotes/.
[16] See www.ibervillechamber.org/about.html.

from 1999 to 2005, Armstrong's team shared a $400,000 prize in the Tour de France bike race. For the purpose of this exercise, let's ignore the money that Armstrong made from endorsements and other sources and assume that the prize money was divided evenly among Armstrong and his nine team-mates. In which year did Armstrong make the largest contribution to GDP? In which year do you think he had the lowest level of individual welfare? In which year do you think he had the highest level of individual welfare? Discuss the relationships among income, output, and your own happiness.

4. Categorize each of the following items as being *in* or *out* of U.S. GDP in the relevant year:
   a. Lance Armstrong's winnings in the Tour de France
   b. the used toboggan you bought on eBay
   c. the Whopper you bought for lunch
   d. the massage you bought your dad for Father's Day
   e. the Monet painting you bought your mother for Mother's Day
   f. the coffee beans that Starbucks roasted in December but didn't sell until the following year

5. How could leisure time be included in a measure of social welfare? Can you think of measurable values that coincide with leisure?

CHAPTER 22

DOES THE MONEY
SUPPLY MATTER?
Money, the Fed, and the Debate
Over Optimal Monetary Policy

Money gets a bad rap. The proverb that money is the root of all evil is at least as old as the Bible.[1] The coins and bills that constitute money for most people are called *fiat currency* because they would have little use if not for the government decree, or "fiat," that makes them valuable. They are adopted merely as a convenience. Without dollars, there would be no less greed, but every type of commerce for every reason would be carried out with less convenience. When fiat currency is unavailable, buyers and sellers resort to cumbersome bartering and the use of *commodity money*, such as precious metals, shells, salt, or anything else that has practical value as a commodity. Inmates can't hold fiat currency in prison, but the number of cigarettes it takes to buy a tattoo is well known in the prison yard.[2] Some summer camps don't allow campers to hold fiat currency, but no small amount of commerce goes on between campers for commodity money, such as candy bars.

A more tenable concern over money might be that the central bank, the Federal Reserve or "Fed," has made too little (or too much) of it available in the economy at a particular time. There is considerable disagreement about the real and lasting

---

[1] See I Timothy 6:10.
[2] I have verified this while conducting economic research at prisons. See http://bkmarcus.com/cache/POW/ for a study of cigarettes as currency in a prisoner of war camp.

effects of fine-tuning the money supply. As trading consultant Howard Simons notes, "The question of how those influences occur, and to what extent, can ignite the closest thing to a barroom brawl among practitioners of the dismal science."[3] This chapter provides an overview of money, the Federal Reserve System, and the battlefield of economic theory on which the Fed strategizes about monetary policy.

SHOW ME THE MONEY

Money serves three primary functions:

- It is *a medium of exchange*. Rather than carting products around to trade for other products, which can be difficult if you're in the refrigerator business or if the person who has what you want doesn't want what you have, people use money, which is easy to carry around and is accepted by all.

- It is *a store of value*. You can hold cash in your pocket or bury it in a pickle jar for use in the future, whereas storing value in output, such as lectures or tomatoes, simply doesn't work.

- It is *a unit of account*. Dollars, yen, baht, and other units of currency provide standard ways of measuring expenditures.

The money supply has several components, beyond cash and standard bank deposits, that deserve mention. A *money market mutual fund* is made up of short-term, low-risk financial securities, such as Treasury bills, certificates of deposit, and municipal notes. *Time deposits* (such as certificates of deposit) are deposits that can't be withdrawn for a specified period without a financial penalty. *Eurodollar deposits* are large (usually more than $1 million) time deposits denominated in U.S. dollars and held either by banks headquartered outside the United States or by foreign branches of banks headquartered within the United States. A *repurchase agreement* (repo) is a way for an investor to make short-term loans. The investor gives money in exchange for an asset, such as a Treasury bond. At a specified time, the loan recipient returns a higher amount of money (the loan amount plus interest) to the investor in exchange for the asset.

M1 = Cash + Checking account deposits
M2 = M1 + Savings accounts + Time deposits + Retail money market mutual funds
M3 = M2 + Institutional money market mutual funds + Eurodollar deposits + Repurchase agreements + Time deposits more than $100,000

As exhibited in the accompanying table, the money you can literally grasp in your hands as cash or a check drawn on deposits is called M1. M2 is the roughly $1.3 trillion worth of M1 plus about $5 trillion worth of savings accounts, time deposits, and retail money market mutual funds. M3 is M2 plus $2.9 trillion worth of money mar-

[3] See www.thestreet.com/options/futuresshocktsc/10124905.html.

ket mutual funds held by institutions, Eurodollar deposits, repurchase agreements, and time deposits more than $100,000.

Does the money supply matter? At the microeconomic (individual) level, there are issues of whether individual wealth really matters in the pursuit of happiness because the conventional wisdom is that "the best things in life are free." This chapter describes the basics of how the Fed can alter the money supply and takes on the macroeconomic (big picture) issue of whether adjustments in the money supply influence gross domestic product (GDP) and unemployment.

THE FEDERAL RESERVE SYSTEM

The *Federal Reserve System*, which serves as the central bank for the United States, has the mission of formulating monetary policy to achieve price stability and economic growth. The Fed oversees a *fractional reserve banking system* in which only a fraction of bank deposits are actually retained by the banks; the remainder is loaned out. Banks earn profits on the difference between the interest rates they pay depositors and the higher interest rates that loan recipients pay the banks. The board of governors of the Fed determines the *reserve requirement*, which is the minimum fraction of deposits that a bank must retain either in the vault or in a reserve account at the Fed. When a bank falls short of the necessary or desired level of reserve balances, it can borrow in the *federal funds market* from banks that have more than enough reserves. The interest rate that banks pay each other in this market is called the *federal funds rate*.

The Fed has three primary tools for influencing the money supply. The main line of attack is open-market operations, by which specialists at the Federal Reserve's Open Market Desk in New York manipulate the supply of reserves. To increase the supply, the folks at the Open Market Desk purchase government securities, such as Treasury bonds, on the market that is open to banks and investors. To pay for the securities, the Fed increases the seller's reserve account by the amount of the purchase.[4] To decrease the supply of reserves, some of the Fed's portfolio of more than $700 billion worth of Treasury securities could be sold to commercial banks, which would result in debits against the banks' reserve accounts. In practice, sales of securities in the open market are rare. Instead, when the Fed wishes to decrease reserves, it usually simply purchases fewer than its usual quantity of securities, resulting in less than the usual supply of reserves. These acts of buying and selling (or buying fewer) securities on the open market to change the supply of reserves are called *open-market operations*.

The Fed sets the wheels of monetary policy in motion by altering the level of reserves. With fewer reserves, banks have less money to lend out and the amount of money in circulation decreases. As our knowledge of supply and demand would predict, a decrease in the supply of reserves also causes the price of borrowing reserves—the federal funds rate—to increase. This makes it more expensive for banks to borrow from each other and triggers subsequent increases in interest rates paid by bank customers. The result is less borrowing and spending in the economy. When the Fed buys securities, payments from the Fed increase reserve levels, the federal funds rate

[4] When the seller is a private securities dealer rather than a bank, the Fed credits the reserve account of the "correspondent bank" that performs banking services for the seller.

and other interest rates drop, and more money flows into the economy. These monetary policy transactions are orchestrated by the Federal Open Market Committee, which consists of the 7 members of the Fed's board of governors and 5 of the presidents of the 12 Federal Reserve System banks.

The Fed's control of the reserve requirement constitutes a rarely used but powerful second tool with which to influence the money supply. If the reserve requirement is 10 percent, $100 out of a $1,000 deposit must be set aside, whereas $900 can be lent out. If that $900 loan is deposited by its recipient or by those from whom the recipient made purchases, $90 must be held and $810 can be lent out. Under the simplifying assumptions that each loan is subsequently deposited and every bank lends out as much as the Fed will allow, the $1,000 deposit ultimately creates $9,000 worth of new loans (the $900 plus the $810 and so on) before no more loans are possible because the entire $1,000 is sitting in bank vaults as 10 percent of a total of $10,000 worth of deposits.

The process that generates up to $10,000 in deposits out of $1,000 in cash is called *money creation*. The amount of money created from each $1 of new deposits is called the *banking multiplier*, and it equals 1 divided by the reserve requirement. With a reserve requirement of 10 percent, or 0.10, the multiplier is $1/0.10 = 10$, which explains why the $1,000 created $10 \times \$1,000$, or $10,000 in deposits. Because the Fed controls the reserve requirement, it controls the amount of money created in this process. If it changed the reserve requirement to 20 percent, the banking multiplier would become $1/0.20 = 5$ and a $1,000 deposit would create $5 \times \$1,000 = \$5,000$ in deposits. The banking multiplier is diminished when money leaks out of the cycle of loans and deposits, as when people hold significant amounts of money as cash, banks hold excess reserves, or expenditures are made on imports.

As the third tactic for controlling the money supply, the boards of directors of the 12 regional Federal Reserve banks, in consultation with the board of governors of the Fed, control the interest rate paid by banks and other depository institutions when they borrow money from their regional Federal Reserve bank. This rate is called the *discount rate,* and the lending facility within each Federal Reserve bank is called the *discount window.* When the discount rate is raised, less money is borrowed, and so there is less money in the economy. Although the availability of funds from other sources limits the direct influence of discount rate changes, a change in this rate is considered an important signal of the intent of Fed policy.[5] The Fed also uses the informal power of *moral suasion*—pressure or persuasion without force—to convey its policy interests and intentions through public statements, published studies, educational programs, and conferences.

The Fed uses combinations of these tools to address the amount of the money supply. To the Fed's consternation, the money-creation process has grown more complex in recent decades because banking functions have spread beyond banks. The 1980 Depository Institutions Deregulation and Monetary Control Act made it possible for credit unions and savings and loan institutions to offer checking accounts and a wider variety of loans. Retail firms, such as Sears; insurance companies, such as John Hancock; and securities firms, such as Merrill Lynch started offering banking serv-

---

[5] See www.chicagofed.org/consumer_information/the_fed_our_central_bank.cfm.

ices in the mid-1980s, and financial innovations, including *commercial paper,* now allow corporations to borrow from investors by selling *promissory notes,* which are unsecured[6] promises for repayment. In the early 2000s, growing levels of nonbank lending and excess capacity (the ability of firms to produce more with existing factories than was demanded) led to record low levels of commercial and industrial lending as a percentage of GDP. This decrease slowed the money-creation activities of the Fed in ways that were hard to control. The money multiplier works best when all loanable funds are lent out, and any excess reserves represent idle dollars that could otherwise be creating more loans and deposits.

The restructuring of banking services also led to difficulties with the traditional measures of money. During the past century, the proportion of the money supply made up of M1 has fallen, indicating a growing number of alternatives to cash and checks. In response, the St. Louis Federal Reserve created a new measure of the money supply called *money with 0 maturity (MZM)* to provide a better snapshot of available funds. MZM is money that is redeemable immediately at face value, so it includes cash, checking and savings accounts, and money market mutual funds. In some years MZM increases even as M1 decreases and vice versa.

One more term is relevant to the money supply and the debate over its importance: the *velocity of money.* This is the number of times each year that the same money is spent and is measured by dividing M2 by GDP. An increase in velocity means that the existing money is being respent more often and that a smaller money supply is needed to support a particular level of spending.

MONEY MATTERS, BUT DON'T MESS WITH IT

> *Money does matter.*
>
> —*Milton Friedman*[7]

The most famous money-supply adversaries are the monetarists and the Keynesians. The monetarists, championed by Milton Friedman and following in the footsteps of the classical economists before them, focus on policy implications in the long run, after the economy has had time to adjust to changes. Monetarist and classical economists believe money is *neutral,* meaning that the level of output is independent of the money supply in the long run. At the center of this debate is the *equation of exchange*:

money supply $\times$ **v**elocity of money = **p**rice level $\times$ **q**uantity of output

or, more concisely

$$MV = PQ$$

---

[6] Unsecured loans involve no *collateral,* which is something of value that the lender gets if the loan is not repaid. In other words, if the borrower doesn't pay back the money, the lender is out of luck. Most loans are secured with collateral. For example, the collateral for a mortgage loan is a house. If a mortgage loan is not repaid, the lender gets the house.

[7] "The Quantity Theory of Money: A Restatement," in Milton Friedman (ed.), *Studies in Quantity Theory* (Chicago: University of Chicago Press, 1956).

The right-hand side of this equation represents the expenditure on goods in a year, which must equal the amount of money multiplied by the number of times per year that the money is spent. That is, 2 oranges could be purchased for $1 each with a money supply of $2 and a velocity of 1, or with a money supply of $1 and a velocity of 2—the same dollar being spent twice. According to the *quantity theory of money,* the velocity of money and the quantity of output are relatively fixed, so that with any increase in the money supply, the equation must be balanced by an increase in the price level. Thus, in the long run, Fed policies to alter the money supply would affect the inflation rate but not the growth rate of output.

Monetarists question the Fed's ability to fine-tune the economy and achieve short-run stability by using monetary policy. Although they acknowledge that variations in the money supply can have a short-run bearing on demand and output, they are skeptical of the Fed's ability to adequately master the complex dynamics of the economy and yield the desired result. Even if the Fed accurately assesses a downturn in the economy and flawlessly carries out a monetary expansion, monetarists argue, by the time the additional money reaches the hands of those who will spend it to give the economy a boost, the economy may have already corrected itself, and the monetary policy will only worsen a period of high inflation. Monetarists prefer a more passive "monetary rule" of letting the money supply grow steadily at the rate of real GDP growth rather than making adjustments in response to short-run demand problems.

THE EVOLUTION OF MONETARY POLICY

Classical economists and, more recently, the monetarists believed that the economy could heal itself in a reasonable amount of time. The Great Depression of 1929–1939 convinced John Maynard Keynes that the economy sometimes needs a nudge from changes in taxes and government spending, which economists call *fiscal policy.* Keynes reasoned that inflexible, or "sticky," wages and prices would prevent the economy from adjusting swiftly to equilibrium at full employment (full employment is defined not as 100 percent employment but as the absence of cyclical unemployment caused by a downturn in the business cycle). Wages might be slow to adjust because of multi-year contracts and because it is difficult to tell workers that their wages will fall. Prices might be sticky because it is a hassle to make price adjustments in catalogs, price lists, and menus. Keynes focused on total, or "aggregate," demand as the driving force behind output and employment and on policies that would raise aggregate demand in the event of a recession.

In Keynes's view, monetary growth would be transmitted to output growth as follows: An increase in the money supply would decrease the price of borrowing money, which is the interest rate. A lower interest rate would spur investment, which is a component of aggregate demand. With higher aggregate demand, the price, GDP, and employment levels would all increase. Keynes pointed out that this chain of events could be broken at several points. If the demand for money is relatively flat, an increase in the supply will not cause the interest rate to fall. And if the demand for investment isn't responsive to the interest rate, investment won't increase even if there is a substantial decrease in the interest rate. These are among the reasons why the money supply might not matter and why Keynes preferred to adjust fiscal policy rather than monetary policy.

The monetarist transmission mechanism is more direct: An increase in the money supply leaves consumers with more money than they want to hold on to, so they spend some of it. However, the monetarist economists disliked meddling with aggregate demand. One argument was that increases in aggregate demand would be *crowded out* by two effects that work against the intended increase in expenditures. First, government expenditures to increase aggregate demand might substitute for private expenditures. For example, when the government expands libraries, private individuals might purchase fewer books on their own. Second, when the government borrows money to make some of its expenditures (as it currently does), it increases the demand for loanable funds, thereby causing the interest rate to rise. Monetarists claim that the higher interest rate and resulting cuts in private investment can lead to either *complete crowding out*—a total offset of the government expenditure by decreases in private expenditure—or *incomplete crowding out* that diminishes but does not eliminate the size of the expenditure boost from the government.

Keynes said that inflation could be countered with higher taxes or less government spending, either of which would lower aggregate demand. Unemployment, conversely, could be remedied by lower taxes or higher spending to boost aggregate demand. Named after British economist William Phillips, the proposed trade-off between unemployment and inflation is known as the *Phillips relationship*. But in the 1970s the United States experienced *stagflation*: high rates of inflation accompanied high levels of unemployment. Just as the Great Depression made people question the laissez-faire (hands-off) policies of the classical economists, stagflation created concern over Keynesian policies. How could aggregate demand be used to moderate the economy if the Phillips relationship did not hold and unemployment and inflation both increased? An increase in aggregate demand might cure the unemployment problem, but the corresponding inflation would go through the roof. It would be a futile contradiction to apply *expansionary policy* to boost employment and *contractionary policy* to limit inflation at the same time.

Skepticism about Keynesian policy in the 1970s left an opening for alternative schools of thought. Nobel laureate Robert Lucas wrote that *rational expectations* would undermine monetary or fiscal policy. His theory was that individuals and firms would anticipate policy responses to upturns and downturns in the economy. For instance, at the onset of a recession, people would anticipate the government response of increasing aggregate demand and the subsequent price increases. They would respond with price and wage increases that increased the cost of production, decreased the quantity demanded, and negated the influence of the expansionary policy.

In the late 1970s and early 1980s, the Fed policy more closely resembled the monetarists' suggestion of steady monetary growth without countercyclical responses. During that period, the alarming inflation rate came down, but the economy remained sluggish. Friedman argued that monetary policy was not applied in the way that it should have been, but that's another story. In the 1980s, there was much fanfare for *supply-side economics,* which emphasized shifting aggregate supply with tax cuts rather than attempting to move aggregate demand. The results were mixed, with inflation under control but another recession in the late 1980s and a burgeoning government debt.

Although Keynes himself did not favor adjustments in the money supply to moderate the economy, the activist, Keynesian approach to policymaking was gradually coupled with the classical belief that the money supply does matter. The outcome was the *neoclassical–Keynesian synthesis*—a hybrid of the previous schools of thought that embraces activist fiscal and monetary policy. Throughout the 1990s and beyond, both types of policy were used in efforts to moderate the economy, with modest success.

Don't think the synthesis compromise is the end of the story. As they say, everything old is new again, and a neo-Keynesian school of economics is also afoot. The new Keynesians have improved arguments for the existence of sticky wages and prices that prevent the economy from self-adjusting to full employment. The reasons include the following:

- **Menu costs:** The expense of printing new menus, catalogs, signs, and price lists makes people reluctant to change prices frequently.

- **Efficiency wages:** Some firms pay amounts in excess of the market wage, called efficiency wages, in order to hire, retain, and encourage the best workers.

- **Staggered pricing:** If firms have staggered pricing schedules and can't all change their prices at the same time, there is a disincentive to raise prices by very much because the first firms to charge more risk losing customers to firms that keep their prices steady.

Neo-Keynesians also argue that sticky wages and prices debunk the rational-expectations hypothesis because stickiness means that prices can't easily be adjusted to a level that negates the influence of policy changes.

With each of these schools of thought having gone through the wringer of bad times and policy ineffectiveness, none is as strong as it once was. Today, there is plenty of activist countercyclical policy on both the monetary and fiscal sides. And although they are tame relative to the Great Depression, wide swings in the economy still occur, so economists are still tinkering with these theories to try to find the best possible bases for stabilization policy.

CONCLUSION

Whether the money supply should be manipulated for the sake of employment and growth depends on a larger set of puzzles: How rigid are prices, wages, the velocity of money, and the level of output? How responsive are interest rates to changes in the money supply, and how responsive are investments to changes in interest rates? Can the economy heal itself? And can the central bank or the government act quickly and accurately enough to rescue an economy in trouble? These are some of the battlegrounds of macroeconomics. Disagreements continue in earnest, fueled by periods of economic history that support each contention. The salient question is this: Whose favored assumptions will hold in the years ahead?

Monetarists and their champion, Milton Friedman, believe that money matters to long-run inflation rates but not to long-term growth. Their concern that unchecked inflation creates uncertainty and inefficiency in the economy leads them to advocate steady growth in the money supply that is in line with GDP growth. Although they see the money supply as having a short-term influence on business cycles, monetarists do not favor short-run adjustments in the money supply as a remedy for economic instability. As reasons against activist policies, monetarists cite policy lags and the possibility of unintended results stemming from the Fed's inability to master the structural complexities of the economy.

Keynes favored policy responses to undesired swings in the economy. He suggested expansionary fiscal policy to bolster sagging aggregate demand, saying that the transmission mechanism between the money supply and aggregate demand may be disjoined. Neoclassical economists, neo-Keynesians, supply-siders, and believers in rational expectations have their own perspectives on appropriate policy. (Of course, using these labels oversimplifies the situation; there is a range of beliefs within each camp.) Of greater importance is an understanding of the issues and dilemmas that surround the money supply because there is much progress to be made and handsome benefits to be had from improvements in macroeconomic policy.

DISCUSSION STARTERS

1. On the basis of the simple banking multiplier discussed in this chapter, calculate how much money would be created by an influx of $1 billion of cash into our economy if the reserve requirement is 10 percent. Explain how the money-creation process works and discuss several reasons why the amount of money created might be less than the largest potential amount.

2. On a graph that measured M1, M2, and M3 on the vertical axis and time on the horizontal axis, would any of the three lines ever cross? Why or why not?

3. Which of the economic theories discussed in this chapter do you think is closest to the truth? Explain your answer with reference to real-world economic phenomena.

4. What remedy would subscribers to each of the following schools of thought suggest for a period of high inflation and low unemployment?
   a. Keynesian
   b. neoclassical–Keynesian synthesis
   c. monetarist

5. Since 2002, the velocity of both M2 and MZM has decreased. How does this trend affect efforts by the Fed to improve the economy by increasing the money supply?

CHAPTER 23

WHAT'S TO LIKE ABOUT OUTSOURCING?

The Influence of International Labor Markets

On February 9, 2004, Greg Mankiw, Harvard economist and chair of the president's Council of Economic Advisers (CEA), described the outsourcing of jobs from the United States to other countries this way:

> Outsourcing is just a new way of doing international trade. More things are tradable than were tradable in the past, and that's a good thing.

Two days later, Senator Hillary Rodham Clinton (D-NY) responded this way:

> I don't think losing American jobs is a good thing. The folks at the other end of Pennsylvania Avenue apparently do.

U.S. Representative Donald Manzullo (R-IL) called for the resignation of Mankiw, saying

> I know the president cannot believe what this man has said. He ought to walk away, and return to his ivy-covered office at Harvard.

President George W. Bush was a believer after all, as he explained in a speech on March 11, 2004:

> People are saying, well, we'll stop jobs from going overseas by making sure we put up walls and barriers between the United States and the rest of the world. That's lousy policy. Consumer prices will go up if we wall ourselves from the rest of the world. Economic isolationism is bad economic policy, and it will cost people jobs.

This chapter investigates the outsourcing (or offshoring) of jobs and the reasons why Mankiw describes this phenomenon as "the latest manifestation of the gains from trade that economists have talked about at least since Adam Smith."[1]

OUTSOURCING: FOR BETTER OR WORSE?

In a typical year, the United States imports about $1.8 trillion worth of goods and services that were produced elsewhere. Most of these items could be produced domestically, and many of them had been produced here in the past. Chapter 28 includes a discussion of the more general issue of who benefits from foreign trade. This chapter examines the particular effects of the decisions by various U.S. companies—including Delta Airlines, American Express, Sprint, Citibank, IBM, and Levi's—to move call centers, manufacturing, or other operations to other countries. CEA chair Mankiw suggested that the outsourcing of jobs is beneficial to the United States. Was the ivy really pulled over the Harvard professor's eyes? And why would economists from Bill Clinton adviser Martin Baily to former Fed chair Alan Greenspan agree that outsourcing isn't something to be feared? Economists seldom concur on something so controversial; might Mankiw's message have merit?

Some people may view outsourcing as a way to help people in developing nations. Those who seek world peace may see that trade and the exchange of jobs provide strong incentives for civility among nations. Followers of some religions labor to love their neighbors as themselves. Stockholders may relish the efficiency gains for their corporations. But what about those of us who simply want to keep our jobs?

There is a perception that the United States is hemorrhaging jobs as a result of outsourcing, but much of the economic research is reassuring. The current unemployment rate of about 5 percent is comfortably below the 50-year average of 5.8 percent. Rates could always be lower, but of course we're recovering from a recession, a dotcom bust, and a string of corporate ethics scandals. After all that, businesses are slowly regaining the self-confidence they need to take risks and create jobs. Federal Reserve chair and former Princeton economist Ben Bernanke estimates that during the past decade, about 15 million jobs have been lost in the United States each year, that about 17 million jobs have been created each year, and that outsourcing was to blame for only 2 percent of the jobs that were lost. "In other words," Bernanke notes, "for the typical job loser during the past 10 years, the chances are 98 percent that some factor other than competition from imports was the principal reason for displacement."[2] In concurrence, the U.S. Department of Labor reported that 2.5 percent of the "mass layoffs" (50 or more people laid off for at least a month) in the first quarter of 2004 resulted from outsourcing. Seventy percent of the nonseasonal layoffs in the Department of Labor study were attributable to internal restructuring, including changes in ownership and bankruptcies.[3] These findings suggest that to blame other countries for our unemployment woes is to lose focus on more relevant problems at home.

[1] See www.useu.be/Categories/Trade/Feb1304JobOutsourcing.html.
[2] See www.federalreserve.gov/boarddocs/speeches/2004/20040330/default.htm.
[3] See http://offshoregroup.com/pressnew.asp?idnew=60.

Fears about outsourcing are nothing new. Since at least the 1950s, there has been talk of losing low-wage jobs to foreign rivals, first to Japan, then to Mexico, China, India, and a host of other Asian countries. The actual damage was not as expected. With improved trade and commerce in developing countries came higher wages and a growing appetite for goods and services from the United States, not to mention an improved standard of living here and abroad. Japan is now a high-wage country that imports more than $50 billion worth of goods and services from the United States each year and operates more than 2,000 of its own manufacturing operations in the United States. Toyota alone has created more than 100,000 U.S. jobs.

The international labor market allows firms to make better use of the world's array of workers with varying availability and skills. As explained further in Chapter 27, when workers in one country can produce something at a lower opportunity cost than workers in another country, the first country enjoys a *comparative advantage*, and it is more efficient for goods to be made where such a comparative advantage exists. For example, textile manufacturing and other labor-intensive jobs tend to migrate to labor-abundant places, which makes sense if you think about it. Meanwhile, the world's most productive workforce continues to draw more and better jobs to the United States, where 30 percent of global output is produced by 5 percent of the world's labor force.[4]

HOW DOES OUTSOURCING CREATE JOBS?

To begin with, remember that what goes around comes around. Foreign trade enlivens developing economies and gives their consumers the ability and desire to import products from us. For instance, the United States has lost manufacturers, such as Fruit of the Loom, to Mexico, but Mexico buys more than $100 billion worth of U.S. products every year, including computers and electronics, transportation equipment, chemicals, food, plastic and rubber products, machinery, and paper. The United States exports more goods and services than any other country in the world.[5] If policymakers in the United States create barriers to trade and job creation overseas, our trading partners will do the same. A protectionist stance would harm 6.4 million U.S. workers who get their paychecks from foreign firms, and these *insourced* jobs pay 16.5 percent more than the average domestic job.[6]

There is understandable concern that outsourcing will diminish domestic employment opportunities, but considerable evidence points in the opposite direction. A study by Global Insight concludes that information technology (IT) outsourcing results in a net gain of jobs in the United States.[7] India's finance minister, Shri P. Chidambaram, makes the point this way: "What do [Americans] outsource? They outsource low-end jobs, call centers, and help centers. What do they insource? They insource orders for capital goods, for technology, for design, for brands, for trademarks, for intellectual property."[8] The McKinsey Global Institute finds that for every dollar

[4] See www.jsonline.com/news/editorials/sep04/256511.asp.
[5] See www.whitehouse.gov/news/releases/2002/05/20020517-13.html.
[6] See http://www.ncpa.org/pub/ba/ba480/.
[7] See www.globalinsight.com/About/PressRelease/PressRelease855.htm.
[8] See http://washingtontimes.com/upi-breaking/20041213-095125-4941r.htm.

spent on outsourcing to India, the U.S. economy gains at least $1.12.[9] The dollars saved by outsourcing bring consumers better prices and allow companies to invest in research and development—a critical factor because mature industries do relatively little for job creation; innovation is the real engine for job growth. The United States also gains jobs from trade in services, such as health care, tourism, and education. For example, the state of Kentucky currently welcomes 5,018 international students to its college campuses, and they and their families contribute about $85 million to the state's economy yearly.

Consider the effect that higher trade barriers would have on U.S. prices and global competitiveness. Fundamentally, firms that don't minimize costs are swept away by those that do. As an example, Kent International, Inc., of Parsippany, New Jersey, sells bicycles made overseas (mostly in China) through Wal-Mart, Toys R Us, and more than 1,000 other U.S. retailers. One of their road bikes sells for about $150. U.S.-made bicycles are available from such domestic manufacturers as Trek and Cannondale for prices starting at about $1,000. What would happen if Kent's 1,000-plus retailers switched to strictly domestically produced bikes or if policies prevented them from purchasing bikes from companies that outsource bike production? Few bikes would be sold, many jobs at Kent and its retailers would be lost, and many American would-be cyclists would be out of luck. Dartmouth College economist Matthew Slaughter found that as U.S. affiliates of multinational corporations, such as Kent, added 2.8 million workers to their payrolls overseas between 1991 and 2001, that didn't mean that they lost 2.8 million domestic workers in an example of substitution; rather, they actually added 5.5 million U.S. employees to their payrolls.[10] This lose-one–gain-two effect on jobs suggests, again, that the efficiencies of outsourcing create benefits all around.

Some job loss is part of any healthy economy. Outsourcing, like computerization and automation, eliminates jobs for some but improves the employment picture for most workers. The U.S. Bureau of Labor Statistics anticipates the creation of 18.9 million new jobs in the United States during the next 10 years, a majority of which will be in occupations that pay more than the average U.S. salary of about $30,000.[11]

HELPING THOSE WHO ARE HURT BY OUTSOURCING

In response to these strains and the dislocations [outsourced jobs] cause, a new round of protectionist steps is being proposed. These alleged cures would make matters worse rather than better. They would do little to create jobs; and if foreigners were to retaliate, we would surely lose jobs.

—*Alan Greenspan, former chair of the Federal Reserve*[12]

If economic theory and the evidence previously described is to be believed, outsourcing is a win–win situation for the countries involved. In the short run, however, it is

[9] See www.mckinsey.com/mgi/publications/win_win_game.asp.
[10] See http://mba.tuck.dartmouth.edu/pages/faculty/matthew.slaughter/MNE%20Outsourcing%200304.pdf.
[11] This salary figure is adjusted for inflation. See http://www.bls.gov/oco/oco2003.htm and www.whitehouse.gov/ask/20060407.html.
[12] See www.federalreserve.gov/boarddocs/speeches/2004/20040312/default.htm.

a win–lose situation for domestic workers who lose their jobs. When the Ohio Art Company closed its plant at 1 Toy Street in Bryan, Ohio, and began producing its Etch-a-Sketches and Betty Spaghetti dolls in China, about 190 workers remained to work in the corporate offices. Some other workers moved to other departments or plants, and a few were ready to retire. But about 100 workers lost their jobs and may have had difficulty transferring their skills to existing positions, making them structurally unemployed.[13] Regardless of whether more jobs are created than are lost as a result of outsourcing, those who become unemployed are dealt a difficult and unfortunate card.

One would hope that the society that benefits from international trade and the outsourcing of jobs will want to supplement its trade policy with safety nets for those who do become unemployed as a result. Several provisions are already in place; more, particularly for educating and training the unemployed, are needed. Unemployment insurance provides most workers with about two-thirds of their weekly incomes (up to a maximum amount determined by each state) for 26 weeks or longer. The Trade Adjustment Assistance (TAA) program provides up to 2 years of retraining and financial aid to eligible manufacturing workers, farmers, and fishers who have lost their jobs because of outsourcing or foreign competition. President Bush tripled the funding for TAA between 2002 and 2004, bringing it up to $1.3 billion. Funding decreased slightly in 2005; moreover, the program currently is not open to service workers.

Proposals for additional avenues of support are on the table. Six members of Congress, including U.S. Representative Adam Smith (D-WA), have introduced variations of the Trade Adjustment Assistance Equity for Service Workers Act that would provide tuition assistance, job training, extended unemployment benefits, and health-care assistance to service workers who lose their jobs to outsourcing. As part of the Jobs for America Act, former Senator Tom Daschle (D-SD) proposed that employers who offshore 15 or more jobs should be required to provide at least 3 months' notice of their intentions to terminate domestic workers. Additional concerns include inadequate public transportation for workers whose new jobs require commutes, the continuation of health-care and pension benefits, and the cost of child care that stands in the way of retraining for many parents. Efficiency dictates that the benefits from outsourcing are worthwhile only if they exceed all these associated burdens. With most employment transitions being relatively short lived, and given the prospects for employment growth, lower prices, and improved living standards as the result of outsourcing, economists, including Greg Mankiw, foresee a net gain.

CONCLUSION

Workers are the heart of any economy and a top priority in the eyes of voters and policymakers. As employers come and go, job losses must be minimized and safety nets promoted, including unemployment insurance, training and education programs, trade adjustment assistance, and transferable health and retirement benefits. Outsourcing to dodge environmental regulations, human rights standards, or taxes is deplorable. But barriers to appropriate matchmaking between employers and work-

---

[13] See www.careerjournal.com/columnists/inthelead/20031022-inthelead.html.

ers are chiefly counterproductive and hurt the country and its workforce. President Herbert Hoover learned this lesson well after his administration attained a pinnacle of protectionism with the Smoot-Hawley tariffs of 1930: A firestorm of retaliatory strikes ensued, wounding the economy and deepening the Great Depression.[14] Policies that allow outsourcing are critical to efficiency, affordability, and competitiveness. They force difficult adjustments for some workers, but the size of the threat is often exaggerated, and the alternative of economic isolation is far worse for everyone involved.

DISCUSSION STARTERS

1. What do you think is the single best argument for outsourcing? What is the best argument against it?

2. We all face the choice between lower-priced goods that create jobs elsewhere and higher-priced goods that create jobs domestically. Look at the labels on your shoes, backpack, clothing, and electronics. What items that you own are produced overseas? Why did you purchase them?

3. Have you paid higher prices to purchase some items from domestic producers? If so, how much and for what products? As consumers, how should the desire to help American workers be balanced with the desire for low prices and competitive industries?

4. Put yourself in the shoes of a U.S. worker whose job might be lost as a result of outsourcing. Describe the program of assistance, retraining, and adjustment that you think would be appropriate and fair for taxpayers to support.

5. Explain in your own words why prominent economists, such as Mankiw and Greenspan, believe outsourcing is part of a healthy economic system with favorable employment prospects.

[14] Perhaps the most damaging retaliation came from our largest trading partner, Canada, in the form of "countervailing duties" on 16 products imported from the United States. For more on the Smoot-Hawley tariffs, see www.state.gov/r/pa/ho/time/id/17606.htm.

CHAPTER 24

DO TREE HUGGERS DETER GROWTH AND EMPLOYMENT?
Myths, Labor Markets, and Environmentalism

> Time and time again, U.S. citizens working to clean up the environment . . . banged into the same argument: cleaner and safer production standards will hurt U.S. business competitiveness and cost jobs.
>
> —*Robert Weissman, The Multinational Monitor*[1]

> It is crucial for decision makers to profoundly understand the possible repercussions of sustainability policies on the global employment profile.
>
> —*Harn Wei Kua, World Student Community for Sustainable Development*[2]

> The U.S. debate about environmental protection often assumes that saving natural resources means losing jobs. . . . Our survey of the environmental-protection employment climate led to the opposite conclusion.
>
> —*Roger Bezdek and Robert Wendling, Management Information Services*[3]

As these quotations indicate, there is considerable disagreement about the existence and extent of trade-offs between jobs and the environment. This chapter highlights myths and realities in the debate about economic growth and environmental protection.

[1] See http://multinationalmonitor.org/mm2005/012005/weissman.html.
[2] See www.wscsd.org/ejournal/article.php3?id_article=58.
[3] See www.nature.com/nature/journal/v434/n7033/full/nj7033-678b.html.

THE CONTROVERSY ABOUT ENVIRONMENTAL POLICY

Julia "Butterfly" Hill spent 738 days living in the canopy of an ancient redwood tree to try to prevent the Pacific Lumber Company from harvesting a forest that had stood for 1,000 years.[4] Similar struggles concerning deforestation are taking place around the globe. The issue came to a head in the United States when President George W. Bush signed the Healthy Forests Restoration Act in 2003, allowing loggers more freedom to harvest trees in national forests.[5] What appears to be a simple trade-off between lumber-related jobs and protection of wildlife is, in fact, a far more complicated situation. To begin with, many types of employment in addition to those that rely on lumber are involved. Forests and wildlife are a major draw in the global tourism industry, which directly provides 76 million jobs and indirectly supports 145 million more.[6] The national park system in the United States generates 273 million visits per year,[7] creating employment in restaurants, gas stations, and hotels along the way, not to mention jobs for people making and selling recreational vehicles and camping equipment. It is said that one-quarter to one-half of all medicines contain rainforest products,[8] making forests integral to jobs in hospitals, doctors' offices, pharmacies, pharmaceutical companies, and research labs everywhere. Then there's the fact that, through a process called *carbon sequestration,* trees absorb carbon dioxide pollution that would otherwise contribute to global warming[9] and release the oxygen people breathe to survive.

An honest assessment of the value of trees cannot discount the facts that humans need a critical mass of vegetation in order to live another day and work another shift, and that the planet is currently experiencing a period of rapid deforestation. Because standing trees are so important to life on earth, the World Bank and the Global Environment Facility are working with several clients in South and Central America to develop payment mechanisms for the "global environmental services" provided by forests that are left intact.[10] It is the job of environmental and natural resource economists to bring to light all the potential costs and benefits of environmental policies so that efficient decisions can be made. The next section provides a case study of policy dilemmas that pit employment against the environment.

TOUGH CALLS AND DIFFICULT TRADE-OFFS IN THE WAKE OF HURRICANE KATRINA

In 1972, officials began closing the beaches on Lake Pontchartrain near New Orleans because of harmful levels of pollution in the water. Jobs in the neighboring chemical

---

[4] See www.circleoflife.org/inspiration/julia/.
[5] For two perspectives on this law, see www.whitehouse.gov/infocus/healthyforests/ and www.sierraclub.org/forests/fires/healthyforests_initiative.asp.
[6] See www.world-tourism.org/tsunami/news/67.pdf.
[7] See www2.nature.nps.gov/stats/abst2005.pdf.
[8] See, for example, www.dnr.state.mn.us/forestry/rainforests.html.
[9] For more on global warming, see www.climatecrisis.net/thescience/.
[10] See www.thegef.org/ and http://web.worldbank.org/WBSITE/EXTERNAL/TOPICS/EXTARD/EXTFORESTS/0,content MDK:20869381~menuPK:985797~pagePK:64020865~piPK:149114~theSitePK:985785,00.html.

and oil industries gained precedence over the environment, but with the environmental decline came a commercial decline as well. In 1983, the Pontchartrain Beach Amusement Park, with its famous Zephyr ride, closed, as had the Lincoln Beach Amusement Park years earlier. These and related losses of enjoyment and jobs led to the formation in 1989 of the Lake Pontchartrain Basin Foundation to remediate the environmental damage. The policymaking pendulum swung toward health and wildlife and away from jobs in 1992, when new leases for oil and gas drilling in the lake were banned in a move to prevent further harm from oil spills, dredging, and habitat destruction. By July of 2005, swimming was again allowed in some areas, and large groups of endangered manatees swam in the waters.[11] Then on August 29, Hurricane Katrina devastated the Gulf Coast, and Lake Pontchartrain bowed once again to greater needs. After the storm, billions of gallons of toxic floodwater were pumped into the lake to help make New Orleans livable and commercially viable again.

Halfway between Lake Pontchartrain and the French Quarter of New Orleans is the former Agriculture Street Landfill, where a century's accumulation of industrial wastes, including lead, arsenic, dioxin, and DDT, were buried beneath a mat barrier and 2 feet of topsoil. Hurricane Katrina's floodwaters surrounded this and other toxic repositories; picked up fuel, paint, and cleaning solvents from approximately 168,000 homes; and swept through countless vehicles and industrial sites. After weeks of being submerged under water that contained heavy metals and other toxins, environmentalists said, the soil in New Orleans would be laden with dangers. Having decided to use Lake Pontchartrain to support jobs rather than endangered species, policymakers now had to decide when to allow seafood, livestock, and other agricultural products to be harvested from the area. If they can't be sold and eaten, potentially tainted shellfish don't create jobs for fishers, truckers, wholesalers, and restaurant workers.

Policymakers also had to decide when to permit residents to return, when to allow businesses to reopen, and how much to spend to restore the safety of the land in and around New Orleans.[12] The city's mayor, Ray Nagin, and President Bush disagreed over when to allow people to return to the city, with Nagin wanting to give the green light sooner rather than later. In mid-September business owners were allowed back into the French Quarter and other areas of the city that had not been flooded, and residents of some neighborhoods began to return in late September. The area became one of the most expensive cleanup sites ever, with the total price tag estimated at about $200 billion.[13] Of course, every dollar spent on cleanup was a dollar earned by an employed worker. The decision to return New Orleans to the ways of cleaner days was both a boon to health and environmental concerns and a boost for an economically depressed area.

[11] See www.saveourlake.org.
[12] In the landmark 1979 case that incited the Comprehensive Environmental Response, Compensation, and Liability Act, the Environmental Protection Agency spent $101 million (later reimbursed by parent company Occidental Petroleum Corp.) to clean up the Love Canal dumpsite of Hooker Chemical Co. near Niagara Falls in western New York. After homes and a school were built over the dumpsite, at least 82 toxic chemicals had seeped into the soil, causing severe health problems and displacing 700 families.
[13] See www.msnbc.msn.com/id/9358118/.

PIECING TOGETHER BETTER COST–BENEFIT ANALYSIS

The discussion of the value of human lives in Chapter 15 is relevant to environmental policy debates, although there is no consensus on a particular value among current decision makers. The Environmental Protection Agency (EPA) has valued each life at $4.8 million when evaluating Clean Air Act amendments[14] and at $6.3 million in the assessment of deaths caused by viruses in contaminated groundwater.[15] Other government agencies use a range of values between $1 million and $7 million per life.[16] Tammy Tengs and a team of other researchers estimated the cost of saving 1 year of a human's life via 500 actual or potential regulations, many involving the environment, such as limits on chloroform releases from paper mills. They reported a range of costs from 0 to $99 billion per year of life saved.[17] This vast range highlights the fact that policymakers can't simply set priorities in the order of, for example, human lives, jobs, and the environment. Our entire national income would not be enough to save all the threatened human lives at billions of dollars per person each year. Where individuals draw the line in terms of willingness to trade dollars for lives and the environment determines which regulations are deemed appropriate by cost–benefit analysis. (Economists' recommendations for this value—about $9 million per life—are discussed in Chapter 15.)

One would think that environmental dilemmas, such as the prospect of drilling in the Arctic National Wildlife Refuge, would be straightforward because the environmental threat is farther from tourists and unlikely to cause human injury, but diverse sources of human happiness make such issues complex in ways that are important to understand as well. Humans place value on more than work and health. *Use values* come from the firsthand enjoyment of natural resources and their by-products. Users of forests benefit from hiking trails and natural beauty. Some people never enter a forest or see a particular animal species but nonetheless place a *nonuse* or *passive-use* value on them. Passive-use values can be divided into the *option values* that people place on the option to use a resource in the future and *existence values* that are unrelated to any possibility of ever using the resource or its by-products. Existence values include the *bequest value* of knowing that preservation allows others to use a resource and the *sympathy value* of knowing that a resource is alive and well. Bequest values are evident in the efforts of recyclers, conservationists, and environmentalists, and they are epitomized by the work of Johnny Appleseed, who planted trees to benefit another generation. Sympathy values drive the establishment of nature preserves with no human access and motivate protests against the cutting of trees in remote areas. The cost–benefit analysis of any environmental policy should include all losses of employment and convenience among the costs and all types of values among the benefits.

[14] See www.cato.org/pubs/regulation/reg19n4c.html.
[15] See www.ers.usda.gov/publications/mp1570/mp1570d.pdf.
[16] See http://aei-brookings.org/admin/authorpdfs/page.php?id=973.
[17] T.O. Tengs et al., "Five Hundred Life-Saving Interventions and Their Cost-Effectiveness," *Risk Analysis* (1995), *15*, 369–390.

GREEN POLICY CAN CREATE JOBS

In his book, *Jobs, Competitiveness, and Environmental Regulations* (1995), Robert Repetto reports that environmental regulations have not caused the loss of jobs or reduced the international competitiveness of U.S. companies. Although many efforts to protect the environment involve trade-offs between health and employment, it is unfair to characterize environmental policy in general as a threat to jobs. Many types of environmental policies create jobs, and the conflict is over who gets the money. Consider the Clean Air Mercury Rule issued by the EPA in 2005, which permanently caps and reduces mercury emissions from coal-fired power plants, and the National Highway Traffic Safety Administration's proposed increase in the corporate average fuel-economy standards for smaller light trucks from the 2006 level of 21.6 mpg to 28.4 mpg by 2011. Compliance with these regulations demands that power utilities support workers in the smokestack scrubber industry and that automobile manufacturers hire people to develop more efficient engines and explore alternative technologies, including biodiesel, turbo diesel, and hybrid-electric engines. Opposition to the policies comes because the power and automobile makers don't want to spend money employing these workers. In essence, it is because they *do not* want to create new jobs in environmental areas that they fight the policies.

Most major environmental-remediation efforts are performed by paid workers. Under the Comprehensive Environmental Response, Compensation, and Liability Act, more commonly known as the Superfund, environmental disaster areas across the United States are identified and cleaned up. These cleanups create $1.5 billion worth of income each year through direct expenditures, and the former danger zones become sites for restaurants, supermarkets, and other sources of employment opportunities. The reclamation of any polluted land or waterway, like the production of any smokestack filter or geothermal heating system, creates employment. Roger Bezdek and Robert Wendling have found that environmental protection is to thank for 5.1 million jobs in the United States.[18]

A final myth related to jobs and the environment is that "tree huggers," who favor less materialism and seek lighter use of natural resources, are inherently seeking the demise of employment opportunities. It is true that current manufacturing jobs rely heavily on the use of nonrenewable resources, including fossil fuels, metals, and plastics. However, the U.S. Bureau of Labor Statistics estimates that service-providing jobs will constitute 18.7 million of the 18.9 million new jobs created between 2004 and 2014.[19] Categories of service-sector jobs that rely less on nonrenewable resources include everything from authors, analysts, and educators to programmers, physicians, and zookeepers. Many more scientists, artists, clergy, historians, massage therapists, chefs, dietitians, police officers, musicians, park rangers, coaches, and museum curators could be employed, and the quality of our lives would improve along with employment opportunities.

Many types of service jobs actually reduce our reliance on manufacturing. When you employ a cobbler to stitch up your old shoes rather than buying a new pair, you

[18] See www.nature.com/nature/journal/v434/n7033/full/nj7033-678b.html.
[19] See www.bls.gov/oco/oco2003.htm.

support one type of employment rather than another and you spare the resource depletion caused by the production of a new pair. The same goes for any type of repair and for the purchase of a more durable car, lawn mower, or dishwasher. The manufacture of alternative-fuel and energy-efficient vehicles, and the use of recycled products, solar panels, windmills, and compost bins is also proenvironment if these items replace other products that deplete resources at a faster rate.

CONCLUSION

You don't have to hug a tree if you don't want to, but economists find that standing trees and a healthy natural environment create and support employment in ways that should not be neglected in cost–benefit analyses. Fortunately, "green growth" is not an oxymoron. Environmental cleanups, ecotourism, low-impact construction, and the manufacture of earth-friendly products create millions of jobs, and the service sector of low-resource-use employment is booming. Jobs can be lost if environmental policies make production prohibitively expensive, but evidence suggests that policymakers do not go to that extreme. Although few regulations come free, expenditures on compliance create jobs in cutting-edge industries, and efficiency guidelines require that the benefits of a regulation exceed the costs. In making those comparisons, the astute policymaker will recognize both the importance of jobs and the reliance of businesses on the ecosystem that supports life and provides our productive resources.

Environmental economists argue that the ideal amount of pollution is not 0 but the level at which marginal benefit no longer exceeds marginal cost. The important thing is that *all* the repercussions of a policy are considered. A recent study by meteorology professor Kerry Emanuel of the Massachusetts Institute of Technology found that global warming—a result of carbon dioxide releases, human-made and otherwise—has caused hurricanes to grow in size and destructive power by 75 to 100 percent during the past 30 years. The effects of environmental degradation, including global warming, should thus be factored into decisions about fossil-fuel policy and use. Similarly, wetlands act as sponges to absorb floodwaters, so by destroying wetlands for development on the Gulf Coast, environmental conditions were created that allowed Katrina to subsequently destroy much of the development. Ultimately, economic efficiency requires an understanding that what goes around comes around.

DISCUSSION STARTERS

1. When an old-growth forest is harvested, jobs are created in the short run and the environmental benefits from that forest are lost for several generations. When fossil fuels are burned, their benefits are no longer available to future generations. One proposal for working toward efficient harvesting, drilling, and mining decisions has been to levy a tax on natural-capital depletion, the tax payment being a percentage of the value of the resources removed, as a disincentive to overindulge. Would you be in favor of such a tax? If so, what tax rate (what percentage of the value of extracted materials) would you suggest?

2. Some foes worry that the government will adopt environmental policies that will ultimately force power companies and large portions of the manufacturing sector to shut down. Do you think that government policymakers would adopt such policies? Explain your answer.

3. Select Steel, Inc., proposed to build a $175 million plant in Genesee County, Michigan. After protests that pollution would fall disproportionately on the poor in Genesee County, the plant was built in relatively affluent Ingham County, Michigan. In Genesee County more and poorer people would have been near the pollution but would also have gotten the 200 jobs the plant created. Would you have located the plant where the jobs are more needed or where the pollution would affect fewer people? Explain your answer.

4. Suppose your friend claims that solar power is less efficient than energy from coal-fired power plants because the price of a solar panel divided by the electricity it will generate during its lifetime exceeds the price of electricity from the local coal-fired power plant. How would you explain the missing pieces in your friend's cost–benefit analysis?

5. What is the largest number of mature redwood trees that you would sacrifice to lower the unemployment rate in your state from 5 to 3 percent? Ten trees? One hundred? One thousand? How would your answer change if the unemployment rate would fall from 25 to 23 percent?

6. How many human lives would you sacrifice to lower the unemployment rate from 25 to 23 percent? Remember that any significant level of production and transportation is likely to result in some loss of life, so a refusal to make any trade-off between lives and jobs would require quite a lifestyle change.

7. Suppose that consumption of the local agricultural products immediately after a nuclear accident would cause 1 death with certainty and that the likelihood of a resulting death would decrease by 1 percent each week thereafter. (After 1 year, for example, the likelihood of a death would be 100 − 52 = 48 percent.) If you were a typical farmer, how many weeks would you voluntarily go without income before selling your crops? If you were a policymaker, for how many weeks would you require farmers to wait before selling their crops? If you were a consumer, for how many weeks would you wait before buying the crops if you had the option to purchase food from other sources? Explain your reasoning and any assumptions you made to resolve factors that would be crucial to your answer.

CHAPTER 25

HOW MUCH DEBT IS TOO MUCH?

Expenditure Smoothing, Ricardian Equivalence, Crowding Out, and Investments for the Future

The surplus is not the government's money. The surplus is the people's money. . . . Now is the time to reform the tax code and share some of the surplus with the people who pay the bills.

—*President George W. Bush*[1]

First [President Bush] described a budget-busting tax cut . . . as a modest plan to return unneeded revenue to ordinary families. Then, when the red ink began flowing in torrents, he wrapped himself and his policies in the flag, blaming deficits on evil terrorists and forces beyond his control.

—*Economist Paul Krugman*[2]

THE DEBT AND THE DEFICIT

Attractive as it may sound to live within our means—spending no more than we earn—strict adherence to that policy would prevent many worthwhile exceptions. Income tends to arrive in fits and starts for individuals, businesses, and governments alike. Work opportunities fluctuate, and sales and tax revenues rise and fall with the seasons, the economy, and consumer sentiment. For example, department stores and jewelry stores make about 15 and 25 percent of their sales, respectively, in the month of

[1] From his speech to the 2000 Republican National Convention. See http://www.2000gop.com/convention/speech/speechbush.html.
[2] *The Great Unraveling* (New York: Norton, 2003), p. 133.

December,[3] whereas expenditures on inventory must be made months in advance. To establish a household, start a business, or defend a democracy, money is needed up front, but the returns can be a long time coming. The inevitable mismatch in timing between expenditures and revenues necessitates borrowing, deficits, and debt. This chapter explores theories relevant to the decisions of whether and when to borrow.

A *deficit* is the amount by which expenditures exceed revenues in one period—usually a year. If revenues exceed expenditures, there is a *surplus*. Over time, *debt* accumulates as the sum of past deficits minus past surpluses. Individuals, businesses, and nations can carry sizable debt loads without much trouble if their assets and incomes are sufficient. And debtors are abundant—the average household's personal debt is $85,000[4]—and stand in good company. Actress Kim Basinger went into debt after purchasing the town of Braselton, Georgia, for $20 million and fighting a legal battle over her broken oral agreement to act in the movie *Boxing Helena* (1993). Known as the world's highest-paid nightclub entertainer, Wayne Newton accumulated more than $20 million of debt in the early 1990s. Corporations routinely amass billions of dollars of debt, as with Ford Motor Company's $158 billion in long-term debt in the second quarter of 2005. And at 65 percent of gross domestic product, the United States's national debt ranks 34th among nations of the world.

National debt in the United States was $0.9 trillion in 1980, $3.2 trillion in 1990, $5.7 trillion in 2000, and more than $8 trillion in 2006. Government debt is used to finance expenditures in excess of tax collections. About 58 percent of the U.S. debt is held by the public. This includes individuals, corporations, state and local governments within the United States, foreign governments, and other entities outside the U.S. government. Anyone can help finance the debt by purchasing U.S. savings bonds, state and local government series securities, or Treasury bills, notes (T-notes), bonds, or inflation-protected securities (TIPS).[5]

DEBT AND DECISION MAKING

After his financial difficulties, Wayne Newton signed a contract with the Stardust Hotel in Las Vegas to perform for $625,000 per week; after hers, Kim Basinger earned $5 million for acting in *I Dreamed of Africa* (2000). The question is this: Should people with debt, such as Wayne and Kim, go out and splurge with their new income? It would be sensible to eliminate accumulated debts before treating current surpluses as available money, although even the U.S. government follows an alternative plan at times. In light of projected federal budget surpluses totaling $5.6 trillion over 10 years starting in 2001, President George W. Bush gave large sums back to taxpayers (see the chapter-opening quote). What followed was a series of tax cuts, the largest being a $1.35 trillion rebate in 2001. Unfortunately, even when the government runs annual surpluses, it may still have a large debt. The accumulation of past deficits

---

[3] See, for example, www.census.gov/Press-Release/www/releases/archives/facts_for_features_special_editions/000766.html.

[4] See www.usatoday.com/printedition/news/20041004/1a_debtcovxx.art.htm.

[5]To learn more about U.S. savings bonds, see www.publicdebt.treas.gov/sav/sav.htm. For more on state and local government series securities, see www.publicdebt.treas.gov/spe/spe.htm. For information on Treasury bills, notes, bonds, and TIPS, see www.publicdebt.treas.gov/sec/sec.htm.

amounted to a $5.8 trillion debt in 2001, so the entire projected surplus amount could have been devoted to repaying the debt and the United States would still have owed money. As the projected surpluses evaporated and the government began running deficits again, President Bush stopped talking about giving back people's money and started talking about tax cuts to spur the economy. That Keynesian brand of expansionary fiscal policy is potentially worthwhile: Debt-financed tax cuts may stimulate consumer spending and investment and help the economy rebound. Later in this chapter you will learn arguments about why this may or may not happen.

Milton Friedman's *permanent income hypothesis* suggests that it makes sense for individuals to smooth expenditures and spend a relatively constant portion of their lifetime income each year. Many of those who invest in higher education spend roughly the first third of their lives going to school and earning very little, the second third earning sizable incomes, and the last third earning very little again. Rather than living in poverty during the early and late stages of life, many people borrow enough during the early years to live comfortably, pay back their debts and become net creditors (lenders) during the lucrative years, and then live on their accumulated surpluses during retirement. For example, a professional who earns an average of $100,000 a year for 30 years of work has lifetime earnings of $3 million. If she expects to live 90 years, the permanent income hypothesis suggests that this individual would spend $3 million / 90 = $33,333 (adjusted for inflation) each year of her life. Reduced needs for spending during youth, and uncertainty about future income and longevity, are among the reasons why expenditure levels aren't truly even throughout one's life, but a glance at the student parking lot at any elite college confirms that those who plan to earn a lot begin spending their lifetime earnings before the flow of revenues actually begins.

The concept of expenditure smoothing makes sense for other entities as well. Rather than missing out on opportunities to grow when they need to grow, prudent corporations and governments accumulate debt if doing so creates benefits that exceed the burdens of borrowing. The trick is to stop borrowing before that trend is reversed.

Whether to finance tax cuts, wars, education spending, or hurricane relief, there are several valid rationales for a government to accumulate debt. One of the fathers of classical economics, David Ricardo, claimed that it made no difference whether government expenditure was financed with debt or taxes because citizens treat their share of the government expenditure as a liability regardless of whether it is collected immediately in taxes. The idea, called *Ricardian equivalence*, is that when the government borrows money, taxpayers know they must repay the loan eventually, and they increase their savings by enough to repay the borrowed funds plus interest at the appropriate time. If the government borrows $300 billion to finance something like the Iraq war, according to this theory, each American would place his or her $1,000 share of this debt into an account where it would accumulate interest at about the same rate as the government's loan. Then, when the government collects taxes to repay the $300 billion plus interest, the citizens will have the appropriate amount ready to send in.

Because U.S. citizens hold about 56 percent of the publicly held debt themselves, the process is often more direct: Rather than depositing more money into savings, many citizens invest in the very bonds used to finance the debt. If you purchase a

$1,000 Treasury bond, your investment goes directly to finance government expenditures. When the government raises taxes to repurchase the bond, what you receive for the bond will be enough to cover your share of the taxes used to retire it. Whether you hold the debt directly in the form of a government bond or deposit funds into an account that will cover the tax repayment, Ricardian equivalence would mean that the debt burden could be carried and repaid without undue trauma for those who must pick up the check.

To the extent that it holds, Ricardian equivalence also has the simplifying result that tax-financed expenditures and debt-financed expenditures have the same effect on the economy. Employing expansionary fiscal policy, the government may try to increase demand by spending money on, say, a national highway system, as President Franklin D. Roosevelt did, or a hydroelectric dam, as President Herbert Hoover did during the Great Depression. In today's dollars, Hoover Dam cost about $2.7 billion. If the government paid $2.7 billion to build a new dam by raising taxes by $2.7 billion, consumers would have that much less to spend and save. If, instead, the dam was paid for by selling $2.7 billion worth of Treasury bonds, Ricardian equivalence suggests that taxpayers would collectively sock away $2.7 billion for a future tax day. Either way, the fiscal policy has the same effect.

Despite the logic of the theory, and more recent support from economist Robert Barro and others, tax cuts and swelling deficits have not stimulated high savings rates in the 2000s. One explanation is that taxpayers would save enough to repay the debt if they expected the burden to fall squarely on them, but instead they anticipate that another generation will foot the bill, and they do not care quite as much about the next generation as they do about themselves.

Debt can be justified even when it is more consequential than under Ricardian equivalence. For instance, the generations that completed the transcontinental railroad in 1869 and the transcontinental highway in 1935 created liabilities that passed through generations, but those who ultimately repaid the debts probably valued the ability to travel and transport goods across the country more highly than the amount of debt they shouldered. The same may be true for expenditures on new medicines, environmental protection, education, peace, political stability, technology, and research in any number of areas pertinent to future generations. When a 7.6 magnitude earthquake ripped apart the infrastructure of Pakistan in 2005, recovery costs were estimated at $5 billion, adding to a Pakistani government debt of almost $250 billion.[6] Even if the funds aren't repaid until 2015 or 2025, many of the citizens who help repay that debt at that time will enjoy homes, schools, roads, hospitals, and utilities made possible by the debt.

THE DOWNSIDE OF DEBT

The payment of interest on the national debt amounts to more than $1.1 billion per day, $405 billion per year, and $1,350 per person each year.[7] Without the debt, those interest payments could instead be spent on favored programs or returned to the cit-

---

[6] See http://newsfromrussia.com/world/2005/11/11/67459.html.
[7] See www.cbo.gov/ftpdocs/57xx/doc5773/08-24-BudgetUpdate.pdf.

izens. The National Priorities Project[8] reports that out of each dollar of tax revenues (excluding trust fund outlays, as for Social Security),

30 cents goes to military spending

20 cents goes to health services

19 cents goes to pay interest on the debt

7 cents goes to income security

4 cents goes to education

3 cents goes to veterans' benefits

3 cents goes to nutrition programs

2 cents goes to housing

2 cents goes to the management of natural resources

0.4 cent goes to job training

11 cents goes to miscellaneous other purposes

Thus, if we didn't have a debt to pay interest on, we could spend almost twice as much on health, 5 times as much on education, or 10 times as much to manage natural resources without raising taxes. When drawing the line between too much national debt and not enough, opportunity costs such as these should be weighed against the benefits of debt, as discussed in the previous section.

With Americans holding 56 percent of the publicly held debt,[9] we can be consoled that a majority of the interest payments goes to Americans. Of course, it would be nice if we could make these payments in exchange for needed goods and services instead of needed debt financing. There is also the problem that, even if the payments remain within the country, taxation to pay interest on the debt redistributes money from taxpayers to relatively wealthy creditors.

Ricardian equivalence would take the bite out of the debt burden, but the question is, Do you have $28,000 set aside to repay your individual share of the national debt? If not, debt repayment may cause a jolt to your way of life. The economy as a whole may also reel from the repayment of what is now $2 trillion owed to foreign purchasers of the U.S. debt. In 2005, for example, Japan and China owned $679 billion and $224 billion worth of U.S. debt, respectively.

The Bush tax cut, like many other debt-financed policy measures, was eventually defended as a means of expansionary fiscal policy.[10] Even if Ricardian equivalence is off base, the intended boost in demand from this debt creation is also threatened by increases in interest rates that dampen investment expenditures. In a process called *crowding out*, government borrowing competes with private borrowing to drive the interest rate up and investment expenditures down. As mentioned in Chapter 22, the supply of and demand for money determine the interest rate paid to borrow money, just as the supply of and demand for espressos determine the price paid for espres-

[8] See http://natprior.org/auxiliary/somePdfs/taxday2005/ms.pdf.
[9] See http://en.wikipedia.org/wiki/U.S._public_debt.
[10] See www.cnn.com/2003/ALLPOLITICS/01/28/sotu.transcript/.

sos. When the government increases its demand for money, the price of money—the interest rate—increases. This makes it more expensive for private borrowers to obtain money for investments in businesses, homes, factory expansions, technology upgrades, and so on. With *full crowding out,* each dollar of debt-financed government spending raises the interest rate enough to eliminate, or "crowd out," $1 of private spending. In reality, we usually experience only *partial crowding out,* meaning that each dollar of debt-financed government spending raises the interest rate enough to crowd out less than $1 of private expenditure.

Government debt also has a detrimental effect on the domestic savings rate and the exchange rate between the U.S. dollar and foreign currencies. Former Federal Reserve chair Alan Greenspan said, "reducing the federal budget deficit (or preferably moving it to surplus) appears to be the most effective action that could be taken to augment domestic savings."[11] To finance a government debt, dollars that could otherwise be saved must be spent on government securities—those Treasury bills, T-notes, and so on mentioned in the opening section. About $2.7 trillion worth of U.S. government debt has been purchased domestically, not including debt held within government trust funds, revolving funds, other special funds, and Federal Financing Bank[12] securities.

It is the foreign-owned debt that poses a particular threat to exchange rates. If foreign investors for some reason lost confidence in their purchases of U.S. debt, they would sell their securities and exchange the dollars they received for their home currencies. The subsequent increase in the supply of dollars and increase in the demand for other currencies would cause the exchange rate of the dollar to fall. There is a related problem with the U.S. *current account,* which measures imports, exports, transfers, and returns on foreign investments (rents, interests, and profits). In 2005, the United States imported $1.99 trillion worth of goods and services and exported $1.27 trillion worth of the same.[13] In order to have enough foreign currency to spend $720 billion more on imports than other countries spend on its exports, the United States must have a $620 billion surplus in the *capital account* that measures flows of money into and out of the country from lending instruments, such as stocks and bonds. Thus, foreign currency flowing into the United States to purchase its debt ends up filling the gap between the foreign currency needed to purchase imports and the foreign currency received when selling exports. If foreigners decreased their holdings of U.S. debt, consumers in the United States would not be able to purchase as many foreign-made goods, including cars, toys, and apparel.

In response to the assortment of problems with a large debt, many valiant attempts have been made to harness government expenditures. President Ronald Reagan introduced the Balanced Budget and Emergency Deficit Control Act of 1985 this way: "This legislation will impose the discipline we now lack by locking us into a spending reduction plan. It will establish a maximum allowable deficit ceiling beginning with our current 1986 deficit of $180 billion, and then it will reduce that deficit in equal steps to

[11] See http://money.cnn.com/2004/11/19/news/economy/fed_greenspan/.
[12] Congress created the Federal Financing Bank as a government corporation in 1973 to centralize and reduce the cost of financing the debt. For details see www.washingtonwatchdog.org/documents/usc/ttl12/ch24/index.html.
[13] See www.bea.gov/bea/newsrelarchive/2006/trad0306.pdf.

a balanced budget in calendar year 1990."[14] As deficits continued to grow, the Balanced Budget and Emergency Deficit Control Act of 1987 was enacted with the intention of balancing the budget by 1993.[15] The Budget Enforcement Act of 1990, extended in 1993 and 1997, replaced the previous system of deficit limits with two independent enforcement mechanisms: caps on discretionary spending and a pay-as-you-go requirement for direct spending and revenue legislation. The legislation was there, but, regrettably, the hoped-for discipline was not. The deficit (even factoring in the surplus in the Social Security account) was $221 billion in 1986, and it didn't fall below $100 billion until 1997, when it was $22 billion. Rather than balancing the budget, Congress raised the limits and enacted emergency spending bills. More recently, the ceiling on national debt rose by $450 billion in 2002, by $984 billion in 2003, by $800 billion in 2004, and by $781 billion to a total of $8.965 trillion in 2006.

CONCLUSION

It is a mistake to pass up the opportunity to borrow seed money for tomorrow's gardens. Debt creation can be an appropriate way for individuals, businesses, and governments to accommodate differences in timing between revenues and worthwhile expenditures. The line between too much debt and not enough comes when another dollar of debt-financed purchases does not justify the burden imposed on those who must repay the debt. Expenditures on research and development, health, education, infrastructure, conservation, and diplomacy are often among those that adequately serve current and future generations. Government debt can also be used for the purpose of expansionary fiscal policy, although the effects of crowding out and Ricardian equivalence weaken the intended influence on the economy.

The considerable assets and credibility of the U.S. government allow it to carry a sizable debt for extended periods with impunity not available to smaller entities. However, the validity of limited debt financing can invite overindulgence at every level. Reporters for *USA Today* used government data to calculate that the total debt and "unfunded liabilities" of U.S. federal, state, and local governments is $53 trillion, or about $475,000 per household—and that's on top of the $85,000 in personal debt that the average household carries.[16] By all reasonable standards, this level of debt warrants concern, making debt repayment a priority among many economists and policymakers.

DISCUSSION STARTERS

1. Does your behavior support the permanent income hypothesis? That is, do you borrow money so that you can spend more as a student than do people who have similar current income but inferior future income potential? Do you borrow less than do people who have strong intentions to pursue

[14] See www.reagan.utexas.edu/archives/speeches/1985/100485a.htm.
[15] For specific yearly targets, see www.cbo.gov/showdoc.cfm?index=5311&sequence=0.
[16] See www.usatoday.com/printedition/news/20041004/1a_debtcovxx.art.htm.

a career that will be more lucrative than your own intended career? What factors, other than current income and expected lifetime income, do you think influence people's decisions of how much to borrow?

2. Discuss the advisability of each of the following items. From the standpoint of the people who will repay the debt created by these projects, how do you think the benefits will compare to the costs?
   a. the Iraq war
   b. the restoration of New Orleans after Hurricane Katrina
   c. the Bush tax cut
   d. NASA's Mars exploration program

3. If the United States eliminated its national debt and no longer had to spend 19 percent of each tax dollar on interest payments, how would you recommend that the country reallocate the $405 billion per year that would be saved on interest payments?

4. Does your behavior correspond with Ricardian equivalence? How much do you have in savings for the purpose of paying your share of the national debt? If you don't have enough to pay your share, explain your reasoning. What would happen to your standard of living if you had to repay your share of the government debt during the next 5 years?

5. How do you explain the reelection of so many lawmakers who dodge legislation designed to impose fiscal responsibility and balanced budgets?

CHAPTER 26

WHAT IS THE ROLE OF GOVERNMENT?

Political–Economic Systems, Snags
in Private Solutions, and Remedies
with a Role for Government

During the time men live without a common power to keep them all in awe,
they are in that condition which is called war. . . . In such a condition there
is no place for industry; . . . no arts; no letters; no society; and which is worst
of all, continual fear, and danger of violent death; and the life of man soli-
tary, poor, nasty, brutish, and short.

—*Thomas Hobbes*[1]

That government is best which governs least.

—*Often attributed to Thomas Jefferson, used by Henry David Thoreau*[2]

Because I [keep hostile possession of the sea] with a petty ship, I am called
a robber, whilst thou who dost it with a great fleet art styled emperor.

—*A pirate speaking to Alexander the Great in
Saint Augustine's* City of God

THE MAKINGS OF GOVERNMENT

Saint Augustine points out that in perilous times, the principal distinction between a
government and a gang may be a matter of scale. Strength and acceptance also con-

---

[1] From *The Leviathan* (1651), Chapter 13. See http://oregonstate.edu/instruct/phl302/texts/hobbes/leviathan-contents.html.
[2] See www.monticello.org/library/reference/quotes.html and http://www.bartelby.net/73/753.html.

vey authority, and a *government* is a body with the authority to lead and govern. Any type of authority can stray from economic and social goals, although democratic elections help to provide incentives for even the most selfish leaders to serve their constituents' interests. Political–economic systems parade in myriad forms. These systems determine how markets operate and how resources are allocated in nonmarket contexts. This section and the next provide a (necessarily simplified) juxtaposition of several prominent systems and philosophies so that fundamental differences and similarities can be readily identified.

Under a *market* or *capitalist* system, land, capital, and other factors of production are owned predominantly by individuals and corporations. Business owners make investment decisions and compete in the pursuit of profit. As explained in Chapter 3, buyers and sellers come together in markets that determine prices on the basis of supply and demand. When supply is low relative to demand, high prices motivate self-interested entrepreneurs to innovate, take risks, and organize businesses that help satisfy the interests of consumers. Wages are determined by negotiations between employees or labor unions and management. Within most market systems, government has the power to protect rights, regulate businesses, and provide tax-supported social benefits.

Communism and *socialism* are *command systems,* meaning that decision making is centralized. The intent of these systems is to eliminate material inequities via the collective ownership of property. Under communism, legislators from a single political party—the Communist party—establish wages, oversee production, and divide wealth for equal advantage among citizens. The pitfalls of communism include a lack of incentives for risk taking and innovation. The critical role of the central government in allocating wealth and setting production quotas makes this system particularly vulnerable to corruption.

Socialism shares with communism the goal of fair distribution and the stumbling block of inadequate incentives. However, in contrast to the practice under communism, a single political party does not rule the economy, and wages are not controlled by the government. Under the most basic socialist system, economic decisions are made collectively by groups of citizen participants, including general assemblies and councils of workers and consumers, sometimes in cooperation with a centralized government. For example, the distribution of revenues from production processes is determined by workers' councils. Quasi-socialist systems exist in Britain, Canada, and Sweden, among other countries.

IS GOVERNMENT NEEDED?

Debates over government's role have long divided political philosophers. The opening quote expresses philosopher Thomas Hobbes's sentiment that government is essential. Karl Marx contended that government is simply an instrument of class domination and would "wither away" with the abolition of distinct classes under communism. To generalize several broader philosophies for the purpose of comparison: *Authoritarians* question the practicality of self-government and look to centralized government for the advancement of society. *Conservatives* express concern about government's size and efficiency. *Libertarians* call for self-government, believing that government's role should be limited to protecting citizens from coercion and violence. *Anarchists* believe that all forms of government are oppressive and should be abolished.

Classical liberalism is a political philosophy that espouses freedom from church and state authority, free-enterprise economics, and individual freedoms. It was the foundation of parliamentary democracy in Britain and the dominant philosophy among the founders of the United States. The Ludwig Von Mises Institute[3] in Alabama is a modern incarnation of circles of economists and others who subscribe to classical liberalism. In contrast, *modern liberals* are sometimes characterized as favoring more government rather than less and as advocating a mild form of socialism or populism.

Advocates of a *laissez-faire,* or *free-market,* approach have long trumpeted the virtues of a market unfettered by government intervention. Classical conservatives, such as Edmund Burke, believed that classical liberals placed too much faith in human rationality. Noting that people are prone to bouts of unreasonable behavior, irrational passions, and immorality, classical conservatives called for adherence to societal traditions and standards, the institution of government, and the church to resist what they saw as the inevitable result of freewheeling human impulses—chaos.

The nineteenth century brought with it amplified problems with monopolies, fraud against consumers, gross economic inequities, and the exploitation of workers. Modern liberals, like classical conservatives, became leery of the laissez-faire approach. They believed that without the influence of regulations and liability, firms would not take adequate precautions to ensure the safety of their products; they also believed that without greater incentives, pertinent information held by firms was less likely to be passed on to customers. Led by Thomas Hill Green in the late nineteenth century and by the likes of Woodrow Wilson and Franklin D. Roosevelt in the early twentieth century, modern liberals championed organized labor, education, the environment, freedom of speech, and freedom of the press. As a result of their efforts, government took on significant new roles in regulating markets, tempering market power, requiring the dissemination of product information, and managing externalities (side effects that are experienced by people other than those causing them) and free-rider problems.

WON'T YOU BE MY NEIGHBOR? THE THEORY AND PRACTICE OF PRIVATE SOLUTIONS

Even neighbors (perhaps especially neighbors) have disputes that drain away sizable amounts of time, happiness, and expense. Neighbors scream, create smells, have barking dogs, cut down trees, erect walls, neglect their lawns, house farm animals, select offensive colors for roofs and walls, and in other ways annoy each other on a grand scale. The Web site www.theneighborsfromhell.com documents many such disputes. The site was created by the Gapski family, whose neighbor's dog drove them out of the neighborhood but not before eliciting the construction of a $1,000 fence and allegedly driving the asking price for their home down by $25,000.[4]

[3] See www.mises.org.
[4] See http://money.cnn.com/2005/03/30/pf/neighborsfromhell/.

Nobel laureate Ronald Coase put forth the popular theory that private negotiations can lead to efficient outcomes under the right circumstances. For example, Coase would expect the Gapskis to negotiate with the neighbors about their dog. If the dog caused the Gapskis $25,000 worth of harm, it would be rational for the Gapskis to be willing to pay the neighbors up to $25,000 to get rid of the dog. If the dog was worth less than $25,000 to the neighbors, say $15,000, any payment between $15,000 and $25,000 would make both parties better off than would the noncooperative solution of the Gapskis moving away. As one possibility, if the Gapskis paid the neighbors $20,000 to get rid of the dog, the Gapskis would lose $25,000 − $20,000 = $5,000 less than if they moved away, and the neighbors would gain $20,000 − $15,000 = $5,000 over the value they place on keeping the dog. This *Coasian bargaining*, therefore, would make everyone better off than the noncooperative solution, and the efficient outcome—removing a dog that causes more harm than good—would be reached. Notice that if it was efficient for the neighbors to keep the dog because they valued its presence by more than the value of the harm to others, the efficient outcome of keeping the dog would also result from Coasian bargaining. For example, if the neighbors received $27,000 worth of happiness from the dog, they would refuse the highest payment that the Gapskis would be willing to make—$25,000—and the dog that caused less harm than good would remain.

If Coasian bargaining could indeed yield efficient outcomes in a broad range of cases involving externalities, there would be little need for government taxes, subsidies, and restrictions conceived for the same purpose. However, efficient private solutions such as those proposed by Coase are less likely in the presence of several complicating factors. In reality, multiple sources of an externality (as with exhaust fumes from thousands of automobiles) make it difficult to know with whom to bargain. Multiple victims make it difficult to organize and collect funds from the affected parties. Incomplete information about the costs or benefits of an externality makes it difficult to know how much to pay or accept in negotiations. Arguments over exactly how much money should change hands doom the bargaining process. Time lags between the cause and the effect of externalities can make it difficult to identify externalities and their sources. The location, availability, and opportunity costs of time for the parties involved can make it difficult to assemble the parties for negotiations. And cultural norms make it strange and uncomfortable for the creators and victims of externalities to come together and negotiate financial payments.

Although many of these complicating factors are common, existing social mores may make the other factors moot. Our society has developed few efficient private approaches to financial negotiation over the behavior of others. It is awkward enough to ask one's hall mates to stop playing music while others are studying, much less offering them money to do so. Have you ever offered someone a bribe to stop smoking in a restaurant? Neighborhoods are replete with residents who are bothered by each other, but do the complainers ever knock on their neighbor's door with an offer of $100 in exchange for a less offensive color of house paint? When development or industry threatens a natural habitat, the difficulty of organizing those involved and negotiating an agreement makes a private solution even less likely.

REMEDIES WITH A ROLE FOR GOVERNMENT

In support of the very existence of markets, government can establish property rights, maintain law and order, and enforce contracts. If others could freely take what is yours, ownership and the transfer of property rights via market transactions would have little meaning. Issues of market failure provide additional rationale for government involvement. In Chapter 11, it was explained that externalities, imperfect information, imperfect competition, and public goods can impede the efficiency of markets. In this section, government solutions to market failure, among other problems, are explained.

The Enforcement of Property Rights

In the context of externalities, the benefits of enforced property rights go beyond allowing people to keep their purchases. The second type of benefit stems from the human instinct to be self-centered. With some exceptions, humans take better care of things that belong to them than of things that belong to others. People are unlikely to litter in their own yards, to dump toxins into their own ponds, or to overhunt their own forests. Americans spend almost $40 billion each year tending to their own lawns and gardens,[5] whereas publicly held lands frequently fall victim to abuse. Biologist Garrett Hardin called this problem the *tragedy of the commons*, citing the tendency for herders to overgraze their cattle in "common" (community-owned) pastures where the herders receive all of the benefits but the damage is borne by the broader community. If there were no government to enforce property rights, disputes over land would become more problematic and fewer places would receive the level of respect granted by private property owners.

Pigou Taxes and Subsidies

Everyone makes decisions on a daily basis that unintentionally affect others. For instance, in the United States we obtain 86 percent of our energy from fossil fuels, the burning of which releases carbon dioxide and contributes to global warming. As one of many repercussions of a warmer planet, tropical storms draw their strength from warm ocean water, and warmer oceans result in more, and more intense, storms.[6] However, the devastation caused by Hurricanes Katrina, Wilma, and Beta in 2005 had little to do with the 30 percent increase in atmospheric concentrations of carbon dioxide that has occurred since the Industrial Revolution.[7] To the extent that fossil fuels contribute to air pollution and global warming, it is a role of government to seek an efficient level of fuel consumption.

Efficiency in gasoline consumption can be achieved if consumers are required to bear both the *private marginal cost* (what they pay) and the *marginal external cost* (the external cost imposed on society) of each gallon of gasoline they purchase. *Social marginal cost* is the term used to describe the sum of private marginal cost and marginal

---

[5] See http://assoc.garden.org/press/press.php?q=show&id=2317&pr=pr_nga.
[6] See www.sciencemag.org/cgi/content/full/309/5742/1807.
[7] See www.ecn.ac.uk/Education/climate_change.htm.

external cost. The private marginal cost of gasoline to users is the price they pay at the pump—say, $3 per gallon. Consumers will continue to purchase gasoline until the marginal benefit from the last gallon consumed falls to $3. If the marginal external cost of a gallon of gasoline is $1, making the social marginal cost $3 + $1 = $4, then, by purchasing until the last gallon is worth only $3, consumers will overconsume and purchase some gallons of gasoline that cause more harm than good.

Most estimates of the marginal external cost of gasoline, including health and environmental costs and subsidies received by the oil industry, fall in the range between 40 cents and $15 per gallon.[8] The government can impose taxes that bring consumption closer to the efficient level. Taxes meant to fill the gap between private marginal cost and social marginal cost are called *Pigou taxes*. The federal gasoline tax is currently 18.4 cents per gallon and the average state tax is 22 cents per gallon, so if the conservative end of the externality estimates is correct, the average combined gasoline tax of 40.4 cents brings consumers to fully internalize the cost of their fuel use and to make efficient choices regarding fossil fuels. If the higher estimates are correct, gasoline is overconsumed, and somewhat higher Pigou taxes would result in a more efficient level of use.

Governments can also address positive externalities. Consider the market for immunizations against measles, polio, whooping cough, diphtheria, and other contagious diseases. The benefit to an individual of getting immunized is that he or she will not catch the disease. There are also external benefits because no member of society will catch the disease from the immunized individual. Without intervention, the individual would purchase immunizations until the private marginal benefit no longer exceeded the marginal cost. Because the private marginal benefit of another shot falls below the social marginal benefit by the value of the marginal external benefit (the benefit to others), individuals will choose to purchase less than the efficient level of protection against disease.

Is it true that people would not protect themselves adequately against diseases without government assistance? Probably. In fact, large numbers of children don't even get the mandatory, government-subsidized immunizations currently available. For example, the Illinois State Board of Education reported recently that 37,425 children in that state were out of compliance with immunization requirements in at least one disease category.[9] With hopes of reaching more efficient levels of performance, the U.S. government currently subsidizes immunizations, along with education, scientific research, alternative energy, the arts, and public transportation, among other sources of positive externalities.

The Provision of Public Goods

Chapter 11 introduced public goods as nonrival and nonexcludable goods and services that would be over- or underproduced if private individuals were left to their own devices. Police and fire protection, national parks, the military, and public schooling are among the services that would be underprovided without government assistance

---

[8] See www.distributiondrive.com/Article4.html. For a survey of many different estimates, see http://www.vtpi.org/tca/tca0512.pdf.
[9] See www.isbe.state.il.us/research/pdfs/immun_03.pdf.

because "free riders" would misrepresent their interests and seek benefits from the purchases of others. Government's role here includes the provision of public goods, the collection of taxes to pay for them, and the enactment and enforcement of regulations designed to protect them. For more on public goods, see Chapter 18.

Laws and Regulations

Government systems that create, interpret, and enforce the law can restrict market power; mandate information sharing; and impose limits, taxes, or subsidies on behaviors that cause externalities. Garrett Hardin favored legislation beyond property rights as a solution to the tragedy of the commons. Like the nineteenth-century economist Thomas Malthus, Hardin believed that overpopulation would lead to starvation and disease. He dismissed technical and scientific solutions as essentially "too little, too late," and he argued that governments must regulate population size. In his words, "To couple the concept of freedom to breed with the belief that everyone born has an equal right to the commons is to lock the world into a tragic course of action."[10] Late in the twentieth century, the Chinese government tried Hardin's solution, limiting couples to having at most one child. This degree of regulation is extreme, as the United Nations indicated in its Universal Declaration of Human Rights.[11] However, less invasive regulations provide meaningful protection for the public. Examples include limits on occupational noise exposure, mandated information labels on food products, and requirements that the repair histories of preowned cars and homes be disclosed to prospective buyers.

Education and Moral Leadership

So many people throughout the world look to the United States for a lead on the most crucial issues that face our planet and indeed the lives of our grandchildren. Truly the burden of the world rests on your shoulders.

—*England's Prince Charles to President George W. Bush*[12]

Education and moral leadership are desirable means of spreading information and promoting societal goals, in part because they elicit social consciousness and wise decisions without unpopular taxes, laws, or coercion. Government leaders serve as role models, and government actions set examples for others to follow. When a president prohibits road construction on 40 million acres of national forest, as Bill Clinton did; erects solar panels on the roof of the White House, as Jimmy Carter did; resolves international disputes with force, as George W. Bush did; or asks citizens to focus on community service, as John Kennedy did, that action sets a tone for the country, and sometimes the world.

Government is also the principal provider of education, with public schools educating 88.5 percent of all secondary school students in the United States. Positive externalities are among the benefits of schooling. Education is a means of affecting the skills and attitudes of society. Education can teach students to be aware of the con-

[10] From "The Tragedy of the Commons," *Science 162* (1968), p. 1246.
[11] See www.un.org/Overview/rights.html.
[12] See www.cnn.com/2005/US/11/03/royal.visit/index.html.

sequences of their actions and to think creatively about solutions to the world's problems. And education creates more productive workers, more informed voters, and citizens who can share their wisdom with others. Given these external benefits, we should expect that, as with immunizations and solar panels, too little education would be purchased in the absence of government subsidies.

Dispute Resolution

Government can work to limit the expense, incivility, and uncertainty of dispute resolution. Courts have little influence without the backing of a stalwart government, and international conflicts reveal the dangers of limited authority. With no worldwide enforcer of civilized resolutions, eight major wars and up to two dozen lesser conflicts were ongoing as of mid-2005.[13] The United States has lost 693,930 citizens to international conflicts since 1775.[14] And as a result of a shortfall of the strength and acceptance that convey authority, the International Court of Justice administered by the United Nations has a checkered history. For example, Argentina rejected a 1977 ruling by the court to grant possession of the islands in the Beagle Channel to Chile, and the United States refused to follow through with proceedings when the Sandinista government of Nicaragua alleged misdeeds by the U.S.–supported *Contra* rebels in 1984. Government-backed judicial systems typically achieve more civilized resolutions to disputes than are seen on the global scale where there is no accepted authority.

Governments eliminate some of the disputes that would otherwise occur—for example, zoning laws clarify where businesses, farms, and homes of different types can be situated. Governmental bodies, including neighborhood associations, also place restrictions on boats and cars parked on lawns, unkempt yards, unsightly buildings and fences, livestock, and other sources of externalities. Cities such as Sedona, Arizona, go so far as to enact codes that limit the size of commercial signs, prohibit light pollution at night, and require buildings to have color schemes that match those in the natural surroundings. Even the McDonald's in Sedona matches the reddish-brown rocks around it. Governments also set up strict procedures for dispute resolution, sometimes requiring the parties to make attempts at mediation or arbitration and, when necessary, to proceed to trial and appellate courts.

CONCLUSION

The efficiency with which resources are allocated depends largely on who controls the resources. There are possibilities for market failure under both public and private systems of control, and strengths can be drawn from models that vary from libertarian to authoritarian. Free-market mechanisms can allocate resources to those who value them the most, encourage the production of goods until the marginal benefit equals the marginal cost, and price goods to reflect a combination of value and scarcity. As a resource becomes relatively scarce, its price will rise, inducing greater efforts to supply that resource or to find viable replacements. This pricing mechanism goes on dis-

---

[13] See www.globalsecurity.org/military/world/war/.
[14] See www.infoplease.com/ipa/A0004615.html.

play every time rising oil prices motivate research into alternative energy, energy conservation, and new discoveries of oil.

Free markets have a harder time allocating resources efficiently in the presence of imperfect information, imperfect competition, externalities, or public goods. Some goods, such as air and river water, have no formal markets to address their allocation. When markets are inefficient or nonexistent, government can sometimes provide needed remedies. If markets are mismanaged, government can also bring excessive bureaucracy, ineptitude, misguidance, and corruption.

Being the product of human will, government is both potent and pliable. History has seen some of the most malevolent, domineering regimes replaced with relatively benign assemblages of authority. This was the case in many Eastern European nations during the 1990s and in several African nations in the early 2000s. The message is that people with courage and insight can indeed shape government. In a democracy, if voters and leaders understand the potential virtues and blunders of government, they are better prepared to exercise collective authority and to generate the efficient public policy so crucial in the many contexts in which government plays the starring role.

DISCUSSION STARTERS

1. Suppose you were studying in the library and a loud gum chewer sat next to you and disrupted your concentration. How would Ronald Coase expect this situation to be resolved? In your experience, what really happens in situations such as this? What might a governing authority, such as a librarian, be able to accomplish in this situation that private individuals cannot?

2. What examples of the tragedy of the commons have you observed?

3. Do you believe that your government embodies an appropriate mix of libertarian and authoritarian policies? Which elements of other forms of government appeal to you? Explain your answers.

4. From your own perspective, how could your government help to achieve greater efficiency for society as a whole? Are there laws that you would like to add or eliminate?

5. Suppose a definitive study on gasoline externalities confirmed that their cost is at the high end of current estimates, amounting to $15 per gallon. What options are available to the government to elicit the efficient level of gasoline consumption? Which of those options would you choose if you were the governmental leader in charge of this decision? Explain your answer.

6. Do you think that the efficient level of immunizations could be reached in the absence of government? If so, how?

CHAPTER 27

IS GLOBALIZATION A BAD WORD?
Comparative Advantage, Culture Clashes, and Organizations Meant to Make the Most of Global Markets

The Reverend Martin Luther King, Jr., said of global interdependence: "We are all caught in an inescapable network of mutuality, tied into a single garment of destiny. . . . Did you ever stop to think that you can't leave for your job in the morning without being dependent on most of the world?"[1] In all likelihood, he explained, the sponge you reach for in the bathroom is "handed to you by a Pacific Islander." Your soap comes from a French person. Your coffee, tea, or cocoa at breakfast comes from South American, Chinese, or West African citizens. Your toast comes "at the hands of an English-speaking farmer, not to mention the baker." And before breakfast is over, you have reaped benefits from work performed by people around the globe. Interdependence is nothing new; spices, slaves, and silk were traded across the oceans centuries ago. But as clipper ships were replaced by ocean liners and airlines that crisscross the globe every day, the cross-pollination of cultures intensified, as did the scrutiny of the resulting mutual influences. This chapter demystifies the nebulous concept of globalization and explains its benefits, such as economic incentives for cooperation and toleration, and its costs, such as exploitation and homogenization.

[1] "A Christmas Sermon on Peace," in *A Testament of Hope: The Essential Writings and Speeches of Martin Luther King, Jr.*, ed. James M. Washington (New York: HarperCollins, 1986), p. 254.

WHAT IS GLOBALIZATION?

One can now travel from one continent to another in the time it used to take to travel from one end of Manhattan Island to the other, and the modes of transportation are only getting faster. The Japan Aerospace Exploration Agency has completed successful tests of a supersonic jet plane that will someday carry 300 passengers from New York to Tokyo in less than 6 hours. New technologies allow instantaneous communication of information and overnight transfers of people and products around the globe, giving goods and influence a worldwide reach. In a nutshell, *globalization* is the creation of a worldwide scope for markets, communications, transportation, and ideas. The term has been used to convey a number of associated concepts, which include the following:

> *internationalization*—the increase of international trade and interdependence
>
> *supraterritoriality*—the deemphasis on territorial boundaries
>
> *universalization*—the spread of common ideas and goods across the globe
>
> *Westernization*—the migration of Western culture

British political scientist Jan Aart Scholte argues that, of these, supraterritoriality is central to the meaning of globalization, citing Milton Friedman's observation that it has become possible "to produce products anywhere, using resources from anywhere, by a company located anywhere, to be sold anywhere."[2] For example, Deere and Company produces tractors in Waterloo, Iowa, for export to 110 countries on 6 continents. Parts in its Augusta, Georgia, assembly plant come from 12 other countries. Deere also produces machinery in China for the Middle East, in Brazil for Europe, and in Germany and India for the United States. In all, the company does business in more than 160 countries.[3]

WHAT CAN BE GAINED FROM GLOBALIZATION?

> *Our company buys denim in North Carolina, ships it to France where it is sewn into jeans, launders these jeans in Belgium, and markets them in Germany using TV commercials developed in England.*
>
> —*Robert D. Haas, board member and former CEO, Levi Strauss & Co.*[4]

Levi's jeans, like many other goods, are shuttled around the globe during the production process for several good reasons. As one of the first places in the world to use a cotton gin to separate seeds from fiber, North Carolina has more than 200 years of experience in the efficient production of high-quality cotton products. Barthelemy Thimonnier patented the first commercial sewing machine and ran the world's first

---

[2] See http://www.mtholyoke.edu/acad/intrel/scholte.htm.
[3] See www.deere.com/en_US/compinfo/speeches/2005/050419_lane.html.
[4] "The Corporation without Boundaries," in M. Ray and A. Rinzier, eds., *The New Paradigm in Business: Emerging Strategies for Leadership and Organizational Change* (New York: Tarcher/ Perigee, 1993), p. 103.

garment factory in France in the 1830s.[5] Having given the world denim as well, France knows a thing or two about sewing jeans. Belgium and England may not have enjoyed a first-mover advantage in commercial laundering or advertising—Texas claims the first Laundromat and New York claims the first advertising firm[6]—but they benefit from available resources and expertise in these tasks.

When one country can make a good at a lower opportunity cost, meaning that it gives up less of other goods for each unit, it has a *comparative advantage* in producing that good. When a country can make more of a product than another country with the same resources, the more productive country has an *absolute advantage*. David Ricardo reasoned that each country should specialize in the goods and services that it can produce most readily and cheaply and should trade those goods and services for those that foreign countries can produce more efficiently. For example, India excels in information technology (IT) services, and, because of this, about half of the Fortune 500 companies are clients of Indian IT firms.[7] Chile's warm winters and hard-working, low-paid workers give that country an advantage in the labor-intensive production of fresh fruits and vegetables, and Chile grows more than 1 million metric tons of fresh table grapes each year, mostly for export.[8] The American Midwest has a comparative advantage in wheat production: Thanks to its rich soil and moderate temperatures, the region exports 28.5 million metric tons of wheat annually.[9]

One of Ricardo's insights was that whenever a country has a comparative advantage over another country in the production of a good, it is a certainty that *both* countries can benefit from specialization and mutual trade. Consider the trading partnership between Canada and Japan. Both of those countries can produce cars and paper. However, Canada has millions of square miles of forested land and established systems of efficient forest management that yield high volumes of wood pulp for the production of about 20 million tons of paper per year.[10] Japan has focused on the development of an automobile industry that produces cars quickly and efficiently and produces more than 10 million cars per year.[11]

Suppose that Canada could produce 20 million tons of paper if it made no cars and that by devoting all its resources to making cars instead, it could make 20 million cars and no paper, thus giving up 1 ton of paper for each car made. Suppose also that Japan could make 10 million cars if it made no paper, and if it devoted all its resources to making paper instead, it could make 2 million tons of paper for an opportunity cost of 5 cars per ton of paper made. Canada's relative abundance of forests means that by releasing the labor, machinery, and other inputs required to make 1 car, it can make 5 times more paper than Japan can per car given up. Although Canada

[5] See www.ismacs.nct/smhistory.html. Ironically, tailors eventually ran Thimonnier out of the country, fearing that his invention would cause them to lose their jobs.

[6] See http://www.jwt.com/contacts.html.

[7] See www.atimes.com/atimes/South_Asia/GK04Df02.html.

[8] See www.fas.usda.gov/htp/horticulture/Grapes/Table%20Grape%20Situation%20and%20Outlook%202005.pdf.

[9] See www.nationmaster.com/country/us/Agriculture.

[10] See www.cofi.org/reports/factbook2000/Pages%20from%20FACTBOOK%202000-12.pdf.

[11] See www.findarticles.com/p/articles/mi_m3012/is_7_184/ai_n6140525.

could make more of either good than Japan, the comparative advantage in car production is held by Japan, where each car causes the loss of one-fifth ton of paper compared to the loss of a full ton of paper per car in Canada. Canada has a comparative advantage in paper production, with each ton of paper causing the loss of 1 car instead of 5. Because a comparative advantage exists, both countries can benefit from trade.

If Canada trades paper for cars at a rate of, say, 2 cars per ton of paper, Canada gets twice as many cars per ton of paper as it could attain without trading (on its own it can make only 1 car per ton of paper given up), and Japan trades 2 cars per ton of paper rather than giving up 5 cars per ton of paper, as it would without trade. Suppose that acting independently, Canada would produce 10 of each product and Japan would produce 1 ton of paper and 5 cars. As an example of the mutual benefits attainable with trade, Canada could produce 13 tons of paper and 7 cars, Japan could produce 10 cars and no paper, and then 2 tons of paper from Canada could be traded for 4 cars from Japan. That would leave Canada with $13 - 2 = 11$ tons of paper and $7 + 4 = 11$ cars, whereas Japan would have 2 tons of paper and $10 - 4 = 6$ cars. As summarized in the accompanying table, trade allows both countries to have more of each product.

		MAXIMUM PRODUCTION (WITH COMPLETE SPECIALIZATION IN 1 PRODUCT)	EXAMPLE OF NO-TRADE OUTCOME	EXAMPLE OF TRADE OUTCOME
Canada	Cars	20	10	11
	Tons of paper	20	10	11
Japan	Cars	10	5	6
	Tons of paper	2	1	2

The benefits of globalization extend beyond the efficiency of specialization and trade. Shared information serves as a public good for those who would otherwise have to reinvent solutions, cures, products, and processes on their own. International collaborations can contribute to the success of projects of grand importance, as with the International Space Station, efforts to track and propagate endangered species, and cures for deadly diseases. Cooperation also permits the spreading of risk. International organizations can pool funds and disburse them for relief from disasters, including oil spills, droughts, cyclones, famines, and floods. When a devastating tsunami hit Indonesia in 2004, international disaster-relief teams from more than 80 established organizations arrived to provide assistance.[12] Cooperative educational efforts include the work of the United Nations Educational, Scientific, and Cultural Organization (UNESCO). UNESCO's nearly 200 member nations have the goal of "education for all" by the year 2015.[13]

[12] See www.cnn.com/2004/WORLD/asiapcf/12/28/tsunami.aidsites/.
[13] See www.unesco.org.

Finally, economic cooperation is a strong disincentive for bloodshed between nations. France and the United Kingdom (U.K.) have an ongoing spat, but it's unlikely to come to military strikes because the two nations are economically interdependent. France receives more than $35 billion in annual trade revenues from the U.K. and purchases more than $32 billion worth of U.K. goods.[14] When contemplating aggression against each other, these countries would have to add the enormous trade revenues and benefits from imports to the other economic and political ramifications of war before deciding to take that route. Growing interdependence thus provides growing disincentives for avoidable belligerence.

WHAT ARE THE OBJECTIONS TO GLOBALIZATION?

It's not free trade, it's stupid trade.

—*Craig Romero, Republican candidate for Louisiana's 3rd congressional district, on the Central American Free Trade Agreement*

Despite the potential gains from cooperation, there is fervent opposition to globalization in many circles. Critics worry that the influence of multinational corporations rivals or trumps that of democratically elected representatives and concentrates power among those driven by profit. Intensified globalization might lead to a relatively homogeneous world market, causing cultures to lose their identities. And production might be shifted to countries that have low environmental or humanitarian standards, so that the exploitation of human and natural resources might be increased. This section explores the potential harm that could stem from the current trends in globalization.

The expansion of some cultures has led to the contraction of others. Some languages and dialects have been lost forever, and people in 121 countries now can eat food served by McDonald's. To critics of globalization, fast-food franchises are symbolic of a broader dissemination of unhealthy and unsustainable Western lifestyles. Seductive corporate advertising and contagious materialistic values could create a world in which everyone consumed at the rate of Western countries—and that would require the resources of at least five planets similar to earth.[15] Other things being equal, we might expect high-consumption countries also to be on the receiving end of influence, gaining ideas about how to live simply from countries with more sustainable economies. However, with an imbalance in marketing savvy, such a balance in influence is less likely. Aside from health and resource issues, homogeneous cultures would be dull.

Critics also argue that, in practice, globalization has perpetuated the imbalance of economic benefits rather than spreading the benefits far and wide. In the 1990s, the share of global income going to the poorest people in the world dropped from 2.3 percent to 1.4 percent.[16] Without adequate policies to prevent the practice, profit-maximizing firms could shop for production sites in countries where labor or environmental protection standards are low. In this respect, Dong-Sook S. Gills found

[14] See www.fco.gov.uk/Files/kfile/UK-France%20trade%20in%202004%20-%20June%202005.pdf.
[15] To learn how many planets would be needed if everyone lived like you, see www.myfootprint.org/.
[16] See http://news.bbc.co.uk/1/hi/special_report/1999/02/99/e-cyclopedia/711906.stm.

that increased globalization has led to the exploitation of female workers in Asia,[17] and Susmita Dasgupta, Nlandu Mamingi, and Craig Meisner found that globalization promoted pesticide use in Brazil, particularly on export crops.[18] Modern trade agreements, such as the North American Free Trade Agreement (NAFTA) and the Central American Free Trade Agreement (CAFTA), typically include provisions meant to protect humanitarian and environmental interests; the difficulty of monitoring and enforcement, among other problems, has meant limited success. (For more concerns about CAFTA and other free-trade agreements, see www.stopcafta.com.)

Some workers believe that, by deemphasizing international boundaries, globalization invites levels of immigration and outsourcing that threaten domestic employment. The importance of these contentious topics warrants dedicated coverage of outsourcing in Chapter 23 and of immigration in Chapter 30.

WHAT ORGANIZATIONS HELP TO KEEP PROBLEMS IN CHECK?

The power and influence of governments tend to erode outside of national boundaries, causing a relative void of authority and changing the formula for successful policy initiatives at the international level. Even the strongest armies have difficulty enforcing policies among rogue nations, and international law is only as binding as the multinational commitments to support it. At the same time, vital interests in the benefits of economic cooperation, in the ethical treatment of labor, and in the avoidance of global environmental catastrophes have spawned several organizations of considerable strength and controversy to offer international oversight.

The United Nations

The United Nations (UN) was founded in 1945 with 51 member countries and a charter "to maintain international peace and security; to develop friendly relations among nations; to cooperate in solving international economic, social, cultural and humanitarian problems and in promoting respect for human rights and fundamental freedoms; and to be a centre for harmonizing the actions of nations in attaining these ends."[19] The organization now boasts 191 member countries, 15 agencies, and an extensive array of programs and bodies. The UN "family of organizations" includes the Global Program on Globalization, Liberalization, and Sustainable Human Development; the Inter-Agency Committee on Sustainable Development; the International Seabed Authority; the UN Food and Agriculture Organization; and the UN Environment Program. At the 2001 World Economic Forum in Switzerland, UN Secretary-General Kofi Annan challenged world business leaders to "embrace and enact" the principles of the UN Global Compact.[20] Covering human rights, labor, and the environment, the compact's principles include the development and use of environmentally friendly technologies, initiatives to promote greater environmental re-

---

[17] "Globalization of Production and Women in Asia," *Annals of the American Academy of Political and Social Science* (2002), *581*, 106–120.

[18] "Pesticide Use in Brazil in the Era of Agroindustrialization and Globalization," *Environment and Development Economics* (2001), 6:4, 459–482.

[19] See www.un.org/aboutun/basicfacts/unorg.htm.

[20] See www.un.org/Depts/ptd/global.htm.

sponsibility, and support for a "precautionary principle" of erring on the safe side when dealing with uncertain outcomes. The latest activities of UN organizations are summarized on-line at http://www.unsystem.org/.

The World Trade Organization

The World War II–era General Agreement on Tariffs and Trade (GATT) reduced barriers to the international trade of merchandise, which now represents 40 percent of global production and 80 percent of global trade. In 1995, the World Trade Organization (WTO) replaced GATT as the global authority on rules of international trade. The WTO administers GATT principles and extends them with policies negotiated among its 144 member nations. Among these, the General Agreement on Trade in Services (GATS) is the service-industry equivalent to GATT. The objectives for GATS and GATT are to create "a credible and reliable system of international trade rules; ensuring fair and equitable treatment of all participants . . . ; stimulating economic activity through guaranteed policy bindings; and promoting trade and development through progressive liberalization."[21]

The WTO has come under fire for allegedly placing commercial interests ahead of environmental protection. The Working Group on the WTO/Multilateral Agreement on Investment claims, for example, that WTO rulings have relaxed the environmental standards for Venezuelan oil refineries, undercut U.S. requirements that shrimp be caught using specific turtle-safe excluding devices, and neglected precautionary policies that call for the WTO to prepare for the worst in the context of environmental concerns. Whatever the intent and result of current WTO actions, the repercussions of globalization were certainly on the minds of its architects. The preamble to the 1994 Marrakech Agreement establishing the WTO states that

> relations in the field of trade and economic endeavor should be conducted while allowing for the optimal use of the world's resources in accordance with the objective of sustainable development, seeking both to protect and preserve the environment and to enhance the means for doing so in a manner consistent with their respective needs and concerns at different levels of economic development.[22]

In support of this goal, umbrella clauses, such as Article 20 of the GATT, permit countries to act in the defense of human, animal, or plant life or health and to conserve nonrenewable natural resources.

The World Bank

Financial ministers from 45 governments gathered in Bretton Woods, New Hampshire, in 1944 as architects of the modern international economy. With fresh wounds from the Great Depression and World War II, they sought economic stability and revitalization for their countries. One result was the creation of the World Bank to assist with rebuilding war-torn Europe. With that task completed, the World Bank turned to less-developed countries, aiming to envelop them in the global economy and to reduce poverty by pro-

[21] See www.wto.org/english/tratop_e/serv_e/gatsqa_e.htm.
[22] See www.econ.iastate.edu/classes/econ355/choi/wtomara.htm.

viding low- or no-interest loans for education, health, infrastructure, and communications. The World Bank and its 184 member countries also work together to combat negative repercussions of globalization, such as the spread of avian flu across borders.[23]

As with all other international organizations and agreements, the World Bank has no shortage of detractors. There are charges that the World Bank actually exacerbates the problems of globalization by hastening development, promoting materialism, and neglecting environment health.[24]

The International Monetary Fund

Like the World Bank, the International Monetary Fund (IMF) was conceived as part of the Bretton Woods agreement. It serves as a stabilizing force for the currencies and economies of its 184 member countries by overseeing exchange-rate policies, lending to countries with balance-of-payment problems, and assisting with the development of monetary and fiscal policy.[25]

The IMF defends globalization, saying that it transformed East Asia from one of the poorest areas to an area of greater prosperity: "And as living standards rose, it became possible to make progress on democracy and economic issues such as the environment and work standards. By contrast, in the 1970s and 1980s when many countries in Latin America and Africa pursued inward-oriented policies, their economies stagnated or declined, poverty increased and high inflation became the norm."[26]

Critics of the IMF, such as the Global Exchange organization,[27] claim that the IMF and the World Bank trap countries by luring them into debt and then placing unwarranted demands on them. There are also concerns that the IMF causes poor countries to promote sweatshops and to accept exploitative inroads by large Western corporations. What is certain is that these organizations have come to symbolize desired order and assistance for some and the pursuit of selfish ideals for others.

CONCLUSION

Innovations in travel and communications make the world's distances easily surmountable, and sharing has become commonplace in what communications theorist Marshall McLuhan dubbed "the global village"—a world made smaller by electronic media. Globalization brings with it the efficiency of specialization based on comparative advantage, an information superhighway leading in the direction of better understanding, and incentives for the civilized resolution of disputes. It also creates threats to the status quo, a longer reach for powerful multinational corporations (Microsoft Corporation now writes software that runs 95 percent of the world's computers),[28] and an extended scope for uncivilized disputes (32 countries have current or impending access to long-range ballistic missiles[29]).

[23] See www.worldbank.org/.
[24] See www.worldbankboycott.org.
[25] See www.imf.org.
[26] See www.imf.org/external/np/exr/ib/2000/041200.htm.
[27] See www.globalexchange.org/campaigns/wbimf/facts.html.
[28] See www.bloomberg.com/apps/news?pid=10000086&sid=aZLWBOYKBK.o&refer=latin_america.
[29] See www.armscontrol.org/factsheets/missiles.asp.

Perspectives on whether globalization provides a net gain depend on the observers' interests and priorities. With the aim of making the most of globalization, the world's nations seek policy guidance from international organizations with good intentions but checkered histories. The UN, IMF, WTO, and World Bank face the ever-present possibility for corruption and the daunting challenge of reconciling differences in a world in which the ability to meet face-to-face has grown faster than the ability to see eye-to-eye.

DISCUSSION STARTERS

1. In what ways did you benefit from globalization by the time you finished breakfast this morning? Did you eat fruit from a tropical island, drink a beverage derived from foreign leaves or beans, put on clothes made in China, or use electronics made in Japan? In what other ways do you gain from globalization?

2. What, in your opinion, are the worst aspects of globalization?

3. Suppose that in one year Belize can produce 1 million oranges, 500,000 telephones, or any combination in between at a trade-off of 2 oranges per telephone. Suppose also that Israel can produce 3 million oranges, 2 million telephones, or combinations in between at a trade-off of $1^1/_2$ oranges per telephone.
   a. Which country has an absolute advantage in orange production? How do you know?
   b. Which country has an absolute advantage in telephone production? How do you know?
   c. Which country has a comparative advantage in orange production? How do you know?
   d. Which country has a comparative advantage in telephone production? How do you know?
   e. Which country should specialize in oranges? Which should specialize in telephones?
   f. What is one rate of exchange (a number of oranges paid per telephone) that would make both countries better off than they would be without trade?

4. Intense controversy revolves around the WTO, the IMF, the UN, and other organizations that were formed to limit the negative aspects of globalization and promote its strengths. What standards—for example, along the lines of fairness, enforceability, sustainability, and cultural appropriateness—would you prescribe for new policies coming out of such organizations?

5. Suppose you're the new president of the WTO. What is the first new policy measure you would advocate to make the world a better place? Why, do you suppose, hasn't this measure been adopted yet?

CHAPTER 28

WHY ARE SOME NATIONS RICH AND OTHERS POOR?
Growth Models, Miracles, and the Determinants of Economic Development

. . . the causes of the wealth and poverty of nations—the grand object of all enquiries of Political Economy.

—*Thomas Malthus in a letter to David Ricardo, January 26, 1817*[1]

The Europeans, they say, were smarter, better organized, harder working; the others were ignorant, arrogant, lazy, backward, superstitious. Others invert the categories: The Europeans, they say, were aggressive, ruthless, greedy, unscrupulous, hypocritical; their victims were happy, innocent, weak. . . .

—*David Landes*[2]

Adam Smith . . . showed convincingly how the principles of free trade, competition, and choice would spur economic development, reduce poverty, and precipitate the social and moral improvement of humankind.

—*Eamonn Butler, Director, Adam Smith Institute*[3]

---

[1] *The Works and Correspondence of David Ricardo,* ed. Piero Sraffa with the collaboration of M. H. Dobb (Indianapolis: Liberty Fund, 2005), vol. 7, p. 122.

[2] *The Wealth and Poverty of Nations: Why Some Are So Rich and Some So Poor* (New York: W. W. Norton, 1998), p. xxi.

[3] See www.adamsmith.org/smith/won-intro.htm. The full title of Adam Smith's most famous book is *An Inquiry into the Nature and Causes of the Wealth of Nations.*

DEVELOPMENT AND GROWTH

With more than 850 million people worldwide going to bed hungry each night,[4] and with the richest 16 percent consuming 80 percent of the world's resources,[5] the determinants of wealth and poverty constitute pieces in one of the world's most important puzzles. As the pieces come together, the goal is to promote *economic development*, which is a sustained increase in the standard of living experienced by a country's population. In order to compare development levels in different countries, Pakistani economist Mahbub ul Haq created the *Human Development Index* (HDI) on the basis of life expectancy, adult literacy rates, school enrollment rates, and GDP per capita.[6] Since 1993, the United Nations Development Program has used the HDI as a gauge of well-being in its annual reports. In the 2005 report, Norway received the highest HDI value of the 177 countries studied, Niger received the lowest, and the United States came in 10th.[7]

Economic growth, commonly measured by increases in GDP, is necessary but not sufficient for economic development. Advances in health and education require expenditures that increase the level of growth. However, as explained in Chapter 21, GDP also increases with expenditures on crime, disease, and natural disasters and fails to capture leisure, income distribution, and some resource depletion problems. Despite these flaws, the relative objectivity and purely financial basis of GDP and other growth measures make them prominent in economic studies.

SCHOOLS OF THOUGHT

Economists have looked at the available data and tried to identify patterns of characteristics among rich and poor nations. Varying findings and interpretations have generated several broad schools of thought, with emphases that include technology, skills and knowledge, geography, outside influences, and governance.[8]

The Solow Model

Economist Robert Solow set forth the neoclassical conception of growth in developing countries.[9] Solow's model attributes growth to technological change, and each country is assumed to have the same technology. Thus, productivity differences among countries are explained by differing amounts of capital per worker. Solow suggested that productivity in poor countries would catch up to that in rich countries because resources are allocated to the place where they are valued most highly, and (as implied by diminishing marginal returns, explained in Chapter 7) capital would be more valuable in countries that have little of it.

---

[4] See www.pbs.org/wgbh/rxforsurvival/series/diseases/malnutrition.html.
[5] See www.cnn.com/US/9910/12/population.cosumption/.
[6] For details on the HDI, see http://hdr.undp.org/docs/statistics/indices/stat_feature_2.pdf#aboutthisyears humandevelopmentindex.
[7] See http://hdr.undp.org/reports/global/2005/pdf/presskit/HDR05_PKE_HDI.pdf.
[8] For a concise overview of modern research on this topic, see Elhanan Helpman, *The Mystery of Economic Growth* (Cambridge, MA: Harvard University Press, 2004).
[9] See "A Contribution to the Theory of Economic Growth," *Quarterly Journal of Economics* (1956), no. 70, 65–94, and "Technical Change and the Aggregate Production Function," *Review of Economics and Statistics* (1957), *39:3*, 312–320.

As an example, the first tractor in a country would be employed for the most valued tasks, whereas the 100th tractor would be used for less important work, and the 100th tractor would be more useful than the 1,000th or the 10,000th. Rational, profit-maximizing investors would take tractors as they came off the assembly line and place them into the country that had the highest marginal productivity. Given the higher return from 1 more tractor in poor countries, where many fields are still cultivated by hand, and similarly high returns for other types of capital where it is most needed, this model predicts that capital would flow from rich countries into poor countries, thereby reducing the inequalities between them.

Human Capital

Economist Robert Lucas pointed out the inconsistencies between the Solow growth model and reality.[10] In fact, capital moves mostly among rich countries, and Lucas explained that the marginal product of capital between, as an example, India and the United States differs by a factor of 5, even when differences in *human capital* (skills, education, experience, etc.) are taken into account. So why isn't all the new capital flowing into places such as India? Lucas points out that capital market imperfections, such as taxes on incoming capital and monopolies that control foreign trade, impede the free flow of capital to its most efficient use.

There are also reasons why the marginal product of capital may not be relatively large in poor countries even though they have relatively little capital. Lucas suggests that positive externalities (that is, beneficial side effects, as discussed in Chapter 11) from human capital may equalize the marginal product of capital between India and the United States. The idea is that workers' skills, education, and experience rub off on other workers. One country may have twice the average education level of another, but by working with more knowledgeable people, the workers in the education-oriented country end up with *more than* twice the human capital. By Lucas's estimates, a 10 percent increase in the human capital of your co-workers will increase your own productivity by 3.6 percent.

Human capital and imperfect capital markets are two possible explanations for the difficulty some countries have in attracting capital investment and achieving economic growth. In related research, economists Greg Mankiw, David Romer, and David Weil found that by augmenting the Solow model to accommodate differences in human capital, savings rates, and population growth, they could explain most of the international variation in incomes.[11] However, the development of human capital is no silver bullet: Several other studies have found no association between an increase in the average level of education and economic growth.[12] The following sections provide an overview of alternative schools of thought about productivity differences among nations.

[10] See "Why Doesn't Capital Flow from Rich to Poor Countries?" *American Economic Review* (1990), *80*:2, 92–96.

[11] See "A Contribution to the Empirics of Growth," *Quarterly Journal of Economics* (1992), *107*:2, 407–437.

[12] See Pritchett, L., "Where Has All the Education Gone?" World Bank Policy Research Working Paper No. 1581 (1997); and J. Benhabib and M. Spiegel, "The Role of Human Capital and Political Instability in Economic Development: Evidence from Aggregate Cross-Country Data," *Journal of Monetary Economics* (1994), no. 34, 143–173.

Location, Location, Location

They say that the three things most important to success in business are location, location, and location. The same could be said about growth and development on a larger scale. The fertile heartland of the United States and the oilfields of Saudi Arabia convey advantages not found in impoverished Laos or Haiti. But it is important to note that geographical problems are surmountable. A benefit of globalization is that transportation and communications reach around the world, helping countries with the narrowest comparative advantage in the production of a few goods or services (as discussed in Chapter 27) to trade for virtually anything made anywhere. Japan and Singapore are examples of countries that have used export-oriented economies to overcome resource constraints and become wealthy nations, with per capita GDP levels of $29,400 and $27,800, respectively. Size needn't be a problem, either. Many small countries have very high standards of living, including tiny Luxembourg, where the GDP per capita is $58,900. Undesirable location and size are more than speed bumps on the road to success,[13] but other factors have proven to be more important determinants of a country's potential for development.

Exploitation and Other Outside Influences

Without foreign involvement, poor countries sometimes languish in poverty, but when foreigners do become involved in the commerce of developing nations, the poor countries often get the short end of the stick. Corporations from rich countries sometimes find relatively lax rules or corruptible governments that allow them to exploit the natural resources and labor of poor countries.[14] Consider the experience of countries sarcastically referred to as *banana republics*—generally small, politically unstable countries whose economies are dominated by foreign corporations that produce and export a single good, such as bananas. In 1871, an American named Minor Keith arrived in Costa Rica to build a railroad and soon began planting bananas. Minor went on to found the United Fruit Company (UFCO), whose plantations extended throughout Central America, South America, and the Caribbean. UFCO owned 112 miles of railroad and 11 ocean steamers; in its home-base country, Guatemala, it controlled telegraph lines, mail delivery to the United States, and all shipments in and out of the trade hub of Puerto Barrios. By 1944, the poorest 90 percent of Guatemalans owned only 10 percent of the country's land. When Jacobo Arbenz was elected president of Guatemala in 1950, he proposed a redistribution of some land from the richest to the poorest farmers, including land owned by UFCO. Using its connections— including a U.S. secretary of state whose former law firm represented UFCO, a top public relations officer married to the private secretary of President Dwight Eisenhower, and a board member who was the head of the CIA[15]—UFCO lobbied for U.S. protection, saying that Guatemala was a "satellite" of the Soviet Union. The

---

[13] For a discussion of geographical handicaps in Africa, see www.frontpagemag.com/Articles/Read Article.asp?ID=18760.

[14] In addition, well-intentioned efforts by capital-intensive nations can introduce chemical- and machine-intensive agricultural practices that are less appropriate for the labor-intensive recipients.

[15] See Walter La Feber, *Inevitable Revolutions: The United States in Central America*, 2nd ed. (New York: W. W. Norton, 1993), pp. 120–121.

CIA orchestrated a coup in Guatemala in 1954 and installed a new leader who opposed land reform. UFCO later changed its name to United Brands and, in the 1970s, sold its land holdings in Guatemala to Del Monte Corporation.

It is unfair to assume that all foreign business operations are hurtful to local populations. The United Fruit Company, like many other multinational corporations, created jobs, built schools, and paid its workers well. But the lion's share of the revenues from its operations escaped Guatemala, leaving that country poor. The same phenomenon occurs when Nike shoes are made in Indonesia and Folgers coffee beans are grown in Brazil. Do foreign operators stand in the way of domestic entrepreneurs who would otherwise have created the same jobs and retained the bulk of the wealth at home? The answer is "sometimes." The United Fruit Company controlled critical communications and transportation infrastructure and land, making it difficult for domestic industries to excel. Without such barriers from foreign capitalists, the East Asian countries discussed later in the chapter became wealthy with minimal intervention from foreign entrepreneurs. Elsewhere, foreigners have served as movers and shakers, ushering in advances in health care, agriculture, and technology. For example, the 300-megawatt San Pedro de Macorís power plant in the Dominican Republic received $233 million in financing from Cogentrix Energy, Inc., of North Carolina and Capital Partners of Great Britain, and engineering, procurement, and construction services from both Siemens of Germany and Motherwell Bridge of Scotland.[16] The affordable electricity delivered by this international team is a boon to schools, hospitals, and factories on one of the poorest islands in the Western Hemisphere.

Poorer nations tend to produce primary products in the agriculture, forestry, fishing, and mining industries that have many sources, inviting competition and low prices. Raw materials, such as iron ore, coffee beans, and timber, are purchased by rich nations for processing into automobiles, instant coffee crystals, and fine furniture, which are then sold globally (including back to the poor nations) at a high markup thanks to brand and quality distinctions and a scarcity of substitutes.

Nations that produce primary products also face competition from government-subsidized production in wealthier countries. During the past 10 years, U.S. wheat farmers have received federal subsidies of $19.8 billion, corn farmers have received $41.8 billion, and soybean farmers have received $13 billion.[17] Subsidies encourage the production of commodities even where substantial irrigation and soil enhancement are required, and surpluses are sold to Mexico and other relatively poor countries where farmers have difficulty competing with the subsidized prices. Likewise, Japanese farmers sell subsidized rice in Vietnam and other developing nations. The subsidies keep prices down, but in countries where most of the consumers are agricultural workers, lower prices on imported grains don't compensate for the loss of farm wages needed to purchase everything.

Foreign involvement and farm subsidies are mixed blessings; as highlighted in Chapter 27, the arguments for trade are more compelling. President George W. Bush has suggested a decrease in trade barriers as a means of assisting people around the world. He advocates a Free Trade Area of the Americas (FTAA) that would consti-

---

[16] See www.cogentrix.com/company/article_1.html.
[17] See http://www.healthyschoolscampaign.org/news/media/food/2006-0222_hatin-it.php.

tute the world's largest open market, including more than 800 million consumers. President Bush writes that lowering trade barriers by one-third would "strengthen the world's economic welfare by up to $613 billion and that of the United States by $177 billion."[18] There are currently about 150 free-trade agreements worldwide, less than 25 percent of which involve countries in the Western Hemisphere and only 3 of which involve the United States. It may be that more cross-pollination between rich and poor nations would better serve the interests of both categories, with the important caveats discussed in Chapter 27 about thwarting the negative aspects of globalization and trade.

Governance and Other Internal Influences

Terry S. Semel, the CEO of Yahoo Inc., received $109 million in compensation in a recent year, and the average CEO of a major company earned about $10 million.[19] Some criticize the high salaries of leaders, and some leaders may well be overpaid, but it is difficult to overstate the importance of the person at the top. Leaders of corporations and nations orchestrate success stories, handle setbacks, and set the tone for ambition and morale. Most new businesses fail, and most countries are not wealthy. It took the guidance of CEO Greg Brenneman to turn Burger King around in 2005 and the genius of President Sir Quett Ketumile Joni Masire to lead Botswana through democratization and three decades of rapid economic growth at the end of the twentieth century.[20] In developing nations, leaders also determine whether international aid and trade revenues go toward investments in human and physical capital or into the pockets of corrupt officials. A change in leadership provides troubled countries and corporations with an immediate change in outlook and is often a first step for nations seeking reform.

No positive characteristic is likely to guarantee a country's development and no negative characteristic inevitably spells doom, but a preponderance of either is the ticket to boom or gloom. Just as Hawaii beat the jinx of tropical geography (tropical areas contain a vastly disproportionate amount of the world's poverty) with the triple virtues of extraordinary agriculture, military bases, and tourism, many nations on the continent of Africa struggle with the triple threat of despotic or corrupt governance, disease, and violence. Many nations stand in the middle, with much going for them but enough negatives to halt a developmental breakthrough. The trick, then, is to tip the scale. The next section describes such a transition in East Asia.

THE ASIAN ECONOMIC MIRACLE

Between 1970 and 1996, the historically poor countries of China, Hong Kong, Indonesia, Malaysia, Singapore, South Korea, Taiwan, and Thailand experienced GDP growth that averaged about 8 percent per year, compared to the 2.7 percent average growth rate of the rich industrial countries.[21] The World Bank's 1993 report *The East*

---

[18] See www.whitehouse.gov/news/releases/2002/05/20020517-13.html.
[19] See www.aflcio.org/corporatewatch/paywatch/.
[20] See www.news.cornell.edu/stories/Nov05/botswana.cover.ak.html.
[21] See www.economist.com/surveys/displayStory.cfm?story_id=114999.

Asian Miracle attributes the development of these nations largely to public-policy decisions. The countries had high levels of savings and investment, high-quality labor with an increasing labor force participation rate, and rising productivity based on imported capital and technology. The governments placed a high priority on secondary education in order to improve human capital and on improved infrastructure in order to make transportation and communications networks more efficient. Export-oriented government policies lowered trade barriers for the purchase of raw materials and fostered competition in order to improve efficiency and reduce prices. Budgetary restraint limited the need to print money and kept inflation in check, bolstering investor confidence. Stable prices and government encouragement prompted high household savings rates. Finally, exchange rates were managed so as to avoid sustained overvaluations of the Asian currencies and to promote investment from abroad. Several of the "Asian Tiger" economies were also revved up by cheap credit and, as the Solow model would suggest, vast inflows of foreign capital.

Partly motivated by the economic growth in East Asia, economists Paul Romer, Robert Lucas, Sergio Rebelo, and others developed a new model, dubbed the *endogenous growth model,* in the late 1980s and early 1990s.[22] In contrast to Solow's model, which holds that technological change is determined by forces outside the economy, this model treats the level of technology as *endogenous*, meaning that it is determined within the economic system. For example, private investment in research and development could hasten technical progress. Government policies could assist in that process by promoting education and training programs that build human capital and by providing patents and protecting property rights so that those who innovate and increase the productivity of capital and labor could reap greater rewards.

There is contention over the root cause of Asia's rapid growth. In 1994, economist Paul Krugman wrote an essay called "The Myth of the Asian Miracle," in which he suggested that the growth was the result of increases in the quantities of labor and capital inputs and not because of higher productivity of these inputs, the latter being necessary for sustained economic growth. As predicted, the Asian economic miracle lost its momentum in the mid- to late 1990s when inadequate bank regulation, cronyism, sliding exchange rates, and slow government responses to these problems dealt a blow to the rapid accumulation of capital. As Krugman had posited, existing productivity growth could not compensate for the waning flow of capital. The details of the downturn in Asian economies are outside the scope of this chapter, but the point is that developing nations can indeed become developed nations, regardless of whether they can sustain a rapid rate of growth in the long run.

WHY CAN'T MORE MONEY SOLVE ALL THE PROBLEMS?

Money alone is not the missing piece for a poor, isolated nation aspiring to prosperity. Consider the tiny island of Barbareta off the coast of Honduras, on which there are coconut palms, fish, firewood, and very few people—for simplicity, let's imagine there are only 3. Suppose that by specializing, the first islander can catch enough fish to feed 3 people for a day, the second can harvest enough coconut milk to provide a

---

[22] See http://economics.about.com/cs/economicsglossary/g/endogenous_g.htm.

day's beverages for 3 people, and the third can collect enough firewood for 1 day's cooking and heating fires for 3 people. With no money, the 3 islanders could make in-kind trades for what they want from each other, as long as each wants what the others have.

Money provides convenience as a medium of exchange, a store of value, and a unit of account, as discussed in Chapter 22. With 2 shells apiece that served as money, each islander could purchase the items made by the other 2 for 1 shell per item, and in the end each would have 2 shells again. It is rumored that the notorious buccaneer Sir Henry Morgan buried treasure on the string of islands that includes Barbareta.[23] If our 3 islanders discovered Morgan's buried treasure worth, say, $6 million, they would be "wealthy," with $2 million apiece, but they would not necessarily be better off. Having more money with which to purchase the same goods, they would each simply be able to pay more for their daily rations—up to $1 million per unit of fish, coconuts, or firewood—but this would create nothing but inflation.

This approach, of introducing more money into the equation, has been tried. In Bolivia in 1985 and in Hungary in 1946, for example, the governments printed large amounts of money in attempts to remedy financial crises. The end result was hyperinflation that in Bolivia amounted to 12,000 percent in 1985 and in Hungary reached a height of 200 percent *per day* in July of 1946.[24] Development does not spring from more money chasing the same amount of goods and services. As another example, on the classic situation comedy *Gilligan's Island*, Thurston Howell, III's, suitcases of money couldn't get the marooned characters off a tropical island because, despite all the cash, they simply had no boat.[25] Rather than looking for buried treasure, the Barbareta islanders should focus on improving their production levels and establishing international trade agreements with countries that can supply what the islanders desire, be it food, health care, or a small yacht on which to flee the island. Solving the mystery of income inequality is thus a matter of explaining why poor countries can't make more stuff or improve their prospects for international trade.

CONCLUSION

Keeping in mind the caveats expressed in Chapter 27 about good and bad coming from outside influences and in Chapter 21 about how GDP growth can differ from improvements in social well-being, economists have much to say about recipes for economic development. Under the right conditions, investors would earn higher returns on capital where availability is sparse, and poor countries, therefore, would receive more capital and grow faster than rich ones. However, these conditions include adequacy in the areas of governance, education systems, entrepreneurialism, savings rates, population growth, and inflation control, not to mention compatible cultural, religious, and trade practices. The convergence of income levels predicted by neoclassical economic models is impeded in practice because many poor countries don't meet these conditions.

International aid and the forgiveness of debt can offer short-term relief, but they seldom provide long-term solutions. The eradication of agonizing poverty requires a

[23] See www.roatanonline.com/moreroatan/roatan_treasure.htm.
[24] See www.econlib.org/library/Enc/Hyperinflation.html.
[25] See www.gilligansisle.com/thurston.html.

confluence of changes, considerable time, and care to sidestep the pitfalls of corruption and exploitation. Economist David Landes summed up the chronology of advances in Britain's development this way: "Institutions and culture first; money [for capital investments] next; but from the beginning and increasingly the payoff was to knowledge."[26] Economic growth stems chiefly from improvements in human and physical capital in an environment that is conducive to development.

DISCUSSION STARTERS

1. Consider again the story of Barbareta Island. For each of the following scenarios, explain how you would expect the outcome for the three inhabitants to differ from the original outcome:
   a. One of the islanders found the treasure alone, thus obtaining $6 million for himself.
   b. The treasure chest is filled with cans of tuna fish, which the islanders divide evenly.
   c. The treasure chest contains only a saw, a solar oven, and a spear gun.

2. Luxembourg, the United States, Norway, and Bermuda have the highest levels of GDP per capita of all the countries in the world: between $40,000 and $60,000 per year. On the basis of what you know about these countries, why do you suppose this is true? What might they have going for them?

3. East Timor, Somalia, Sierra Leone, and the Gaza Strip have the world's lowest levels of GDP per capita: between $500 and $600, 1/100 the level of the richest country. What might explain such low production levels? What specific steps would you, as the leader of these countries, take to effect change?

4. Research at Abdou Moumouni University (AMU) in Niger is reportedly hampered by the lack of a communications network.[27] Suppose the McDonald's Corporation wants to invest in a new computer network for one university that is looking into lower-fat substances in which to fry food and that scholars at both your school and AMU are working on the project. Under what assumptions would McDonald's be better off investing in a network at AMU? How does this question relate to the issue of convergence according to the Solow growth model?

[26] *The Wealth and Poverty of Nations: Why Some Are So Rich and Some So Poor* (New York: W. W. Norton, 1998), p. 276.
[27] See www.bc.edu/bc_org/avp/soe/cihe/inhea/profiles/Niger.htm.

CHAPTER 29

POLLUTION: HOW MIGHT ECONOMICS HELP SAVE THE PLANET?

Cap-and-Trade Programs as a Market Solution to Problems Large and Small

Scarcity is the central problem of economics. In our pursuit of happiness, we have too few of virtually everything beneficial—hours in a day, gallons of oil, corner dorm rooms, printing privileges on campus computers—to satisfy our desires. We also have too few of the natural repositories for pollution known as *environmental sinks*. As with a kitchen sink, society can send only a certain amount of "gunk" into an environmental sink before trouble arises. Pollution in limited quantities can be diluted in water, dispersed into air, or absorbed into body fat or soil before problems occur. And by a process called *carbon sequestration*, oceans and vegetation absorb carbon dioxide (CO_2), release the oxygen (O), and store the carbon (C). To deal with scarcity issues, governments could divvy up goods more or less equally and place standard caps on things such as printing and polluting, but the solutions would be inefficient. English majors may value printing privileges more than economics majors do, and power utilities whose plants cannot easily be retrofitted with emissions-reducing scrubbers value the right to pollute more than newer, cleaner plants do. Markets provide alternative mechanisms for allocating scarce goods and services to those who value them the most. This chapter explains how unconventional markets can provide solutions to many of society's most serious scarcity problems.

THE BIG PROBLEMS

Along with the delights of indoor climate control, electricity, motorized transportation, and manufactured goods come the evils of pollution. Industries in the United States release about 4.4 billion pounds of toxic chemicals into the air and water each year,[1] and the Environmental Protection Agency (EPA) recently found 474 counties in 31 states, home to 159 million Americans, out of compliance with its health-based 8-hour ozone pollution standards.[2] The value and proper implementation of policies to limit pollution depend on the type and severity of the problems. This section provides perspectives on some of the pressing environmental issues of the twenty-first century.

Global Climate Change

Global climate change has become *the* hot topic among environmentalists who argue that it should be on everyone's plate of concerns that deserve attention. The so-called greenhouse gases, including carbon dioxide, methane, and nitrogen oxide, hold heat within the earth's atmosphere and keep it about 33°C (59°F) warmer than it would otherwise be. Since the Industrial Revolution, atmospheric concentrations of carbon dioxide have risen by about 28 percent, methane concentrations have more than doubled, and nitrogen oxide concentrations have risen by about 15 percent. These trends, with a debated mix of human and natural causes, may be to blame for the reported 0.5°C to 1.0°C increase in global temperatures during the past century. The 10 warmest years in that period have all occurred since 1985. Global warming has already thinned the snow cover in the Northern Hemisphere and the floating ice in the Arctic Ocean, increased the volume and intensity of rainfall in the United States, and raised the sea level by 4 to 8 inches during the past century.[3]

Continuing changes in the global climate and ensuing alterations in soil moisture, sea level, and weather patterns threaten the health and welfare of life on earth. Ecosystems and agriculture are sensitive to climate change, and densely populated coastal regions could be submerged by rising sea levels. For access to the ships that brought delicacies from afar and picked up goods to sell elsewhere, many of the world's largest cities were built near the sea. Venice and New Orleans are famous examples of cities that already must battle to remain above water. With such high stakes, regardless of whether humans are causing global climate change, it is likely that the benefit exceeds the cost for some finite level of pollution limits that work against it.

Acid Rain

Acid rain and its wind-borne cousin, dry acid deposition, result primarily from sulfur dioxide and nitrous oxides released from coal-fired power plants, motor vehicles, and various types of industry. In these forms, acid is deadly to plants, animals, and humans, and damaging to buildings and automobiles. Soil acidity affects the ability of plants to absorb nutrients, and increases in acidity can mortally starve forests. Beyond its direct toxicity, acid causes the release of copper, aluminum, and mercury

---

[1] See the EPA's Toxic Release Inventory at www.epa.gov/tri/tridata/tri03/brochure.htm.
[2] See http://epa.gov/region6/6ra/air_pc_041504.htm.
[3] See http://yosemite.epa.gov/oar/globalwarming.nsf/content/Climate.html.

from rocks and pipes that would otherwise retain those metals. Acid rain presents an externality problem (as discussed in Chapter 11) because much of the damage occurs far from the causal sources. Dead trees and lifeless lakes in Canada and Norway are attributed to sulfur dioxide emissions from the United States and central Europe, respectively. Although the United States emits 6 times as much sulfur dioxide as Canada, the Environment Canada agency reports 95,000 lakes that will remain damaged even after planned acid rain control programs are fully implemented.[4] And the EPA reports that decreases in fatalities, hospital admissions, and emergency room visits in the United States will bring annual health benefits from the ongoing Acid Rain Program to $50 billion by 2010.[5]

Water Pollution

Water pollution provides the last example of an environmental problem that may deserve careful attention from economists and policymakers. Industrial waste and sewage find their way directly into bodies of water,[6] and pesticides, fertilizers, and gaseous emissions from vehicles and factories are washed into waterways by precipitation. A *watershed* is a land area that catches rain and snow and "sheds," or drains, that water into surface waterways or groundwater. Fifteen percent of U.S. watersheds have "relatively good" water quality; 36 percent have "moderate problems"; 22 percent have "more serious water quality problems"; and 27 percent cannot be characterized because of insufficient information. Another 7 percent of watersheds are considered "highly vulnerable" to degradation below their current levels.[7]

All these pollution threats challenge the creativity of policymakers. The next section describes innovative approaches to a variety of problems, big and small, environmental and otherwise.

MARKET SOLUTIONS

Chapter 6 explained that markets can serve efficiency goals by bringing goods and services to those who value them the most. For example, markets deliver the 1,504 tickets for each night's Broadway production of *Spamalot*[8] to the 1,504 people who value them the most and thus are willing to pay the most for them—an outcome that could not be expected from a ticket lottery among all those who placed any value on seeing *Spamalot* or from a government allotment based on chance or politics.

The efficiency of markets can be tapped by putting more kinds of goods and services up for sale. Dorm rooms, for example, are typically allocated by a lottery that does not necessarily deliver particular rooms to the students who cherish them the most. A more efficient solution would be to auction off dorm rooms. If the corner dorm room on the second floor was worth $100 more to you than to anyone else,

---

[4] See www.ec.gc.ca/acidrain/acidfact.html.
[5] See www.cpa.gov/airmarkets/acidrain/effects/health.html.
[6] For example, in 2006, 48 million gallons of raw sewage flowed into waterways near Waikiki Beach in Honolulu, Hawaii. See http://starbulletin.com/2006/03/31/news/story01.html.
[7] See www.epa.gov/305b/.
[8] *Spamalot*, winner of the 2005 Tony Award for the best musical, is based on the movie *Monty Python and the Holy Grail*.

you would be able to bid a penny more than the next-highest bidder and capture those benefits for yourself. The $100 worth of additional benefits you received from that room wouldn't be created under a lottery system that gave the room to someone else. Similar efficiency gains can be captured by selling the best parking spaces, faculty offices, and other goods to the highest bidder. Concerns about advantages for wealthy bidders can be allayed by allowing people to "purchase" the items with community service hours, high grades, or weeks of perfect attendance. (Of course, wealthy individuals have the same advantage in traditional markets; approaches to income inequality are discussed in Chapter 28.)

Traditional *command-and-control* pollution regulations require uniform reductions or specific technology applications across all sources of pollution. This approach presents problems because there is disparity in the ability of polluters to comply with the regulations, and once they do, they have no further incentive to reduce pollution levels. For example, EPA regulation 40 CFR 63 limits mercury emissions from existing industrial boilers to 10 micrograms per dry standard cubic meter.[9] This rule might be easy for some plants to obey and impossible for others, depending on their age and the adaptability of their equipment. For this common type of dilemma, economic reasoning points to another breed of market solutions: *cap-and-trade* programs.

Cap-and-trade programs were adopted in the United States in 1995 to address the acid rain problem. The Acid Rain Program sets a limit, or "cap," on the quantity of sulfur dioxide (SO_2) that can be released from regulated sources, such as power utilities. Existing polluters then receive a certain number of "allowances," each granting the right to emit 1 ton of SO_2. Total emissions are gradually reduced by granting fewer allowances each year. From a starting point of 17.5 million tons of SO_2 emissions from U.S. electric power utilities in 1980, annual caps are set to decline to 8.95 million tons by the year 2010.[10] The trading of pollution allowances is similar to that of stocks, and sulfur dioxide allowances can be purchased from allowance brokers or at an annual EPA auction conducted by the Chicago Board of Trade.[11]

Allowing firms to buy and sell a decreasing number of pollution allowances results in a more efficient division of pollution rights and a lower overall volume of pollution. With this special market in place, each ton of SO_2 emissions either requires the purchase of another allowance or represents the lost opportunity to sell an allowance to another firm. Regardless of a firm's allowance holdings and emissions level, if further reductions can be made for less than the cost of allowances, the incentive exists to reduce emissions and sell more, or buy fewer, allowances. The market-clearing price in the 2005 auction was $690, and 125,000 allowances were sold. Ameren Energy Generating Co. topped the list of big buyers with a purchase of 40,000 allowances. Among the other successful bidders were the Acid Rain Retirement Fund and environmental groups at Bates, Colby, Hobart, and William Smith Colleges and Cornell University.

Emissions trading programs have three primary benefits:

1. **Flexibility and creativity:** Trading programs make it possible for overall pollution targets to be met while allowing individual firms to satisfy their require-

[9] See www.epa.gov/docs/epacfr40/chapt-I.info/.
[10] See www.epa.gov/airmarkets/trading/basics/.
[11] See www.epa.gov/airmarkets/trading/buying.html.

ments via creative conservation methods, new technology, alternative energy sources, lower-sulfur coal, or the purchase of allowances—whichever is the most feasible and affordable approach for a particular firm. Economists estimate that compliance with command-and-control policies that limit the amount of SO_2 each electric power company can emit cost the utilities more than twice as much as cap-and-trade programs that achieve the same overall level of emissions.[12]

2. **Efficient distribution of pollution rights:** Firms that gain the most from polluting a lot, whether because pollution reductions would be particularly difficult for them or because they produce a highly valued good, can purchase allowances from firms that can more easily reduce their emissions or make goods of lower value.

3. **Incentives for reductions beyond stipulated levels:** Whenever emissions can be cut for less than the market price of allowances, firms have an incentive to make the cuts. That way they can increase their sales or reduce their purchases of allowances. If the market price of an allowance is $500 and a firm can cut emissions by 1,000 tons by spending $400,000 on an emissions scrubber upgrade, they will gain ($500 × 1,000) − $400,000 = $100,000 by making the cut even if they are not using all their allowances because they can sell 1,000 additional allowances in the market.

APPLICATIONS AND PITFALLS

There is no end to the possible applications of tradable allowances. Cap-and-trade programs are currently in place or in the works for sulfur dioxide and nitrogen oxide in California,[13] for sulfur dioxide at the national level, and for carbon dioxide at the national and international levels.[14] Articles 6, 12, and 17 of the 1997 Kyoto Protocol on Climate Change implement emissions trading on a global scale.[15] In the United States, cap-and-trade policies under the Clear Skies Act will reduce greenhouse gas emissions by 18 percent over 10 years. Regarding water pollution, the discharge prohibitions under the Clean Water Act require a permit for the release of designated substances, and the EPA is considering effluent-trading programs for National Pollutant Discharge Elimination System permit holders.

Cap-and-trade programs aren't only for pollution. In the wake of overfishing problems, the National Fisheries Conservation Center reports that tradable permits in the form of *individual transferable quotas* (ITQs) have benefited both fish and fishers.[16] Unlike traditional command-and-control fishing regulations that limit the excursion frequency, crew size, or gear used on fishing boats, ITQs provide the flexibility and incentives of tradable emissions allowances while protecting vulnerable fishing areas. Fishers receive quotas for the volume of fish they can catch, and if their actual catch

---

[12] See www.rff.org/Documents/RFF-DP-00-38.pdf and Curtis Carlson, Dallas Burtraw, Maureen Cropper, and Karen Palmer, "SO_2 Control by Electric Utilities: What Are the Gains from Trade?" *Journal of Political Economy* (2000), *108*:6, pp. 1292–1326.

[13] See www.epa.gov/airmarkets/trading/basics/.

[14] See www.cbo.gov/showdoc.cfm?index=2876&sequence=0.

[15] See http://unfcc.int/resource/docs/convkp/kpeng.html.

[16] See www.nfcc-fisheries.org/ir_pov_c19.html.

falls below the level of their quotas, they can sell their unused ITQs to others who place a higher value on those fishing rights. As another possible application of tradable allowances, in 2002, the National Research Council's Committee on the Effectiveness and Impact of Corporate Average Fuel Economy (CAFE) Standards recommended the adoption of tradable fuel-economy credits for automakers.[17]

Tradable allowances also offer a way to distribute printing privileges efficiently on college campuses. At Centre College, as on other campuses, students can print out 500 pages on school printers without charge. This is great for students who don't have an overabundance of long papers but inadequate for students who do. Imagine if printing rights were tradable. Then chemistry majors, who can easily conserve paper, would have an incentive to do so, enabling the sale of extra printing rights to classics majors.

As with all such programs, allowance trading faces challenges. It may be less successful at the international level than within nations because of monitoring difficulties and the barriers of culture, language, and distance. Some people fear that the focus on developing new emissions-trading systems will distract from efforts to address the root causes of pollution, including immoderate consumption and inefficient transportation systems.[18] Even well-functioning policies to enforce emissions targets are only as good as the choice of those targets. The EPA and analogous agencies in other countries face the contentious task of selecting pollution standards. In this type of policymaking, the tools of cost–benefit analysis and ethical decision making are susceptible to influence by politics, emotions, and imperfect information.[19]

CONCLUSION

Solutions to the problems of scarcity are at hand if we allow the efficient characteristics of markets to work in unconventional ways. The splendor of cap-and-trade programs is that they serve the interests of environmentalists and free-market advocates at the same time. President George W. Bush says that a cap-and-trade program "cuts pollution further, faster, cheaper, and with more certainty, . . . replacing a cycle of endless litigation with rapid and certain improvements in air quality."[20] Liberal ecological economist Herman Daly describes cap-and-trade programs as "a beautiful example of the independence and proper relationship among allocation, distribution, and scale."[21] It isn't often that these two fellows are on the same side of an issue; they agree on this, however, with good reason. Cap-and-trade programs allow flexibility and creativity in pollution reduction, allocate pollution rights to those who get the most value from them, and provide incentives for reductions below individual plant limits, while constraining activities to the level deemed appropriate by authorities.

Market solutions can be applied to problems that threaten life as we know it—problems that we are otherwise far from resolving. They can also solve problems on cam-

[17] This committee's report is available at www.nap.edu/books/0309076013/html/. See, for example, Finding 11 on page 113.
[18] See, for example, www.oneworld.org/ips2/Dec98/07_14_005.html.
[19] For perspectives on ethical and emotional arguments, see http://ecoethics.net/hsev/newscience/200012b-res.htm.
[20] See http://www.whitehouse.gov/news/releases/2002/02/20020214.html.
[21] In *Beyond Growth: The Economics of Sustainable Development* (Boston: Beacon Press, 1996), p. 52.

pus, at the office, or in the household. If someday you have kids who have an unequal availability of free time, you might assign them equal sets of chores but allow them to buy chore transfers from each other. That way, if one has an alternative activity worth $10 and another would pick up the slack for $5, the busier kid can transfer the chore for a payment of, say, $8, and the budding capitalists would both be happier than before.[22] If someday you're the leader of a country and you need to limit the use of toxic pesticides without nixing their most beneficial applications, you can divide the total acceptable quantity by the number of acres of agricultural land and then grant each farmer pesticide allowances for the resulting quantity per acre. Those who can most easily use organic farming methods will conserve on pesticide and sell their allowances to those who get the most out of them. If you think outside the box when applying these tools, you'll probably increase efficiency, and you just might save the world.

DISCUSSION STARTERS

1. Summarize the general pros and cons of market-based and command-and-control approaches to limiting toxic emissions.

2. Suppose that the market price for emissions allowances remains at $690, your local power utility has an ample supply of unused allowances, and it can reduce its SO_2 emissions by 1 ton at a cost of $650.
   a. Should the utility reduce its emissions? Why or why not?
   b. How does your answer change if it costs the utility $700 to reduce its emissions by 1 ton?
   c. How do your answers to parts (a) and (b) change if the power utility has already used all its allowances?

3. The chapter describes several unconventional applications of market-based solutions, including tradable allowances. Can you think of some more? Remember, think outside the box.

4. Some caps on activities can be difficult to enforce. If it is hard to monitor a farm in order to determine how much pesticide the farmer has sprayed on her crop, how else might the cap be enforced? Hint: Think about how the use of antibiotics is monitored.

5. Suppose that your dorm instituted a market for room selections. If you were willing to pay $100 more than anyone else for the corner room on the second floor and the market price for that room (beyond the standard room rate) was $100, would it still be more efficient to have the room-selection market rather than a room lottery? What, in this case, is the net gain to society from the market solution?

[22] Note that this might not be the most efficient outcome if there are positive externalities from each kid learning to work hard at household chores.

CHAPTER 30

IMMIGRATION: HOW WELCOMING SHOULD LADY LIBERTY BE?
The Costs and Benefits of Relatively Open Borders

Give me your tired, your poor,
Your huddled masses yearning to breathe free,
The wretched refuse of your teeming shore.
Send these, the homeless, tempest-tossed, to me:
I lift my lamp beside the golden door.

From "The New Colossus" by Emma Lazarus (1883)

INTRODUCTION

These words, emblazoned at the base of the Statue of Liberty, remind us that the United States is a proud nation of immigrants, whereas the terrorist attacks of September 11, 2001, confirmed that its relatively open borders have costs as well as benefits. Since 1820, more than 70 million immigrants have entered the United States. Foreign-born individuals make up 11 percent of the United States's population, 14 percent of its workforce, 23.7 percent of its doctors,[1] 2.3 percent of its prison inmates,[2] and 15.1 percent of its unemployed.[3] Immigration issues are complex, and entire books are devoted to relevant details that must be omitted here, but this chapter provides an overview of the pros and cons of immigration and of policies to limit the number of immigrants who will be greeted by what Lazarus describes as Lady Liberty's "beacon-hand" of "world-wide welcome."

[1] See www.ama-assn.org/ama/pub/category/211.html.
[2] See www.ojp.usdoj.gov/bjs/pub/ascii/pjim03.txt.
[3] See www.nupr.neu.edu/3-03/immigration_march.pdf.

ARGUMENTS AGAINST IMMIGRATION

Criticism of immigration centers on the drawbacks of population growth, competition for jobs, and overburdened public assistance programs. Although the birthrate among native-born Americans is about 13 per 1,000 people per year, the average among immigrants is 28 per 1,000.[4] Some fear the threat to the status quo posed by immigrants with different social values, languages, and cultures. Anti-immigration sentiment has buoyed support for like-minded political parties in Austria, the Netherlands, Italy, Denmark, France, and Australia. The mix of French- and English-speaking immigrants in Canada has compelled the adoption of bilingual education programs for children and laws that require labels in both French and English on all products.[5] The prospect of similar measures to serve the growing number of Spanish speakers in the United States is met with resistance.[6]

Rapid mass migration, like the flood of emigrants from Europe to North America that took place between 1870 and 1913, can provoke nationalism and increase competition for resources. The Carrying Capacity Network (CCN) considers the current level of immigration into the United States to be "immense," listing among the repercussions traffic congestion, air pollution, water and energy shortages, overcrowded schools, declines in purchasing power, a lower quality of life, tax increases, and soil erosion.[7] These claims are arguable but come from respected sources. The board of the CCN includes such celebrated environmentalists and ecological economists as L. Hunter Lovins, Herman E. Daly, and Robert Costanza.

Despite expenditures of $16 billion annually on border and transportation security,[8] an estimated 8 million illegal immigrants live in the United States, and that number grows by about 500,000 per year.[9] Illegal immigrants place additional stress on budgets for schools, medical care, public transportation, criminal justice systems, and public infrastructure. The burden of illegal immigrants falls disproportionately on border states, most notably California and Florida. The Federation for American Immigration Reform (FAIR) estimates that $1.83 billion is spent per year in Florida on the education, health care, and incarceration of illegal immigrants and their children.[10] The same immigrants pay $920 million in taxes, for a net cost of $910 million per year.

FAIR provides estimates of immigration-related impacts in nonborder states as well. Consider what FAIR identifies as some of the environmental and quality-of-life impacts of immigration in Ohio:

■ **Population:** In 2000, foreign-born residents made up 339,000 of the state's 11.4 million population, and immigration created 16 percent of the state's population growth in the 1990s.

---

[4] See www.fairus.org/site/PageServer?pagename=iic_immigrationissuecenters7d78.
[5] See www.mac.doc.gov/nafta/7602.htm.
[6] See http://spanish.about.com/library/weekly/aa110502a.htm.
[7] See www.carryingcapacity.org.
[8] See www.whitehouse.gov/omb/budget/fy2006/dhs.html.
[9] See www.cis.org/topics/illegalimmigration.html.
[10] See www.fairus.org/site/PageServer?pagename=research_flcoststudy_html.

■ **Traffic:** The average commute in Ohio increased by 11 percent during the 1990s, from 21 to 23 minutes. Traffic congestion causes the loss of an estimated 250 million hours of Ohio motorists' time each year.

■ **Open space:** Development claims 73,000 acres of open space in Ohio each year.

■ **Housing:** There are 74,000 households in Ohio designated as severely crowded by U.S. Census Bureau standards, and the price of homes rose 30 percent between 1995 and 2001.

■ **Air pollution:** Electricity utilities serving Ohio produce about 375,000 tons of nitrogen oxide per year, the equivalent of the emissions from 19 million automobiles.

■ **Poverty:** Fourteen percent of Ohio's immigrants and 19 percent of its noncitizen immigrants live below the poverty level. The ample availability of low-skilled immigrant workers depresses wages in the state.

■ **Education:** Elementary and high school enrollments increased by 6 percent between 1990 and 2000, and schools in Cincinnati and Columbus face overcrowded conditions, including the use of trailer classrooms.

Visit www.fairus.org to see FAIR's summary of immigration-related problems in your state.

About 80 percent of immigrants have less education than the average American and earn correspondingly lower wages. Lower household incomes mean greater reliance on social services, including welfare and food stamps. Current legislation prevents immigrants from collecting food stamps for at least 5 years after entry into the United States, and immigrants can't collect Supplemental Security Income (SSI) from the federal government until they achieve citizenship, which takes at least 5 years.[11] However, there are exceptions for immigrant children within the food stamp program, and most immigrants have been in the country for more than 5 years. U.S. immigration policy caters to potential immigrants with family connections, to refugees, and to workers who have been invited by U.S. employers. An alternative would be to follow the lead of Canada, Australia, and New Zealand by placing more weight on the economic potential of workers and less on family connections when selecting visa recipients. This would place a lighter burden on social services and bring in more workers ready to contribute to gross domestic product.

ARGUMENTS FOR IMMIGRATION

The first human inhabitants of North America are thought to have crossed a land bridge from present-day Russia to Alaska roughly 50,000 years ago.[12] The first Europeans crossed the Atlantic about 1001. Thus, every American is either an immigrant or a descendant of immigrants, without whom the benefits of this great melting pot of ideas, customs, and productivity would be unrealized.

[11] See http://aspe.hhs.gov/hsp/immigration/restrictions-sum.htm.
[12] See www.cnn.com/2004/TECH/science/11/17/carolina.dig/.

Foreign-born workers are to thank for more than half of the U.S. job growth between 2000 and 2003[13] and for more than 90 percent of the job growth in 16 states between 1996 and 2000.[14] Consider Charlie Woo, who emigrated from Hong Kong to the United States in 1968 to pursue an education and a new life. In 1979, he opened a toy wholesaling business in what the Los Angeles Community Development Agency considered a "dead warehouse district."[15] Woo's Megatoys company became the centerpiece of Toytown, the business district that now employs 4,000 workers and earns $500 million in annual revenues. Entrepreneurial immigrants such as Woo bring new ideas, energy, and jobs to the marketplace. Immigrants also fill jobs in rural locations where labor is scarce and in low-paying blue-collar industries, such as textile manufacturing, meatpacking, poultry processing, and crop harvesting, that go largely unfilled by U.S. citizens. In so doing, they contribute to U.S. growth and prosperity.

In many ways immigration represents an ideal source of labor. Beyond providing hard work for low pay, immigrant workers tend to respond to market forces by supplying their services when and where they are most needed. There is evidence that the supply of both legal and illegal immigration fluctuates with business cycles. The Homeland Security Department's Office of Immigration Statistics reports that the number of people caught attempting to cross the southwestern border between the United States and Mexico increased by about 50 percent during the prosperous late 1990s and fell sharply during the recession of the early 2000s. The flow of working-age immigrants into the country also assists "pay-as-you-go" entitlement programs, such as Social Security and Medicare, which collect from current workers to pay for current retirees. Immigration policies such as the H-1B visa program,[16] which admits immigrants who can fill positions for which no available U.S. citizen qualifies, lower the average age of the U.S. population and increase the proportion of people who are working and paying taxes rather than receiving benefits from entitlement programs.[17]

Economists Rachel Friedberg and Jennifer Hunt studied the effects of immigration on host countries and found no evidence of economically significant reductions in employment among native-born workers.[18] These researchers also concluded that a 10 percent increase in a country's share of immigrants reduces wages for natives by, at most, 1 percent. Alan Greenspan, former chair of the Federal Reserve, sees immigration as beneficial, saying that "unless immigration is uncapped . . . the continuous reduction in the number of available workers willing to take jobs . . . would intensify inflationary pressures or squeeze profit margins, with either outcome capable of bringing our growing prosperity to an end."[19] Working in tandem, labor force growth and

---

[13] See www.eurekalert.org/pub_releases/2004-01/nu-nia010804.php.

[14] Abraham T. Mosisa, Bureau of Labor Statistics, *Monthly Labor Review*, May 2002. Available on-line at www.bls.gov/opub/mlr/2002/05/contents.htm.

[15] See www.aworldconnected.org/article.php/300.html.

[16] For details on the H-1B visa program, see www.uscis.gov/graphics/howdoi/h1b.htm. It is also discussed again later in this chapter.

[17] See www.census.gov/prod/2004pubs/p20-551.pdf for statistics on the age of foreign-born and native-born residents. Among the foreign-born there are relatively few children and elderly individuals.

[18] "The Impact of Immigrants on Host Country Wages, Employment, and Growth," *Journal of Economic Perspectives*, Spring 1995, pp. 23–44.

[19] See www.bc.edu/bc_org/mvp/fincon/greenspanspeech.html.

productivity growth allow an economy to grow faster with less inflation, thereby reducing the Fed's need to curtail inflation by raising interest rates and slowing growth.

Harvard economist George Borjas notes that lower wages as the result of immigration need not be a problem at all. Because low wages increase profits for firms and lower prices for consumers, he writes, "If these gains are much larger than the reduction in earnings suffered by less-skilled workers, it should be possible to set up a redistribution scheme that makes everyone in the United States better off."[20] Borjas estimates that immigration into the United States depresses wages by $152 billion annually but increases profits by $160 billion.[21] In theory at least, we could use taxes and transfer programs, such as food stamps and welfare programs, to redistribute some of the gains from corporate profit earners to workers who bear the brunt—primarily those who lack high school diplomas.[22]

The pace of immigration reform changed with the terrorist attacks of 2001. Entry by temporary immigrants became more difficult, and ongoing efforts to liberalize immigration were tabled. This included President George W. Bush's proposed guest-worker program to legalize the status of about 4 million unauthorized Mexican workers in the United States. Also suspended was a proposed increase in the number of H-1B visas granted to skilled immigrant workers each year. The H-1B visa is a 3-year, once-renewable permit for foreign professionals hired by U.S. employers. In 2001, the number of such visas was temporarily raised from 115,000 to 195,000 but then reverted to the 1992 level of 65,000 visas.[23] In 2004, President Bush renewed his call for immigration reform, proposing a new temporary visa to legalize the status of 10 million unauthorized workers and a liberalization of policies for invited H-1B workers and temporary workers seeking permanent resident status.

In the wake of the 9/11 terrorist attacks, a wave of legislation related to immigration was enacted: the USA Patriot Act,[24] the Enhanced Border Security Act,[25] and the Homeland Security Act.[26] By increasing the cost and difficulty of entering the country, these laws provide a glimpse of the effects of more restricted immigration. Groups claiming damage from the new procedures include U.S. companies trying to attract customers from overseas, refugees seeking asylum from oppressive regimes, and educational institutions trying to capitalize on the United States's reputation for academic excellence. Universities are among the institutions that must consider complex visa issues when trying to hire the best employees and attract the best students. Stricter requirements helped reduce the number of student visas issued in the United States from 299,000 in 2001 to 220,000 in 2003. In 2003, the number of refugees resettled in the United States also fell to a 25-year low of about 28,000, and in 2004 it remained below the Bush administration's goal of 70,000 per year.[27]

[20] See www.slate.com/id/2346/entry/2110392/.

[21] See *Heaven's Door: Immigration Policy and the American Economy* (Princeton, NJ: Princeton University Press, 2001).

[22] See www.cis.org/articles/1998/sacPublicInterest.html.

[23] See http://uscis.gov/graphics/services/tempbenefits/cap.htm.

[24] See www.epic.org/privacy/terrorism/usapatriot/.

[25] See www.house.gov/judiciary_democrats/hr3205secbysec.pdf.

[26] See www.whitehouse.gov/deptofhomeland/analysis/.

[27] See www.refugeesinternational.org/content/article/detail/1141/.

As for the burden that immigration places on the border states, a line must be drawn between legal and illegal immigration. Although $910 million may be spent in Florida on illegal immigrants (net of their tax payments), this is not a reason to criticize policies for legal immigration. Illegal immigrants have violated U.S. law, and solutions necessarily involve law enforcement. One relevant question is whether the costs of expanded efforts to patrol the borders exceed the benefits, but reform in law enforcement is a separate issue for another book. Border states absorb much of the expense of educating immigrant children, but as explained in Chapter 28, investments in education are a primary determinant of the productivity and wealth of a region. Thus, Florida's $1.51 billion expenditure on the education of illegal immigrants is likely to contribute significantly to the state's $500 billion share of gross domestic product.

Immigrants don't simply fill a need for blue-collar workers. They also help remedy the severe shortage of medical personnel, particularly in rural areas. The U.S. Department of Health and Human Services estimates that the demand for health-care professionals currently exceeds the supply by 126,000 nurses, 16,000 doctors, 8,500 dentists, and 4,000 mental health workers.[28] The American Immigration Law Foundation (AILF) points out that the "enhanced use of immigration policy" would further ease these shortages.[29] At present, according to the AILF, 1.1 million immigrants account for 13 percent of health-care providers in the United States, including one-quarter of all physicians; 17 percent of nursing, psychiatric, and home health aides; 15.8 percent of clinical laboratory technicians; 14.8 percent of pharmacists; and 11.5 percent of registered nurses.

SORTING OUT THE CLAIMS

Perhaps the best way to sort fact from fiction in the debate over immigration is to weigh the claims against theory and evidence. Despite immigration in record numbers, U.S. crime rates have declined markedly during the past 25 years[30] and the standard of living has remained among the highest in the world by virtually every measure.[31] The U.S. unemployment rate hovers around a low of 5 percent, indicating that immigrant workers are creating jobs or filling labor needs.

Economic theory and data support the contention that ample supplies of manual labor suppress wages for low-skilled jobs. The relative lack of interest among U.S.-born workers in migrant agricultural work and other forms of unpleasant manual labor diminishes the harm to natives, as suggested by the Friedberg and Hunt research mentioned previously. The concurrent benefits are enjoyed by producers and consumers of food, clothing, and other critical goods and services that low-skilled workers provide, and by immigrants, who would generally earn less in their home countries.

Pollution and stresses on natural resources do indeed grow with population, but remember that immigration is a transfer of people from one place to another, not a source of population growth for the planet. The most serious pollution problems, including

[28] See www.ailf.org/ipc/ipf031104.asp.
[29] See www.ailf.org/pubed/healthcare.shtml.
[30] See crime rates per 100,000 population at www.disastercenter.com/crime/uscrime.htm.
[31] See http://en.wikipedia.org/wiki/Standard_of_living_in_the_United_States.

climate change, acid deposition, and ozone depletion, are global problems, and it makes little difference where the pollutants are released. The depletion of natural resources is likewise a global problem, although immigrants who adopt the American lifestyle will use more resources, but have fewer children,[32] than do people in the countries from which most immigrants come—Mexico, China, India, the Philippines, and the Dominican Republic. If we so desire, the productivity gains[33] and the sharing of ideas achieved with immigration will allow us to devote more funds and better policymaking efforts to the ubiquitous issues of resource scarcity and pollution.

CONCLUSION

The central message of this book, and of economics as a whole, is that the wisdom of actions depends on heedful comparisons of costs and benefits, many of which lie below the radar of conventional wisdom.[34] Immigration is no exception. Appropriate policymaking requires an understanding of the contributions and burdens of people who follow the immigrant path of the founders of the United States. The benefits of immigration include job creation, inflation control, and diversity in skills and ideas. Increased expenditures on education, infrastructure, and public assistance are among the burdens.

Income disparities among nations, and skills gaps within nations, intensify the interest in immigration. Natural tendencies to avoid competition for jobs and steer tax dollars away from expenditures on immigrants collide with desires to pay low prices and fill large needs for manual laborers; health-care professionals; and workers with skills in science, math, and technology. Relevant policies touch the lives of would-be immigrants and virtually every U.S. citizen. The best decisions on pending policies will come not from emotional or political decisions but from cost–benefit analyses that go beyond direct tax and profit measures to cover every facet of Lady Liberty's promised welcome.

DISCUSSION STARTERS

1. In your opinion, what are the three largest costs and benefits of immigration?

2. With the United States unlikely to ever close its borders entirely, immigration policy is primarily a matter of degree. Some people argue that the costs associated with additional immigrants exceed the benefits after 100,000 immigrants per year.[35] Others favor limits far higher than the current rate of more than 1 million immigrants per year. On the basis of your personal knowledge, how many immigrants would you welcome into the country each year? Defend your answer.

[32] The exception in terms of birthrates is China, where the birthrate is similar to that in the United States.
[33] See, for example, www.nli-research.co.jp/eng/resea/econo/eco0008b.pdf.
[34] The term *conventional wisdom*, meaning generally accepted explanations or ideas, was coined by economist John Kenneth Galbraith.
[35] See www.carryingcapacity.org/100000.html.

3. Immigrants to the United States are helping to fill persistent needs for workers in health-care and high-tech careers. A national campaign in the United Kingdom is urging residents to close their own skills gaps by seeking additional training in fields that are experiencing labor shortages.[36] Are Americans well enough aware of the skills gap and the role immigrants play? Should a similar informational campaign be run in the United States? Are there alternative ways in which the United States's skills gap could be handled?

4. Many immigrants enter the country with relatively few marketable skills beyond a willingness to perform manual labor for a low wage. Are you aware of unemployed Americans who would be willing to pick crops or perform similar tasks for the minimum wage of $5.15 an hour? Discuss the costs and benefits of paying manual laborers a more desirable wage of $10.30 per hour, which might attract more U.S.-born workers to those jobs.

5. Does a nation of past immigrants have a moral obligation to welcome new immigrants? Explain your answer.

[36] http://news.bbc.co.uk/1/hi/education/1446681.stm.

GLOSSARY

absolute advantage: The ability of a country (or other entity) to make more of a product than another country using the same resources.

ad valorem tax: A tax collected as a percentage of the sales price.

adverse selection: The propensity for those who face greater risks to purchase more insurance.

allocative efficiency: The goal when deciding which goods and services to produce, achieved when no reallocation of productive resources would create a net gain in the well-being of society.

anarchists: People who feel that all forms of government are oppressive and should be abolished.

asymmetric information: An imbalance of information with which some people know things that others do not.

authoritarians: People who question the practicality of self-government, and look to centralized government for the advancement of society.

average fixed cost: The fixed cost divided by the number of units made.

average variable cost: The variable cost divided by the number of units made.

banking multiplier: The amount of money created by each $1 of new deposits as a result of the money creation process.

bequest value: Value resulting from the ability to pass a product or resource on to others.

big-box retailer: A retail establishment that resembles a large box.

blackouts: Complete power outages due to overburdened power grids.

bootlegging: Initially used to describe the illegal production and distribution of alcohol, the term is also applied to the unauthorized recording and distribution of music tracks.

brownouts: Periods of low voltage in power lines that cause lights to dim and equipment to malfunction.

cap-and-trade program: A program that places a cap on the level of pollution emissions and then allows polluters to buy and sell the pollution permits required for each unit of emissions.

capital account: Measures flows of money into and out of a country from lending instruments such as stocks and bonds, and similar assets.

capital consumption expense: The cost of new capital purchased to replace old capital.

capital gains tax: A tax levied on profits from the sale of an asset such as a home or shares of a stock.

capitalist system: A system in which markets determine the prices and quantities of goods and services. Also called a *market system*.

cartels: Groups of sellers who cooperate in attempts to charge higher prices.

cash economy: The subset of the economy that is conducted in cash and is not reported to the government.

ceteris paribus: Other things remaining unchanged.

classical liberalism: A political philosophy that espouses freedom from church and state authority, free-enterprise economics, and individual freedoms.

Coasian bargaining: Bargaining between those with the legal rights to control a situation and those whose desired activities would cause harm to those in control. For example, if a noise ordinance stipulates that outdoor concerts cannot be held without the permission of neighbors, concert promoters could negotiate a payment to neighbors in exchange for the ability to hold a concert.

command system: A system with centralized decision making, as with communism and socialism.

command-and-control pollution regulations: Regulations that require uniform reductions or specific technology applications across all sources.

commercial paper: An unsecured IOU issued by a corporation or bank to satisfy short-term financial needs.

common good: The ethical doctrine that policies should aim for outcomes that are beneficial to all.

communism: A system designed to eliminate material inequities via collective ownership of property.

comparative advantage: The ability of a producer to make a good at a lower opportunity cost than another producer.

compensatory damages: A court-mandated payment to a claimant to compensate for harm the claimant has suffered.

competition, pure or perfect: A market condition characterized by many buyers and sellers, none of whom can influence the market price.

complete crowding out: A complete offset of private expenditures by government expenditures.

conservative: In the context of government, conservatives generally express concern about government growing too large or making inefficient decisions.

consortium: Used to describe companionship, assistance, affection, as well as sexual relations.

consumer surplus: The difference between the value of a good to consumers and the amount paid for it.

contestable market: A market with low enough barriers to entry to allow competitors to enter.

contractionary policy: Policy with the purpose of decreasing aggregate output.

counterfeiting: The making of inauthentic replicas of goods such as albums, watches, or currency.

crowding out: Lower private expenditures that result from higher government expenditures, either because the government expenditures take the place of private expenditures or because borrowing to fund the government expenditures causes the interest rate to increase and the level of private investment to decrease.

current account: Measures imports, exports, transfers, and returns on foreign investments (rents, interests, and profits).

cyclical unemployment: The unemployment of workers who are forced out of their jobs due to a downturn in the cycle of business peaks and troughs.

damage award: An award paid to a successful plaintiff by a defendant in a civil case.

deadweight loss: A loss of consumer or producer surplus that is not gained by anyone.

debt: The accumulation of past deficits minus past surpluses.

defensive goods and services: Goods and services necessitated by problems that make society worse off, such as corruption, natural disasters, disease, and the perils of economic growth, including pollution, congestion, and work-related stress.

deficit: The amount by which expenditures exceed revenues in one period—usually a year.

depreciation expense: The cost of new capital purchased to replace old capital.

derived demand: Demand for an input that is dependent on the demand for the output that is created by that input.

deterrence hypothesis: The hypothesis that as punishments increase, crime rates will decrease.

deterrence value: The amount that must be paid for causing the loss of life in order for decisions that might put life at risk to be efficient.

diminishing marginal product: A decrease in marginal product when another unit of input is added.

discount rate: The interest rate paid by banks and other depository institutions when they borrow money from their regional Federal Reserve Bank.

discount window: The lending facility within each Federal Reserve bank.

distributive efficiency: The goal when deciding who will receive the available goods and services, achieved when no reallocation of goods and services would create a net gain in the wellbeing of society.

econometric analysis: Statistical analysis that helps to determine the influence of variables on each other, such as the influence of study time on grades.

economic development: A sustained increase in the standard of living experienced by a country's population.

economic growth: Growth in the level of gross domestic product.

economic profits: Profits calculated as the difference between revenues and costs *including* opportunity costs.

economies of scale: A condition that exists when the average cost of production decreases as the quantity of output increases.

efficiency wages: Wages set above the market wage rate to attract the best workers, gain loyalty, avoid search costs, and promote better performance.

efficiency: The absence of waste. Efficiency is achieved by carrying out activities until the additional benefit of continuing no longer exceeds the additional cost. With an efficient allocation of resources, it is impossible to make anyone better off without making at least one person worse off.

elastic demand: Demand that is relatively sensitive to price changes.

endogenous: Determined within the economic system rather than by outside influences.

endogenous growth model: A model of economic growth that treats the level of technology as *endogenous*, meaning that it is determined within the economic system.

endowment effect: People value what they have more than what they don't have.

energy conversion efficiency: The percentage of energy input that is converted to work.

energy: The amount of physical work a system is capable of performing.

equation of exchange: The identity that the money supply multiplied by the velocity of money equals the price level multiplied by the quantity of goods and services.

equity: Distribution characterized by fairness, balance, impartiality, and justice.

ethical egoism: The ethical doctrine that personal interests should be pursued without regard to the effects those pursuits may have on others.

Eurodollar deposits: Large (usually over $1 million) time deposits denominated in U.S. dollars and held either by banks headquartered outside of the U.S. or by foreign branches of banks headquartered within the U.S.

excise taxes: Taxes imposed on specific goods or services.

existence value: Value derived from the knowledge that a product or resource exists.

expansionary policy: Policy with the purpose of increasing aggregate output.

expected value: Calculated as the weighted average of possible outcomes, this is the most that a risk-neutral person would pay to participate in an activity such as a lottery with an uncertain outcome.

expenditure approach: A method of calculating gross domestic product by adding up expenditures on consumption, investment, government spending, and net exports (exports minus imports).

externalities: Costs and benefits felt beyond those causing them, such as the effects of loud music or pollution.

federal funds market: A market in which banks borrow and lend excess reserves.

federal funds rate: The interest rate that banks pay each other in the federal funds market.

Federal Reserve System: The central bank for the United States.

fiscal policy: Changes in taxes, government transfers, and government spending used to stabilize the economy.

fixed cost: A cost that does not change as more of a product is made.

fixed inputs: Inputs the quantity of which cannot be changed in the short run.

four-firm concentration ratio: The sum of the market shares of the four largest firms in a market.

fractional reserve banking system: A banking system in which banks retain a fraction of their deposits and the remainder is loaned out.

free-market: Without intervention or government regulation.

free rider: Someone who benefits from a public good without helping to pay for it.

frictional unemployment: The unemployment of workers who have the necessary skills to work but are between jobs in the process of improving their work situation.

general deterrence: One of the reasons for punishment; the deterrence of some criminals that results from punishing other criminals.

General Theory of Second-Best: The theory that, when one of the conditions for perfect competition is not met, intervention to remedy the situation can lead to a better outcome than a hands-off approach, even if every other condition is met.

Gini coefficient: A measure of the equality of income distribution within a country.

globalization: The creation of a worldwide scope for markets, communications, transportation, and ideas.

government: A body with the authority to govern.

green space: Undeveloped land.

gross domestic product: The final value of all goods and services produced within the borders of a country.

guilt burden: The amount one would pay to avoid guilty feelings about a particular action.

heuristics: Rules of thumb.

human capital: Skills, education, experience, and knowledge that improves the productivity of workers.

Human Development Index (HDI): A measure of development on the basis of life expectancy, adult literacy rates, school enrollment rates, and gross domestic product per capita.

imperfect information: Information that omits significant details.

income approach: A method of calculating gross domestic product by adding up the income received by workers and adjusting to include all portions that represent contributions to GDP.

income tax: A tax collected as a percentage of income.

incomplete crowding out: A partial offset of private expenditures by government expenditures.

indirect business taxes: Taxes such as excise taxes, sales taxes, and property taxes, which are part of what is paid for products but not part of income received by workers.

individual transferable quotas (ITQs): An application of cap-and-trade programs in the fishing industry. Fishers receive quotas for the volume of fish they can catch, and if they reduce their catch below the level of their quotas, they can sell their unused ITQs to others who place a higher value on those fishing rights.

inelastic demand: Demand that is relatively insensitive to price changes.

inferior good: A good that is purchased in smaller quantities as income increases.

inputs: Productive resources such as labor, land, capital, and technology.

insourced jobs: Domestic jobs created by a foreign producer.

institutional economists: Economists who believe that economic theory should acknowledge limits on information and rationality among economic decision makers.

institutions: Rules, relationships, organizations, and systems of norms.

insurance value: The amount for which a person insures his or her life.

internalize: To feel costs and benefits personally, such as the costs and benefits of manufacturing and using products.

internationalization: The increase of international trade and interdependence.

justice: The ethical doctrine that fairness and justice are compelling measures of morality.

Kantianism: The ethical doctrine that moral actions are only those that you would choose to be undertaken by everyone.

keystone pricing rule: Double the wholesale price to obtain the retail price.

laissez-faire: Without intervention or government regulation.

law of demand: As the price increases the quantity demanded decreases.

law of diminishing marginal returns: As the amount of one input increases, holding the levels of all other inputs constant, the additional output gained will eventually decrease.

law of diminishing marginal utility: As more of a good is acquired, the utility gained from one more unit of that good will eventually decrease.

law of supply: As the price increases the quantity supplied increases.

liberals (modern): Generally characterized as favoring more government rather than less, and as advocating a mild form of socialism or populism.

libertarians: People who believe that government's role should be limited to protecting citizens from coercion and violence.

loser-pays policies: Legal policies under which the "loser" in a case pays the legal costs of the "winner."

lump-sum tax: A tax of a set amount that does not change with income or revenues.

marginal benefit: The additional benefit gained from one more unit of something.

marginal cost: The cost of making one more unit of a product.

marginal external cost: The external cost of providing one more unit of a good or service.

marginal product of labor: The amount by which total output increases when one more unit of labor is hired.

marginal revenue: The additional revenue gained by selling one more unit of output.

marginal revenue product: The increase in revenues achieved by hiring one more unit of an input.

marital income: The benefits from marriage, which can include love, affection, companionship, cooperation, assistance with chores, children, and a healthier financial situation.

market: A place or system that brings together buyers and sellers of goods or services.

market failure: The inability of a market to achieve an efficient outcome.

market power: The power to influence the price of a good or service in a market, generally held by firms in markets with a limited number of sellers.

market system: A system in which markets determine the prices and quantities of goods and services. Also called a *capitalist system*.

marriage market: The system by which prospective marital partners come together.

menu costs: The costs associated with changing prices.

money creation: The expansion of the money supply as the result of deposits and loans in a fractional reserve banking system.

money market mutual fund: A fund made up of short-term, low-risk financial securities such as treasury bills, certificates of deposit, and municipal notes.

money with zero maturity: A new measure of the money supply that includes money that is redeemable immediately at face value, such as cash, checking and savings accounts, and money market mutual funds.

monopoly: A firm in a market that has no competitors.

moral hazard: The tendency for people who are insured to take more risks because the personal repercussions are relatively small.

moral suasion: Pressure or persuasion without force.

national income: Income earned by the people of a country, including income from labor and capital investment.

natural monopoly: A single firm in a market that could not support more than one firm.

negative marginal product: A decrease in total product when another unit of input is added.

neoclassical economists: In general, economists who rely on the assumptions that people are fully informed, rational utility maximizers and that firms maximize profits.

neoclassical-Keynesian synthesis: A hybrid of the neoclassical and Keynesian schools of thought that embraces active fiscal and monetary policy.

net foreign factor income: The difference between what foreign investors earn on assets in the U.S. and what U.S. investors earn from their assets abroad.

neutrality of money: Implies that the level of output is independent of the money supply in the long run.

newspaper test: A test of moral judgment: An action is acceptable if you wouldn't be embarrassed to have it reported on the front page of a newspaper.

non-excludable: When one person consumes the good or service, other people cannot be excluded from consuming it.

non-rival in consumption: Consumption by one person does not affect the ability for another person to consume the same unit of a good or service, such as military protection.

nonuse or passive-use value: Value that comes from indirect enjoyment of a product or resource, such as the value of being able to pass a resource on to future generations.

normal good: A good that is purchased in larger quantities as income increases.

oligopoly: A market dominated by a small number of firms.

open market operations: The purchase or sale of securities by the Fed on the open market to change the supply of bank reserves.

opportunity cost: The full cost of something, including what must be given up to obtain it.

optimal consumption rule: A rule that stipulates that consumers should purchase more of the good that provides the most utils per dollar until the utils per dollar are equal for all goods.

option value: Value derived from the knowledge that a product or resource could be used in the future.

peak-load pricing: A pricing structure that sets higher prices during periods of high demand.

perfect competition: A market condition characterized by many buyers and sellers, none of whom can influence the market price.

perfectly inelastic demand: Demand for a good or service that does not change as the price changes.

permanent income hypothesis: The hypothesis that people's expenditures are based on their expected lifetime income rather than on their income at any particular time.

perverse incentives: Incentives that create undesired results.

Phillips relationship: The inverse relationship between inflation and unemployment.

poll tax: A type of lump sum tax that requires a specific payment from each adult.

power: The rate of energy transfer per unit of time

price discriminate: To charge different prices for units of the same good or service, as with volume or senior discounts.

price elasticity of demand: The sensitivity of the quantity demanded to the price.

price floor: A minimum below which prices cannot be set.

price taker: A firm so small that it has no influence on the market price and must accept the price as given.

private marginal cost: The cost to producers of providing one more unit of a good or service.

producer surplus: The difference between the payment for a good and the cost of producing it.

productive efficiency: The goal when deciding what mix of resources to use in the production of goods and services, achieved when it is not possible to produce more of any good or service without producing less of another.

progressive tax: A tax that represents a larger share of income for high-income taxpayers than of low-income taxpayers.

promissory note: A document signed by a borrower stipulating the terms under which a loan will be repaid.

property tax: A tax levied on some measure of the value of property such as a home or automobile.

proportional tax: A tax that constitutes a fixed proportion of income at all income levels.

public goods: Goods that are both non-rival in consumption and non-excludable, such as street lights.

punitive damage: A court-mandated payment to punish a person for wrongful actions.

pure competition: A market condition characterized by many buyers and sellers, none of whom can influence the market price.

quantity theory of money: Holds that the velocity of money and the quantity of goods and services are relatively fixed, so that with any increase in the money supply, the equation must be balanced by an increase in the price level.

rational choice theory: Holds that decision makers are able to compare all their alternatives with full information about the ramifications of their choices.

rational expectations theory: A theory that people forecast future events on a rational basis using all available information.

regressive tax: A tax that decreases as a proportion of income as income increases.

rehabilitation: The restoration of physical or psychological health.

repurchase agreement (repos):   A way for investors to make short-term loans. The investor gives money in exchange for an asset such as a treasury bond. At a specified time the loan recipient returns a larger amount of money (the loan amount plus interest) to the investor in exchange for the asset.

restitution: In the context of punishment, an act of restoration or recovery on the behalf of the victim.

Ricardian equivalence: The theory that when the government borrows money, taxpayers know they must repay the loan eventually, and increase their savings by enough to repay the borrowed funds plus interest at the appropriate time.

rights: The ethical doctrine that the morality of an action depends on its adherence to moral duties, such as the duties to treat individuals with dignity and respect.

risk-averse: To care not only about the expected value of an outcome, but also about the range of possible outcomes, and to prefer to minimize the size of that range. For example, a risk-averse person would prefer a coin flip that determined whether $1 was won or lost over a coin flip that determined whether $1000 was won or lost, even though the expected value of each outcome is $0.

risk burden: The amount that a risk-averse person would pay to avoid uncertainty about a particular risk.

risk-loving: To prefer a wide range of possible outcomes over a more certain outcome with the same expected value.

risk-neutral: To care only about the expected value of an outcome and not about the range of possible outcomes.

role models: Examples for others.

sales tax: A tax on the retail price of goods or services, collected by retailers.

short run: The period during which it is not possible to increase the quantity of some inputs, typically capital.

socialism: A system with the goal of fair distribution of resources. Wages are determined by negotiations between trade unions and management, and multiple political parties oversee the economy.

social marginal cost: The cost to all of society of providing one more unit of a good or service. This is the sum of the private marginal cost and the marginal external cost.

social price: The price to be paid in the marriage market, based largely on necessary courting efforts and ease of attraction.

specific deterrence: One of the reasons for punishment; the deterrence of a criminal by punishing that criminal.

stagflation: The combination of an increase in inflation and a decrease in aggregate output (and thus a decrease in employment).

staggered pricing: When different firms have different schedules for when price changes are made.

statistical life: The life of an unidentified person. For example, statistics indicate that lower speed limits would save lives, but at the time of policymaking it is impossible to predict whose lives would be saved, so they are considered statistical lives.

status quo bias: A bias toward sticking with the way things are when faced with equally attractive alternatives.

structural unemployment: The unemployment of workers who lack the skills necessary for available jobs.

sunk costs: Costs that have already been paid and cannot be recovered.

supply-side economics: A school of economic thought that concentrates on shifts in aggregate supply, as can be achieved with tax cuts, as a means of improving the economy.

supraterritoriality: The de-emphasis on territorial boundaries.

surplus: The amount by which revenues exceed expenditures in one period—usually a year.

sympathy value: Value in knowing that a natural resource such as a forest or animal species is alive and well.

time deposits: Deposits that can't be withdrawn for a specified period without incurring a penalty.

tort: A civil, not criminal, wrong other than breach of contract.

total cost: Fixed cost plus variable cost.

total product: The total amount of output produced.

tragedy of the commons: The problem that people tend to mistreat public property.

transitive preferences: Preferences such that if A is preferred to B and B is preferred to C then A is preferred to C.

underground economy: The subset of the economy that is conducted in cash and is not reported to the government.

unit tax: A tax collected as a certain amount per unit of a good or service.

universalization: The spread of common ideas and goods across the globe.

use value: Value that comes from the firsthand enjoyment of a product or resource.

utilitarianism: The ethical doctrine that the sum of everyone's utility should be as large as possible.

utility: A measure of happiness or satisfaction.

utils: Units of utility.

value-added approach: A method of calculating gross domestic product by adding up the incremental change in value from one step in the production process to the next.

value-added tax (VAT): A tax imposed on the increase in the value of a good at each stage of production and sale.

variable cost: A cost that increases as more of a product is made.

variable inputs: Inputs the quantity of which can be changed in the short run.

velocity of money: The number of times a particular unit of money is spent within a set period, typically one year.

virtue: The ethical doctrine that people should learn and practice virtues, which are the middle ground between vices. For example, courage is a moral virtue between cowardice and rashness.

Westernization: The migration of Western culture.

INDEX